CAPITAL BUDGETING
UNDER CONDITIONS
OF UNCERTAINTY

NIJENRODE STUDIES IN BUSINESS

Volume 5

Business is a broad field where science and business reality can and should meet to analyze and discuss old theories and to develop new ones, applicable for modern managers. One of the main objectives of the **Nijenrode Studies in Business** is to give a push to new developments in the multidisciplinary business area, to serve the profession as well as a wider audience.

CAPITAL BUDGETING UNDER CONDITIONS OF UNCERTAINTY

Edited by
Roy L. Crum
University of Florida

Frans G. J. Derkinderen
The Netherlands School of Business

Martinus Nijhoff Publishing
Boston / The Hague / London

Distributors for North America:
Martinus Nijhoff Publishing
Kluwer Boston, Inc.
160 Old Derby Street
Hingham, Massachusetts 02043

Distributors outside North America:
Kluwer Academic Publishers Group
Distribution Centre
P.O. Box 322
3300 AH Dordrecht, The Netherlands

Library of Congress Cataloging in Publication Data

Main entry under title:

Capital budgeting under conditions of uncertainty.

  (Nijenrode studies in business; v. 5)
  Includes bibliographies.
  1. Capital budget—Addresses, essays, lectures.
2. Capital investments—Addresses, essays, lectures.
I. Crum, Roy L. II. Derkinderen, F. III. Series.
HG4028.C4C35   658.1'54   80-11883
ISBN 0-89838-045-6

Printed in the United States of America

CONTENTS

II INVESTMENT ISSUES IN COMPLEX ENVIRONMENTS

III CAPITAL ALLOCATION MODELING

INTRODUCTION

The business environment, particularly after the continuing oil crises of the seventies, can be characterized as evolving rapidly in complex and often unpredictable ways. Such things as high interest and inflation rates, fluctuating exchange rates, volatile commodity markets, and increasing political turmoil have led to a situation in which explicit consideration of environmental dynamics is becoming much more important for successful business planning than was true in the past. Companies are finding that it is no longer possible to conduct "business as usual" under these changing circumstances. Rather, decision makers are having to be more cognizant of the many sources of uncertainty that could have serious impacts on the continued prosperity of the firm, as well as of actions that can be taken so that the company can thrive in spite of these greater uncertainties.

Businesses have responded to these challenges by giving more thorough consideration to strategic issues. Whereas in the past the steady progression of markets and technology was taken for granted, the uncertainties associated with increased worldwide competition, as well as with other exogenous factors, have forced companies to think more about flexibility. This involves not only how best to exploit profitable current options, but also how to position themselves at present to be able to respond appropriately to threats and opportunities as they arise in the future. Unfortunately, in this redirection of outlook, the finance profession has not kept pace. Theoretical issues associated with capital budgeting under conditions of uncertainty still reflect most of the assumptions of data availability and reliability, as well as the unidimensional decision framework that was developed for less volatile and simpler periods. Whether or not these methodologies continue to be applicable has not been seriously investigated. In fact, very few attempts have been made to break out of the general equilibrium mold in which markets are assumed to be complete, efficient, and able to provide all relevant information required to allocate resources appropriately. Thus there appears to be a widening gap developing between financial theory and business practice.

Because of the practical importance of this issue for effective and efficient utilization of scarce resources in the coming years, the Netherlands School of Business hosted a conference entitled Financial Management of Corporate Resource Allocations that investigated the causes of this gap and its ramifications for financial research. Held at Nijenrode Castle in the Netherlands in August 1979, the conference brought together more than forty distinguished scholars and business executives from eleven countries to present research papers on this topic and to participate in round-table discussions. This volume is the first to come out of that conference, and the papers selected for inclusion represent a cross section of views on the subject of capital budgeting under conditions of uncertainty, considering the business environment of the 1980s.

CONTENT OF THE BOOK

The theme of the book is current investment problems in a variety-rich and changing world. It is divided into three parts, which focus attention in turn on different aspects of this important issue. The first part deals with increased complexity in the environment faced by business, as well as with enhanced uncertainty in the investment process, resulting mainly from the intervention of activist governments in the marketplace.

As usually characterized in finance textbooks, the basic investment decision assumes that it is possible to rank two projects in terms of their desirability or at least to accept or reject the one being studied. The decision is placed in the context of capital markets in which a distinction is made between operational and financial cash flows. This also enables the firm to alter the cash flows by suitable policies. The presumed objective of the conventional textbook analysis is to identify the project(s) whose acceptance would maximize the value of the firm. In the first paper, Parés, Sala, and Tornabell assert that if there are sufficient environmental constraints that hamper the firm's freedom to act, the use of analytical techniques based on the above assumptions quickly becomes an exercise of little practical relevance. It is their contention that these types of restrictions now exist in Spain. They show that the market structure in Spain, coupled with the fiscal and industrial policies of the Spanish government, may well have led some private firms to have an investment policy whose main goal could be described as "stay private." Within the context of Spain, this policy may be highly rational, but it is certainly far afield from the situation described in the textbooks. The important point made by Parés, Sala, and Tornabell is that while the usual finance concepts and models are appropriate in many circumstances, they are not universally applicable for all situations. One must carefully temper the analytical methodology to the environment before sound resource allocations can be expected.

This theme is echoed by Gandemo. His essay is based on an empirical investigation of the impact on business decision making of government activities in Sweden. One of the most dirigismic of the developed Western nations, Sweden's government has a strong and growing interest in controlling economic activities within the country through a number of stimulating and restricting economic-political measures. Gandemo shows that these interventions change the operating context in which firms in Sweden must contend so that the practical planning conditions are far removed from the assumptions of markets and internal planning processes encountered in theoretical research. The results of the investigation cast doubt on the effectiveness of these governmental activities in achieving the desired consequences. Not only that, there are indications that some situations with societally undesirable characteristics are being fostered by the reaction of companies to the government actions.

The conclusions of the first two papers are supported by Schneider. From a theoretical perspective, he shows that many common beliefs about the impact of governmental actions, in the form of tax incentives, on risk-taking behavior by firms are built on a foundation of loose sand. In fact, he demonstrates that these effects are largely indeterminant if the conditions set forth in the tax laws are properly taken into account. Schneider further argues that the portfolio models now in use for analyzing the interrelationships between taxation and risk-taking considerably overrate the investor's ability to choose according to the expected utility theorem or its simplifications, such as the mean-variance rule.

Even without, or in addition to, government intervention in the marketplace, there are many other environmental complexities that have a bearing on the capital investment process. Four papers are presented in the second part of the book dealing with other significant investment issues in complex environments.

In the first paper, Bey studies the impact on the mean and variance of net present value (NPV), for both individual projects and portfolios, of incorrectly assuming that project lives are known with certainty. His empirical results indicate that a substantial error in both the mean and the variance of NPV may occur when project life is incorrectly assumed to be certain. Furthermore, when the cash flows are autocorrelated, Bey found that the direction and magnitude of the bias in the estimates of variance of NPV are a function of the direction of the autocorrelation. To overcome these potentially serious problems, a simulation methodology is suggested as a means for allowing both stochastic project lives and autocorrelated cash flows to be included in mean-variance–based capital budgeting procedures.

In the second essay, Bühler goes one step further. Most of the approaches to capital budgeting under conditions of uncertainty assume that the decision maker is able to specify the probability distributions of all uncertain data affecting the investment decision. Practical experience has shown that this assumption is often unrealistic. It is not unusual for managers to be unable to specify probabilities quantitatively, or, if they are forced to, the results of risk analyses based on them are not fully accepted. Bühler does not presuppose an ability to quantify probabilities. Rather, he assumes only that there is sufficient information available to a manager to enable him to specify whether one value of an uncertain variable is more probable than another value. Bühler calls information of this type "qualitative," and it forms the basis of the planning system for allocating corporate resources that is described in his paper.

The last two essays in Part II both address another important issue, but from different perspectives. When one thinks about complex environments, the operations of a multinational firm should come to mind as a paragon. Subjected to many different social, political, legal, and economic systems, the multinational firm must balance carefully a host of often-conflicting variables before reasoned resource allocation decisions can be made. To structure this difficult problem, in the first paper Lessard develops an adjusted present value (APV) approach based on the value additivity principle. This method holds for independent projects in complete capital markets and provides a relatively simple framework for evaluating international projects in a way that is consistent with state-of-the-art financial practice. The applicability of the suggested methodology is restricted by the assumptions to projects that are either wholly owned by the parent or whose equity is shared by investors having access to the same relatively complete capital markets. It does not address the valuation of projects by joint ventures in which equity is shared by investors based in markets segmented by barriers. Nor does it apply to the valuation of particular projects by firms based in countries with relatively complete markets, on the one hand, and by local firms operating in a more restricted capital market, on the other.

Addressing the same issues from a different point of view, Folks investigates some vital aspects of technology of financial analysis of foreign investment projects by the investing firm that are perhaps applicable to a broader range of situations. He offers some suggestions for developing a methodology for the analysis of parent company cash flows. This method puts different, possibly competing, projects on the same analytical footing. Since parent return is a function both of external environmental factors and of managerial decisions, it is shown that failure to standardize assumptions regarding managerial parameters will lead to inconsistent project analysis. Folks makes these suggestions in an attempt to fill a void in the analysis of foreign investment projects, and he views the suggestions as a reasonable starting point for developing standardized corporate procedures.

The emphasis on investment issues in complex environments that characterize the four papers in Part II is carried over to the third part. Part III, however, focuses more directly on specific models for capital allocation that are appropriate aids to the decision-making process. As a lead-in to the topic, Crum and Derkinderen, in an essay written especially for this volume, examine environmental characteristics and behavioral factors that evoke a need to consider multiple criteria to achieve operational reality, if not theoretical validity, in capital budgeting under conditions of uncertainty. The paper investigates how appropriate criteria can be ascertained for these purposes. Through the use of a typological approach, these criteria can be determined as a function of the requirements of the specific problem class. Various methodologies for solving multicriteria problems are also examined, and suggestions are given both for structuring the decision process and for selecting a solution technique that is consistent with the character of the problem.

With the introductory article of the editors as a background, the view of Schmidt that strategies considering the future business environment must attach great importance to economic and social change is explored. Occurring within both the firm and the environment, such changes may give reason not only to revise plans, but also to adapt the entire planning system. In this paper Schmidt concentrates on the influence of changing objectives on the flexibility of the planning system. Starting first with an investigation of the nature of the change process as it affects the objectives of the company, ways to ensure flexibility in a computerized planning system are developed. Finally, corporate planning models are discussed for the case of changing objectives. An illustrative example is given by applying the planning system for mathematical applications (PLASMA) on a dialogue basis.

The need for interactive modeling methods, such as are incorporated in PLASMA, is reinforced in the paper by Spronk. If these methods are based on a mutual and successive interplay between a decision maker and an analyst,

Spronk asserts that they require neither an explicit representation of the decision maker's preference function nor an explicit quantitative representation of tradeoffs among competing objectives. These interactive methods for structuring and reevaluating data are then linked to an integer goal programming algorithm. When this is done, a planning system that is especially suited for capital budgeting and financial planning with multiple goals is effected. Called Interactive Multiple Goal Programming, this approach is shown to be superior to conventional goal programming techniques for the purpose at hand.

The first three papers in Part III all put forth a common theme that interactive mathematical programming models are particularly effective for exploring the ramifications of resource allocations under conditions of uncertainty. To put sophisticated models such as these into proper perspective, in the last paper in the book, Forsyth and Owen report on an empirical study of alternative approaches to the development of a capital investment plan. They compare and contrast the efficiency of two methods of solving the capital rationing problem: a mathematical programming model and a heuristic approach. A series of simulation experiments were conducted. These show that for fairly simple but realistic problems, management can make use of the net present value ranking approach and obtain results that are essentially identical to those obtained with mathematical programming models. As the problems become more complex, with multiperiod resource requirements and constraints, lumpy investments, and project interdependence, the efficiency of mathematical programming approaches increases. However, it still might be possible to design more complex heuristics to prescreen projects so that essentially equivalent results could be obtained. Further study of the problem is required; but as one considers the accuracy of the data estimates in any capital investment process, the need for very sophisticated techniques that offer little improvement over heuristic approaches has to be evaluated very carefully.

This volume starts with and develops the theme of greater complexity and uncertainty existing in today's business environment. It concludes with an in-depth discussion of modeling approaches for structuring and solving complex problems that may deserve consideration when operating under conditions of enhanced uncertainty. Since the stakes associated with playing the game are now higher than ever, it is vital to think through the possible ramifications of these environmental considerations for the firm and to structure the problem analysis correctly. Once this is done, programming models can enhance the decision-making process.

I GOVERNMENT INTERVENTION IN THE INVESTMENT PROCESS

1 INVESTMENT DECISIONS IN THE ELECTRIC INDUSTRY:

The Spanish Case

Antoni Parés
Cristian Sala
Robert Tornabell

ESADE, Spain

The application of investment decision-making rules, based on theoretical developments in economics and finance, has been and is useful to many corporations. Evidence gathered regularly in the United States [2, 4] and Europe [6] indicates an increasing acceptance by executives of the techniques usually described in the textbooks and explained in business school classrooms.

Both practical and academic circles, however, have leveled some criticism at theoretical or pedagogical developments in finance on two counts: First, it seems that some models (CAPM, for instance) have been overemphasized beyond their real-world usefulness. Second, exclusive reliance on available models precludes the consideration of complex real situations entailing a type of constraint, and consequently objectives for decision making, beyond those accepted in the literature and included in the models.

The basic investment decision that is usually contemplated in textbooks assumes the possibility of choosing among different projects, or at least accepting or rejecting the one being studied, the separability of operational and financial cash flows, and some freedom to alter those by suitable firm policies. The decision is also couched in a financial market framework, the objective being to maximize the firm's value. Where some of these (and other) elements are not relevant for the decision maker, the usefulness of analytical techniques based on such assumptions is diminished. Furthermore, if there are environmental constraints that hamper the firm's freedom, the use of the techniques becomes an academic exercise of little use for decision makers.

The electric utility industry exemplifies well the occurrence of complex investment decisions. It is either state owned or state regulated. In all cases, especially since the 1974 oil crisis, production processes have become more capital-intensive, and as a result business risk may for some utilities have changed in scale. Also, the investment is usually accompanied by specific financing. It is extremely difficult or impossible for any firm to stop producing if the rate of return is not sufficient to meet its shareholders' expectations. These and other departures from the usual capital budgeting assumptions are well known and relevant to most private utilities in the world. However, in this paper we want to present the case for private Spanish utilities, which departs from the two typical situations encountered in most countries: state-owned utilities (France, Italy, U.K.), or private utilities with state regulation (the U.S.). In Spain we have both public firms and private firms, all of them regulated by the state.

This market structure, coupled with the fiscal and industrial policies of the Spanish government, may well have led some of the Spanish private firms to have an investment policy whose main goal could tentatively be called "stay private." This may be highly rational, but it is certainly far from the situation described in most textbooks.

We reach our thesis by observing that it is difficult, given current and announced Spanish practices, to obtain acceptable profitability from current and prospective investments in electric utilities. Furthermore, there are indications both in the present government plans, and even more so in the opposition's, of increased control over almost all aspects of utilities, even proposals for nationalization. The latter, a highly ideological issue, has appeared at a time when some private firms are reluctant to follow the nuclear program, being uncertain about their abilities to counter the risks involved, while others (those with a "stay private" objective) are indeed willing to take the risks, and to prove their managerial ability in doing so.

To develop our thesis, we will proceed by first providing an overall view of the electric industry in Spain: its market structure, tariff policy, and the fiscal, financial, and other state policies. Second, we will focus our attention on the National Energy Plan (NEP), with a special emphasis on the nuclear power policy. In the third section, we will analyze the financial alternatives available to the electric industry and particularly to the private firms, vis-à-vis the huge investments they have to make, and explore the consequences of some possible courses of action. Finally, we propose some recommendations for tariff setting.

THE ELECTRIC UTILITY INDUSTRY IN SPAIN

Market Structure

Spain is divided into six geographical areas for the administration of the electric utility industry. Generally each utility operates only in one area. In some areas there are few utilities operating, but there seems to be a certain amount of coordination among them. The Ministry of Industry ensures, for instance, that there is no competition for building hydroelectric plants in any one region, since it allocates new hydroelectric concessions and operating permits. The six largest companies supply roughly two-thirds of Spain's electricity needs. The private sector produces about 83 percent of the national output, but the government, as explained below, plays a determinant role in planning and pricing policies.

Practically all Spanish utilities are joined in UNESA, which serves three main functions:

- It coordinates power exchanges in collaboration with the Ministry of Industry.
- It submits applications for rate increases on behalf of its members.
- It submits modifications to the NEP.

Tariff Policy

For more than twenty years, the price of electricity has been subject to government control. Electricity tariffs are applied on a uniform basis throughout Spain. The bases for determining Spanish tariffs are nowhere stated. Therefore it is not known for certain how the Ministry of Industry proceeds in setting the tariff, which is composed of a capacity factor and a variable factor [8].

The government has consistently used electricity prices for certain economic policies. It is convenient to examine how these policies have affected the electric industry and the economy. In particular, the subsidization of the industrial energy consumers and the setting of the tariff structure and its process of revision are of great importance.

Tariffs for Types of Consumers. Because of the priority given to industrial development, the government has kept industrial prices at a low level, either by explicit subsidy or by charging more to commercial and household consumers. In a study undertaken recently [10], there was a comparison made among all European countries between the prices for industrial and other consumers. The ranking (see Table 5) in 1975, shows Spain as the country offering nearly the cheapest energy for industry and one of the most expensive for other consumers.

Spain has a complex system of tariffs, with four major groups, each one of them with subtariffs (the number of which is shown in parentheses) [8] :

Low-voltage supply:
1. Commercial and household (7)
2. Industrial uses (4)

High-voltage supply:
3. Industrial uses (7)
4. Special supply (public sector and wholesalers) (3)

This variety of tariffs does not correspond to differences in cost and directly affects the revenue of the different companies according to the structure of their markets. In fact, high voltage is billed below cost and low voltage at cost (if industrial) and above (if commercial or domestic). From the consumers' point of view, high voltage is billed as if all its demand were made in off-hours and low voltage as if all demand were made at peak hours. In practical terms, as is apparent in Table 1, there is a billing ratio of 2.75 to 1 between low- and high-voltage consumers.

Table 1. European Countries: Ranking by Electric Tariffs (lowest to highest), 1975

Country	Domestic	Industrial	General
Norway	1	1	1
Portugal	2	4	2
Sweden	4	3	3
Great Britain	3	6	4
Switzerland	6	5	5
Spain	10	2	6
France	9	7	7
Austria	8	8	8
Italy	7	9	9
Finland	5	13	10
The Netherlands	11	11	11
Denmark	13	12	12
Germany	12	13	13
Belgium	14	14	14

Source: UNIPEDE [10]

Change in Tariffs. The increase in oil prices and the level of cost inflation in Spain led the government in February 1977 to apply more realistic prices to industrial consumers by increasing the relevant tariff by 20 percent. Later, in August 1977, both consumer and industrial rates were increased by an additional 5.4 percent, passing on the then latest rise in the cost of oil. Even if increases are submitted by UNESA and negotiated with the Ministry of Industry, an automatic indexation formula has been established that is triggered by increases in the cost of fuel. However, in practice the automatism is less than evident, since only in July 1979 has an increase been finally authorized in spite of repeated hikes in OPEC prices and very high double-digit inflation.

In October 1976 the government introduced a temporary surcharge on tariffs in order to compensate and subsidize some electricity producers and industrial consumers, even at the very low prices prevailing for industrial use.[1]

The utilities facing such a tariff system had already perceived the impact of oil price increases in the income statements of fossil fuel plants. A discretionary redistribution agreement was created among them, with the name of Compensación entre Empresas de Unesa (CEUN). Firms whose increase in revenues has been exceeded by the increase in fuel costs are compensated for the differential by those companies whose increases in revenues have exceeded the negative impact of more expensive fuel. According to this scheme, the net contributors tend to be those companies with important hydroelectric production. Redistributions take place every two months. This agreement allows the utilities to share equitably the results of lacking tariff procedures, but does not allow them to increase their collective ability to finance their expansions, as tariffs inevitably lag behind cost increases.

Fiscal, Financial, and Other State Policies

Even before the current revision of the NEP, the government had offered some incentives to electric utilities to carry out their heavy investment plans. The program of Acción Concertada (Concerted Action), announced in 1975, established a comprehensive framework for supporting and stimulating the electric industry, whereby the utilities would agree to commit themselves to carry out and complete the construction of certain plants, transmission, and distribution facilities during a period ending in 1985. The administration would, in turn, agree to grant the utilities certain benefits.[2] However, it is difficult to evaluate the benefits procedure as currently practiced in Spain.

THE NATIONAL ENERGY PLAN (NEP)

Objectives

Since the Government recognized that the energy supply was the single most important element in guaranteeing the continued industrial development of Spain, the Ministry of Industry established an NEP in 1969. The NEP is updated every two years. A detailed revision, approved recently by the government and awaiting ratification by the Spanish Parliament, covers a ten-year period. Its major objectives [5] are:

- To moderate energy consumption, adapting it progressively to Spain's resources
- To ensure an energy supply sufficient to meet the needs of the expected growth in gross national product
- To reduce dependency on external supplies
- To establish a realistic energy price policy

The rationale for the plan's objectives can be best seen in the following tables. The mix of primary energy sources currently used to generate electricity is presented in Table 2. The table makes patently clear that Spain's primary energy supplies hinge upon oil imports in a proportion that renders energy development practically dependent upon one supplier, OPEC, with the aggravation of the almost intolerable impact on the balance of payments and the uncertainty of prices.

Table 2.   Energy Sources for Spain, 1977

	Demand	Supplied by	
		Domestic Production	Imported
Coal	16.2%	12.6%	3.6%
Oil	66.1	1.4	64.7
Natural gas	1.7	—	1.7
Nuclear energy	2.0	2.0	—
Hydraulic energy	14.0	14.0	—
	100.0%	30.0%	70.0%

Source: NEP

Table 3. International Comparison of Electricity Generating Sources: Spain, EEC, and OECD, 1985-1987

| | SPAIN | | EEC | OECD |
	1976	1987	1985	1985
Coal	22.1%	29.4%	29.2%	31.6%
Oil	43.4	13.3	21.7	17.0
Natural gas	—	—	6.0	8.2
Hydraulic energy	27.0	13.3	8.8	17.0
Nuclear energy	7.5	40.4	34.1	26.0
Other sources	—	3.6	—	0.2
	100.0%	100.0%	100.0%	100.0%

Source: NEP

In an attempt to restore the current imbalances, the NEP proposes the transition from an oil-based to a nuclear-energy-based electricity-generation system in ten years. Table 3 exhibits the structure of this transition and how Spain would compare at the end of the NEP with the rest of the EEC and OECD countries.

Nuclear Power Policies

Nuclear energy has long been viewed as a viable alternative for the Spanish situation and probably the only one able to repair the imbalance in terms of costs, though perhaps not in terms of foreign dependency. In point of fact, it was in 1968 when the first nuclear generating plant went into operation. There are presently three plants in operation, and four others are being built and are expected to be in operation within two or three years, with a total nominal capacity of 6.555 MW. The nationalized firms participate in some of these projects, but the bulk of the investment is being made by the private ones.

From the standpoint of the balance of payments, nuclear energy appears to have an advantage over other sources of energy. Table 4 shows the estimate of the proportion of Spanish inputs in the construction, maintenance, and running of a generating plant. As a result, the proportion of production costs that would have to be paid in foreign currency for different types of generating plants differs widely for each type: 26 percent for nuclear, 56 percent for imported coal, and 66 percent for oil.

Besides the aspects already analyzed, it seems that the example set by a variety of countries who have "gone nuclear," together with the lack of national energy

Table 4.   Structure of National Inputs in Different Types of Electric Plants, 1977

	Type of Plant		
Inputs	Nuclear	Imported Coal	Oil
Capital investment	80%	85%	85%
Maintenance	90%	90%	90%
Fuel	45%	10%	5%

Source: NEP

resources, has led NEP also to adopt the nuclear power alternative. It requires, however, a far greater capital investment than would be needed for conventional thermoelectric plants. The cost structure for the different types of power plants can be seen in Table 5.

Table 5.   Costs of Electricity in Different Generating Plants (at 6000 hours per annum production) in Pesetas per Kilowatt-Hour, 1977

	Type of Plant		
Type of Cost	Nuclear	Coal	Oil
Capital investment	1.70	1.08	0.98
Maintenance	0.10	0.14	0.08
Fuel	0.34	1.30	1.58
Total	2.13	2.52	2.64

Source: NEP
Note: It is readily apparent from the table that the considerable increase in financial burden would have to be supported by those firms currently involved in nuclear projects.

Attitude toward Private Utilities

Up to the restoration of the monarchy in Spain and the legalization of political parties of all persuasions, the status quo was one of control by the administration, with certain competition among utilities expressed in terms of market share; a recurrent lag in tariff setting (oil prices and inflation did not become important until 1973); and a marked advantage to public firms. However, in two successive national elections, political views were expressed for the need for more control by the administration, and even nationalization of the electric industry. As a result, even the winning party, Unión de Centro Democrático, not in favor of nationalization, has produced an NEP that reinforces greatly the control by the administration of all aspects that were controlled earlier, and introduces some more. The tone of the plan is greatly interventionist, as some excerpts will prove.

"Among the most salient aspects of our energy situation we have:
. . . firm fragmentation and lack of Administrative coordination. Overcapacity in almost all energy transformation fields." [5, p. 8]

In order to remedy the first point, the government will implement the optimum national utilization of electric energy (high voltage) through the Repartidor Central de Cargas (RECA), a central dispatching board. RECA is a technical department of UNESA, under the control of the Ministry of Industry. RECA defines programs for the optimum transfer of electricity between the different networks, controls its security, and acts as a clearing house for the accounts generated by the transfers of electricity. There are possible conflicts between RECA's rationality and the needs of a particular utility. In case of a conflict, RECA will have the deciding voice.

With respect to over capacity, NEP points out that the nuclear authorizations have been issued in excess of the needs currently foreseen (1979) for electric demand in the four years to come. Hence, "It is deemed necessary to increase the public participation in the future generation of nuclear energy. This will be considered in programming the new plants which will have to be authorized." [5, p. 90]

This interventionist tone coincides with the lack of concern for the basic financial variables that determine the ability of private firms to finance their expansion. For instance, when discussing their approximate financial needs, NEP considers as sources of funds self-financing, new stock issues, bonds, and loans. For self-financing, composed of retained earnings and depreciation, the plan sets out four financing scenarios, depending only on different depreciation policies. Considerations or even mention of the link between dividend policy, new issues, and stock prices, or of the relationship between tariffs and profitability, are completely missing in the text.

INVESTMENT AND FINANCIAL STRATEGY

Investment Needs

The total investment needs for the electric industry in the revised NEP projections are set at about 390 billion (constant 1977) pesetas for the 1978–1981 period, about two-thirds of which is required for production and one-third for distribution. Investment in nuclear power plants is the largest single item in this projection. In fact, the plan establishes a rigorous order of priority for new plants: hydroelectric, coal, and nuclear. Oil plants are authorized only for the Islands. Therefore, for any given company willing and able to keep pace with the growth in demand, the peculiar resources of its geographical area may force it to invest in a nuclear power plant if other sources are unavailable.

As seen in Table 4, the relationship of capital investment to total costs is much larger for nuclear power plants than for other types. Any one single power plant project of such importance will certainly increase in great amounts both sides of the firm's balance sheet. To illustrate this point, let us take a private firm—FECSA, third in the ranking—as an example [3]. FECSA is currently constructing a nuclear power plant that is expected to go into operation in two phases between 1980 and 1981. The accumulated capital investment not yet in operation runs to 64.3 percent of all the rest of their facilities in operation; 84.4 percent of these works in progress correspond to the nuclear power plant. This means that we are talking about a single project that represents 54 percent of the firm's total capital investment. The magnitude of the outlay may clearly pose some serious financial strain for the utilities.

Financial Resources

Reinvested Earnings and Dividend Policy. This has been a negligible source of funds for the electric industry. In other words, payout policy has been close to 100 percent. Such dividend policy is due to the legal borrowing constraints set by the Ley de Sociedades Anónimas (Limited or Incorporated Firms' Act), Articles 111 and 114, which provide that fully paid capital stock should always be larger than all outstanding unsecured bonds. No amount of reinvested earnings could therefore increase the firm's capacity to absorb unsecured debt.

New Stock Issues. New stock issues provided management with needed funds and debt capacity, but they also created an interest in the Bolsa (stock exchange) since these issues used to be sold at par. The Spanish law prescribes, in all cases, the preferential right of current shareholders to subscribe the issue. Since market price was nearly always above par, there was a substantial value attached to the subscription rights. Many Spanish investors did believe—and still do—that the rate of return on Bolsa investment was obtained by adding up dividends and rights sold. This confused view, adding real return on investment with partial liquidation of shareholdings, had permeated the thinking of many investors in Spain and somehow favored the financial strategy of such firms as electric utilities, which are dependent on new issues for their expansion.

This behavior can only be explained by assuming extremely short-sighted investors interested only in short-run profits and liquidity. The reasons most often hypothesized to account for this investors' choice have been inflation, lack of investors' sophistication, and alternative investment opportunities outside of the stock market (property, for instance).

Whatever the situation might have been in the past, nowadays there are many situations that have put severe constraints on the financing ability of some electric firms. The oil crisis has triggered an increase in energy costs, which, in Spain, has not all been included in the tariffs. Also, double-digit inflation has increased operating costs. The higher capital intensity of the new nuclear power plant makes the cost of depreciation relatively more important. As there have been both an inflation and devaluation of the Spanish peseta, the replacement cost of fixed investment has been increased.

In fact, the Spanish Bolsa's perception of the electric utilities' problems is so acute that the stock price is currently much below par. In part, we have analyzed some factors that may explain such a low price. Also, the fear of the uncertain valuation process resulting from the announced nationalization of the industry had the opposition won in the March 1979 elections may have caused the current price level. The utilities' management is currently in a situation in which it cannot offer any subscription "rights" return to Spanish shareholders, and hence it is in a difficult position to justify the attractiveness of the investment based only on dividend yield. Even for this to be possible, it is necessary to obtain profits. But, as explained before, these are difficult to obtain if no tariff increase is approved. Fortunately for the utilities, they have large capital assets and almost free depreciation policies. It is not inconceivable that, for some utilities, the only possibility of showing profits stems from a "variable" depreciation policy. In fact, it appears that some utilities, not only electric, have been compelled (with the apparent tolerance of the authorities) to build their income statement from bottom to top in order to make sure that, by paying dividends, they will be able to issue new stock and borrow additional unsecured debt, and so finance their new investments.

Long-Term Debt

Spanish Sources. The other usual Spanish sources of funds for electric utilities have been the bond issues, always in preferential terms, subscribed by savings banks, under the direct orders of the Spanish government. We have seen, in the first section, how under Acción Concertada similar financial facilities were promised. However, it is more difficult at present for electric utilities to obtain such funds because of two circumstances: (1) greater difficulties in placing new issues in the market, and (2) the fact that Acción Concertada refers only to one part of their financing needs. Since 1977 there has been a modest liberation of the Spanish financial system. One of the results is that savings banks have much more autonomy in placing their funds, and electric firms have to compete on equal basis with other borrowers. Hence it is now more difficult for utilities to obtain these funds.

Foreign Sources. For any, or both, of the reasons mentioned above, and since Spanish sources are difficult to tap, electric firms have had increasing access to Euro- and other foreign markets. In fact, even if Spanish sources could have been easily obtained, national savings would have probably fallen short of the total investment funds required for the NEP. From a national viewpoint, therefore, it was probably necessary to borrow abroad. From a company point of view, since Euro- or other loans are not bonds, they are not subject to the leverage constraints as expressed in the Spanish law.

However, some limitations have recently been placed by the Spanish authorities on such funds. The conversion of foreign loans was a source of monetary growth, and the objectives set out by the Bank of Spain could not be met if some limitations on this source of money creation were not established. As a result, since a few months ago, 25 percent of the proceeds from new foreign loans have had to be immobilized, at no interest, in the Bank of Spain. Thus the interest cost on foreign loans is greatly increased. This, and more severe limitations on the authorizations to borrow, has greatly reduced the availability of foreign funds.

In summary, the financing sources available for electric utilities are increasingly difficult to obtain: new stock issues because of a depressed market price; Spanish debt because it has to be paid at competitive rates and, given current utilities' profit, the leverage effect might turn out to be unfavorable to the shareholders; and, finally, foreign loans are also temporarily restricted and more expensive.

Although these financial constraints are applicable to both private and public electric utilities, public firms have consistently enjoyed preferential credits and better state guarantees.

Competition between Public and Private Utilities. As an illustration of the marked difference in the ability to compete for funds, we will compare the two largest utilities operating in Catalonia: FECSA, privately owned, and ENHER, with an 80 percent participation of Instituto Nacional de Industria (INI), an autonomous government agency.

Based on the latest public information available, the financial structure of both companies can be seen in Table 6. Observe several interesting aspects:

- Both utilities have a similar financial structure at the beginning, but FECSA's degrades more than ENHER's at the end of the period.
- Both have an increased levered position, due to the new borrowings necessary for the nuclear investment effort and the cost-tariff lag.
- The average financial structure for the period is roughly equal to 50/50 for both ENHER and FECSA. However, ENHER has, on average, half of its debt advanced by INI outside of market conditions. In fact, this is a quasi-equity financing.[3] It can be either repaid or converted into shares. The interest rate of INI's facility is not known. Certainly, if positive in real terms, it would be lower than that for FECSA's loans.

Table 6 shows a practical example of the competitive ability of two electric utilities in Catalonia. Obviously, ENHER has the advantage of 20 percent of its liabilities being, in fact, "free" equity. For the other borrowings, in Spain and outside, ENHER will certainly be favored by the "improved" financial structure as a normal firm and also by the lender's knowledge of its relationships to INI. In Spain this situation holds because saving banks would probably be forced by the administration to subscribe more cheap loans to ENHER than to FECSA. In the Euro- and foreign markets, it occurs because a risk-avoiding lender would rather invest in a quasi-state guarantee than in a private firm. Hence in its foreign financing operations also, ENHER can obtain better spread over LIBOR and other conditions than can FECSA.[4]

Table 6. Comparison of Permanent Funds Financial Structures (in percent): Public versus Private Electric Utilities, 1974-1978 (F = FECSA; E = ENHER)

Source of Funds	1974 F	1974 E	1975 F	1975 E	1976 F	1976 E	1977 F	1977 E	1978 F	1978 E
Equity	53	53	59	52	54	51	45	49	41	49
Long-term debt	47	(19)	41	(24)	46	(27)	55	(32)	59	(32)
Market		(28)		(24)		(22)		(19)		(19)
INI		47		48		49		51		51
Total	100	100	100	100	100	100	100	100	100	100

Source: Banco de Bilbao [1]

Private Utilities' Investment Strategy

Private utilities are given a very narrow scope for action, since the administration has the following controls over the utilities:

- Authorization for any new plant or transmission system
- Authorization for any modification of plants or transmission systems
- Tariffs
- Authorization to decide as to whether electric bonds would be able to benefit from subsidized rates

Besides, there exists an uncertainty about the administration's criteria in tariff setting and its implementation. The severe difficulties encountered in raising funds, coupled with the huge capital outlays involved in the construction of nuclear-powered plants, are not easily digested by the traditional rules of financial management. Yet private utilities are still investing heavily, even when the stock market seems to discount these uncertainties, difficulties, and constraints, rendering the market value well below a hypothetical liquidation value.

Some reasons may be hypothesized to account for this behavior, which apparently does not seem to conform with an orthodox one.

Given the controls mentioned above, the only effective variable that a firm could use to compete (not to extremes) was market share. By applying earlier for new plant or transmission authorizations than their competitors, and long before the consumer needs were felt—an inescapable characteristic of the industry—a firm might be able to serve the new consumers faster and better than their competitors when the demand arose, thus gaining market share. In spite of controls by the administration, and a gentleman's agreement among the different utilities, it seems that certain competition for market share was established. If all firms within one area wanted to keep their market share (this applies, obviously, to those areas, such as Catalonia, where more than one utility operate), all of them would follow an investment strategy of anticipating demand, thus having extra capacity to meet its upsurge. This type of policy was probably the only one on which utilities had some freedom. Since plants have always been rather capital-intensive, the cost of capital would be a critical element in competitive advantage: Those firms having access to cheap (or cheaper) funds would have an edge over their competitors. Private firms cannot allow the market share to decrease in a market growing at an annual rate of 4 percent. If they did allow the public utilities to increase their market share at this stage, they would be "nationalized" in a subtle way by being shifted out of the market in the long run.

Some Recommendations on Tariff Setting

Although the regulatory proceedings are always complex and difficult, as the experience in the United States shows, the Spanish utilities and administration would probably benefit by more clarification of the rules of the game, as is done in the United States. Not only are there many works written on the economics of tariff setting and regulation [9], but there is also a clear procedure for establishing tariffs, a checklist of items that will determine the final outcome. Following a recent article [7] on this topic, it would appear that the main items (about which, nevertheless, there is frequent disagreement between commissions, experts, and judges) are:

- The rate of return on debt
- The "just and reasonable" rate of return on equity holdings
- The appropriate proportions of debt and equity, or financial structure
- The appropriate level of the capital base (what is to be included, during which period, and at which value—historic or "fair")
- The level of operating expenses
- The "sales mix" that will generate a given level of total revenue and the setting of a schedule of rates for each type of service offered by the utility

Together with these financial points, there are clear procedures as to when, how, and in front of which entity revision or complaints may be filed.

Comparing Spanish to U.S. practice, we can see that, first, there is not as much expertise in Spain on this issue of marginal pricing; hence, from a pure economic viewpoint, tariffs could be improved and, probably, use of electricity would correspond more to its real cost. Most importantly, from the utilities' viewpoint there is a lack of financial theory and expertise implicit in the administration's tariff setting. In the United States, there is a clear priority in the reasoning leading to the establishment of a tariff: a fair remuneration of the funds' suppliers by setting tariffs that include such remuneration. In Spain, the rules of tariff setting seem to follow a different path, which is not clearly founded on any financial theory. Labor and financial (only of debt) costs and depreciation are added up and divided by "standard volume." The rate of return on shareholders' investment will really be of "residual" nature under these circumstances.

CONCLUSIONS

We are ready now to summarize the various elements we have discussed so far, restate our thesis, and comment on possible future scenarios.

The investment decisions of the electric utility industry in Spain patently cannot be motivated by the same goals that are implicit in the usual textbook framework. Initial investment is prescribed by the controlling authorities, if and when it is allowed; the return on it will depend on tariff revisions, which are uncertain and which do not seem to include in their procedures an established "just and reasonable" rate of return to shareholders. Financing possibilities, always tipped in favor of public firms, are constrained, by law, for unsecured bonds. Those sources that may increase the firm's total financing capacity—new stock issues and national or foreign loans—are now more difficult and expensive to obtain, either because of market forces—Bolsa stock prices and liberation of the Spanish financial system—or by administrative dispositions, such as the ceiling on foreign borrowings and "free" deposits in the Bank of Spain as a percentage of those authorized.

Not only is the prospective equity profitability of an investment uncertain, given the low return on assets and high financing costs, but even the *possibility* of new authorizations for private nuclear power plants, as NEP remarks, is seriously jeopardized. Thus the strategy of private electric utilities may well have changed from the past one of ensuring a given market share hoping to recoup their investment through future tariffs, in times when a lag of this type was the only important danger for their future, to the present one of "staying private" when the Spanish administration has almost nationalized the industry, *de facto*. The choice seems difficult for private utilities: If they want to stay in business, they have to follow the demand, in spite of all the previous and current difficulties. Should they get discouraged and abandon their investment plans, the administration would have no choice but to actually take over the market. There is also a high probability that under such circumstances, public opinion would favor an outright nationalization of the industry. By keeping active in the market, going on as usual, even if their margin for maneuver is almost nil, utilities may avoid the risk of favoring nationalization. Because the process of valuing the utilities' shares is full of uncertainties and is likely to prove very costly to shareholders (Bolsa stock prices are now at their lowest level ever), a wealth-maximizing behavior would rather favor the present policy of *fuite en avant,* for an investment of random (low) profitability is certainly better than an expropriatory payment at very low prices.

The private Spanish utilities' situation is a dramatic example of the power of the state in redistributing wealth in an arbitrary fashion at all levels of the energy field: consumer and industrial prices; rates of return on public and private investment; and direct and indirect subsidy from one social group to another. We have explained the impact of such arbitrariness on investment decisions in the industry, and there could be many considerations made on the issues of fairness and economic efficiency, but this is not our topic.

In conclusion, we will limit ourselves to emphasizing the very special rationality of the utilities' management under such circumstances. Perhaps they expect that the government will favor a more rational allocation of resources based on market prices (as has happened recently in France) and hence will produce a new environment where a more satisfactory return on investment can be obtained. This is to be expected if the interventionist philosophy of the Spanish government is changed in the future, or if more sophisticated procedures—such as those applied in the United States for utility rate setting—are someday introduced in Spain.

Finally, we would like to emphasize the analytical richness of the particular Spanish situation. Given the "stay private" objective we have described, there needs to be a holistic view of the investment process as regards the "maximization of the firms' value." Investment, financing, and dividend decisions are intimately connected. We believe that this is a particularly suitable example of the need to go beyond traditional capital budgeting techniques and procedures if we want to maintain the relevance and usefulness of our teaching and research.

NOTES

1. This heavy subsidization provides one more element for an exercise in cost-benefit analysis of the state's discretionary intervention in the economy. The Spanish government has opted for industrialization by, among other things, subsidizing both capital (through an extreme control of the financial system) and energy, as presently discussed. Together with a few good results, some claim that Spain has not combined its factors of production optimally, or even sensibly. By subsidizing capital, labor-intensive processes have been disfavored in a country endowed with plenty of labor. Furthermore, most of the industrial exports (steel, ships, cement), are doubly subsidized since they are both capital- and energy-intensive. As a result, when most countries in the present critical times try to save energy and export labor embodied in competitive products, Spain is instead exporting embodied capital and oil-produced energy, both heavily subsidized. These exports are not favorable for a long-term growth of the Spanish economy in the present condition, and the NEP itself [5, p. 33] wonders about the wisdom of such policies.

2. Those benefits would consist of (1) a 95 percent exemption from withholding taxes applicable to interest on loans and debentures, equity issues, and imports of capital goods; (2) 7 percent, fixed-rate, fifteen-year concessionary loans from the Spanish government, through the official credit banks, to finance up to 40 percent of the new hydraulic and coal-fired plants; (3) 7 percent investment tax credits for new utility plant investments; (4) bonds issued by electric utilities (at less than market rates) and subscribed by savings banks to comply with the "investment coefficients" required by the Bank of Spain for such institutions; (5) the depreciation of nuclear plants commencing once half of the construction program had been achieved, and upon completion of a nuclear power plant, the possibility of depreciating it in five years.

3. The NEP explicitly includes as new stock issues INI's loans to their utilities.

4. But public firms have also disadvantages vis-à-vis their private competitors: Inflexible

2. To analyze the influence on corporate investment and financial planning from an increasing turbulence in the business environment
3. To make a few comments on future research based on empirical observations

FINANCIAL DEVELOPMENT AND POLICY

Solvency, calculated as the book values of equity plus 50 percent of untaxed reserves disclosed in the balance sheets as a percentage of total capital, has decreased from an average of about 40 percent in 1967 to approximately 20-25 percent in 1978 for Swedish industrial companies. Another way of describing this trend is as a rise in the debt/equity ratio from 1.5 to approximately 4.0-5.0. This ratio is somewhat lower than the average for companies with more than 500 employees and somewhat higher than the average for small companies with 50-100 employees. The development of different rates of return and the D/E ratio is shown in Figure 1 for the companies quoted on the stock exchange (excluding banks and investment companies).

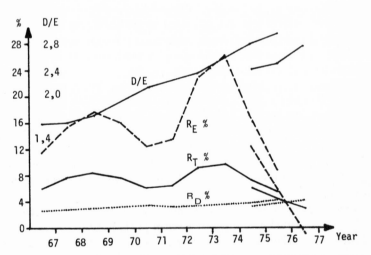

Figure 1. The Relations between Rates of Return and Debt/Equity Ratio for Some Companies Quoted on the Swedish Stock Exchange [25, 1968–1978]

$$R_E = R_T + (R_T - R_D)(D/E), \qquad 1967\text{–}1977$$

Notations: R_E = return on equity, R_T = return on total capital, R_D = average rate of interest on total debts, D/E = debt-equity ratio.

The slight improvement of the D/E ratio occurring in 1975 is attributable to disclosure or approximation of accumulated excess depreciation as untaxed reserves in the balance sheet. This to some extent also affects the rates of return via changes in the amount of the total capital.

External sources of capital have been used to a large extent to provide capital needed for continuously increasing investment in rational production units, stocks, customer credits, research and development, marketing, etc. Since the possibilities of issuing new shares are limited, the most important alternatives remaining are short-term and long-term debts. The leverage effect on R_E had been positive until 1975, but it was zero in 1976 and negative in 1977.

A typical pattern for a single company during the last ten years is a decreasing trend in the operating profit margin with maxima during booms and minima during recessions. This is due partly to sharp price competition both on export markets and domestic markets and partly to an increasing share of fixed costs, especially labor costs, out of the total operating costs. In addition, there have been rising depreciation costs and interest to pay owing to large investment programs financed by external capital. During the last three years, heavy foreign exchange losses have further deteriorated the profit or loss before appropriations and taxes. From aggregated funds-flow analyses (not presented in this report), it appears that the degree of internal financing of the total funds used varies strongly with the general economic situation. It was 78 percent in 1974 and only 50 percent in 1977. Issuing new shares amounts to an insignificant part of the total funds provided (only between 1 and 7 percent). The net increase in long-term debts as a percentage of the total funds provided is low during "good years" and extremely high during recessions, as high as 44 percent in 1971 and 49 percent in 1977. Variations in the need for capital, together with restricting and stimulating credit-policy measures from the government, changes in the official discount rate, and permissions to use international financial markets, have had very strong effects on the corporate propensity to use debts. Structural changes in the domestic credit market in the form of attractive new financial institutions and new forms of financing are also worth mentioning.

From empirical studies of aggregate data [3], detailed analyses of annual report data for individual companies [3, 11], and systematic interviews with company managers [11], some interesting observations may be made. With rising fixed costs—consisting of labor costs, depreciation, and interest—as a proportion of the total costs, R_T becomes very sensitive to even relatively small changes in the sales volume. In combination with rising D/E ratios, the fluctuations from one year to another in R_E could be immense for individual companies. Two examples are presented in Figure 2.

Companies are confronted with great difficulties in determining an optimal capital structure as both the environment and the internal conditions are chang-

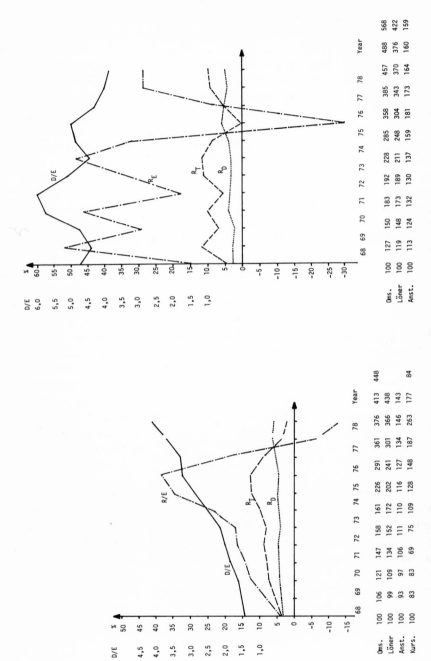

Figure 2. The Relations between Rates of Return and the Debt/Equity Ratio for Two Companies

24

ing. A variable-satisfactory D/E ratio or an acceptable interval often has to be based on more factors than those appearing in theoretical models. Such factors are the risk of being acquired by another company, the risk of losing control over the company if disclosed and hidden reserves are insufficient to cover fixed financial obligations, and unpredictable losses during a long and deep recession. Deviations from a determined long-range corporate financial policy, expressed as a D/E ratio, can of course be allowed for single investment projects because of the size and stability of R_T and for especially attractive financial opportunities concomitant with each project.

The financial risk for lenders is not fully reflected in a rising R_D for borrowers. Assets pledged in the form of mortgages on real estate or general business mortgages result in a stable and proportionately low rate of interest on long-term debts. Guarantees from a solid parent company or the government also keep the rate of interest at a low level. On normal short-term commercial debts and tax credits, usually approximately 50 percent of the sum of untaxed reserves in the balance sheet, there is no interest charge at all. It may of course be included in the prices charged by suppliers. On short-term bank loans, international loans, leasing, etc., the rate of interest varies depending on the financial risk. On the basis of a D/E ratio and a future debt structure, it is possible to estimate an average R_D.

The limited possibilities to determine, in a theoretical sense, an optimal D/E ratio also make it difficult to maximize R_E. Instead, companies try to derive a satisfying R_E before corporate income taxes from normal claims at the stock market. The "shares" of a company must be attractive at the market, and its dividend and expected growth in market value must make both existing and potential new shareholders willing to take part in new share issues. Specific business risks for the company, as well as inflation and economic conditions in general, must be considered when determining the size of R_E. From the formula mentioned in Figure 1, the necessary average rate of return on total capital, R_T, can be derived for a company as a whole. Such a percentage can then be divided into more specific claims on subsidiaries, divisions, markets, products, etc., for use in decentralized budgeting work. This approach can also stimulate a search for new products and customers or initiate strategic actions, such as acquisitions or liquidations. Such behavior is normal in a rapidly changing environment [2].

The course of action described is the opposite of a well-known theoretical approach, where R_T is given, R_D is determined on assumptions of capital investors and their risk preferences, and the goal is to maximize R_E through an optimal capital structure. Theoretical assumptions concerning the influence of the financial environment and the planning process within companies diverge radically from observed practical planning conditions and methods for determining a financial policy. These observations are similar to Donaldson's [8]. He has found "very little evidence that managements have in mind an optimum debt-equity ratio or an optimum dividend payout to generate the maximum earnings leverage on market value. This does not mean that they have no opinions about policies in these areas, where extremes would adversely affect market value" [8, p. 247]. He also states that "financial policy is seen as an evolutionary process of feeling out new positions in a constantly changing world, positions which, it is hoped, will be both safe and successful by whatever yardstick the company sets for itself" [8, p. 249].

CHANGES IN THE FINANCIAL ENVIRONMENT

When explaining the increasing environmental influence on corporate investment and financial planning, it is difficult to express causes and effects more exactly. A gradually decreasing rate of return on total capital leads to a lower degree of internal financing of investments. Corporate and private income taxes discriminate share issues compared to bond issues. Companies have therefore been forced to use external capital to a greater extent for their growth, a favorable way as long as the leverage effect remains positive. Corporate problems have thus changed over time, and so have some external activities for solving the problems. Risk preferences of capital investors and shareholders and their criteria for the evaluation of D/E ratios of companies as a whole, as well as the financing of specific projects, have shifted. New state-owned financial institutes have been started to serve special purposes and to take higher financial risks than commercial banks.

At the same time there have been a rapidly growing public sector and powerful political wishes to obtain control of the allocation of capital in the community. Heavy new taxes on added value and taxes in relation to labor costs have been introduced. A tremendous concentration of capital from companies has also taken place since 1961 in the general pension funds. In the seventies there have been remarkable changes in the financial environment through a very active economic policy, mostly adapted to the current economic situation [20]. To realize such economic-political goals as full employment, rapid economic growth, price stability, balance between regions, and balance in foreign trade, different measures have been used by the government. During the last ten years, a tendency toward less general measures and more selective measures can be observed. This tendency is especially noticeable in employment, credit, and industrial policies. Different measures for the total industry can be assigned to the following groups: general support, special industrial measures, regional policy measures, special measures for small and medium-sized companies, and short-term measures adapted to the current economic situation.

In Figure 3, the structure and duration of some general and selective measures are illustrated from the point of view of their conceivable influence on corporate

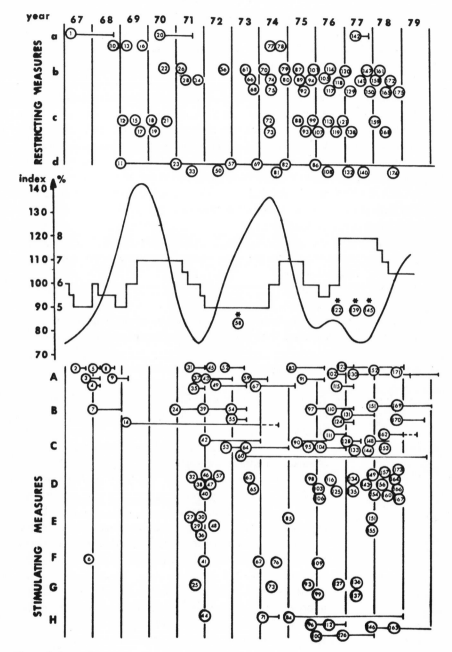

Figure 3. Some Restricting and Stimulating Economic-Political Measures in Sweden, 1967–1978

investment and financial and operative planning (via sales volume, prices, or costs). The measures have been obtained from current economic information from the government [27]. In the center of the figure, there is a continuous curve representing a weighted monthly index of the economic situation for the total industry in Sweden [14]. A discontinuous curve for the official discount rate and marks with an asterisk for devaluations of the Swedish crown represent two general economic measures used. In the upper and lower parts of the figure, a number of restricting and stimulating selective economic measures and their duration are grouped according to their chronology and influence on corporate planning. Measures are marked with circled numbers and sometimes a line showing the duration. The classification method is shown in the appendix to this paper. It is not necessary to know the specific content of each circled measure to see the general structure and to draw conclusions.

Restricting measures include:

(a) Inv. Investment charges and other restrictions on nonpriority investments

(b) Op.   Price regulations; stops, supervisions, duty to announce raises of prices, etc.

(c) Fin. Credit market restrictions, especially on commercial banks

(d) Op.   Raises of direct and indirect taxes and social welfare charges

Stimulating measures include:

(A) Inv.   Releases of investment funds for construction and machinery and for temporary transfers to investments in stocks

(B) Inv.   Special tax deductions and grants for investments, and changes of depreciation rules

(C) Inv/Op. Support to firms with "excess" stocks of semifinished and finished goods, arising from continued production in recessions, to avoid discharges or layoffs of employees who are kept on by firms during recessions; support for export credits; tax deductions for research and development costs

(D) Op.   State grants for industrial orders from central and local governments, contributions to special government investments, grants for new external environmental investments, and improvements of the internal working environment, special measures for crisis industries, etc.

(E) Inv.   Release of additional licenses and other measures for nonpriority building projects

(F) Fin.   Enlarged permission to bond issues for large companies and
                   loan facilities for small and medium-sized companies,
                   including even possibilities to get new equity
(G) Fin.   Release of credit market restrictions for commercial banks
                   and for corporate borrowing in foreign exchanges
(H) Op.   Lowered direct and indirect taxes and social welfare charges

Some interesting observations can be made from Figure 3 and the studies
behind it. Repetition of the same kind of measures can be read horizontally, and
the ingenuity as to new kinds of measures can be read vertically. The total number of measures has increased rapidly since 1971, and the situation seems to be
much more complicated than before. Large doses of both stimulation and restriction are always put into force irrespective of the economic situation. Perhaps the
Swedish government created a "homemade" artificial boom in 1976 through the
extensive use of stimulation measures.

Another interesting observation is that many temporary supporting measures,
such as the release of investment funds within companies, seem to be prolonged
and made almost permanent, with the exception of short interruptions.

The government tried to neutralize the serious recession in 1971-1972 with
new direct measures aimed at investments and operative activities (the groups C,
D, and E) instead of indirect stimulations through the credit market. During the
boom in 1973-1974, price regulation and credit-market regulation were frequently used. This continued through 1975-1978, when several kinds of measures were introduced to stimulate investments and to avoid discharges or layoffs
of employees. Full employment is probably considered to be a more important
goal in Sweden than in many other countries. Instead, inflation has been per-
mitted to rise. During 1976-1978 changes in the official discount rate were
highly influenced by the effects of a sharp rise in foreign financing by the government, local governments, and companies. Three devaluations of the Swedish
crown took place within a year to stimulate export efforts and to solve some of
the problems concerning the balance of payments. This was an important deviation from the previous policy.

CONSEQUENCES FOR CORPORATE PLANNING

Many measures taken by the government are based on aggregate information for
the industrial sector as a whole. The situation for branches and individual companies may differ greatly from the economic situation on average, owing to their
phases (early or late) in booms and recessions, degree of diversification or spe-
cialization, degree of internationalization, size, or planning horizon. In heavy

industry, the time requested for planning and building new capacity is often longer than in light industry. The former does not have the same opportunity to react in the short run and to change its planning to get the benefit of stimulating economic measures.

Certain measures have only indirect effects on industrial companies. Decisions made by banks, local governments, and customers, for example, may result in refusal of loan applications or rejected orders. Other measures have direct effects on companies, and their consequences, as well as normal business planning, must be considered. The profitability of forcing investment projects in order to benefit from temporary stimulating measures must be compared to additional investment costs and the subsequent costs of excess capacity. The attractiveness of support for excess stocks and keeping on unneeded employees must be assessed relative to the possibilities of selling out the excess stocks later on. There are disadvantages like risks for obsolescence or destruction of goods and pressures for price reductions from customers who are well informed of the situation, as well as advantages like more economic lot sizes for production runs and good delivery capacity.

In the manner described above, many stimulating measures are accompanied by claims for services in return from the companies. Investments have to be made within specific periods or allocated to certain regions. Employees have to be kept on and companies in crisis have to promise a temporary continuation of their activities in order to benefit from very attractive tax deductions and financial support.

In the long run, there seems to be a risk that normal planning processes in companies are disturbed by the increasing number of various measures. Companies may be more interested in using the economic-political measures effectively than in reaching real efficiency in their commercial markets. Temporary "homemade" booms, such as the one in 1976, can serve as evidence of such a policy. On the other side, there is the risk that companies who have been accustomed to prolongations and improvements of the announced measures do not want to invest in early stages of recessions. Instead, they wait for still more favorable measures from a more and more generous government, and the effects of the measures become insignificant. There is a risk, too, that normal competition between companies can be distorted. The price regulations, in particular, have been heavily criticized by managers and the Federation of Swedish Industries and considered as a threat against legal security [24]. Furthermore, companies in crisis, saved from bankruptcy, and regions and branches with heavy special support may reach better positions than those without any support at all. The governmental interference in corporate planning can restrain companies from necessary adaptation to changes in environmental commercial markets. There is also the risk that the industrial structure will be preserved.

The real effects on corporate planning of some credit policy measures taken in 1969 and 1970 have been analyzed in a survey [10]. Owing to these measures, small and medium-sized companies seem to change their investment planning to a greater extent than do large companies. There is, however, much work to be done in evaluating the real effects of the economic-political measures, especially price regulation [13].

FINANCIAL RESEARCH FROM A MANAGER'S POINT OF VIEW

Each decade has its own stimulating, purely theoretical advances and intensive debates on investment and financial questions. It is worth mentioning the research on the existence of an optimal capital structure following Modigliani and Miller's famous article in 1958. Other research deals with the theory of portfolio selection, equity valuation models, the use of mathematical programming methods in capital budgeting, the development of corporate planning models [12, 28], and the penetrating studies of the planning process related to organization theory [1, 4, 5, 8].

There is a noticeable time delay between the appearance of many theoretical research results and their practical application in corporate planning. Such a delay is necessary in the transfer of knowledge, as this process takes a long time. The results must be worked at and adapted to current and specific situations for each user. Corporate planning and decision making must, however, be carried out in a permanently turbulent environment. This turbulence appears in various commercial markets, as well as in domestic and international credit markets, as a result of increasing interest from both national governments and international unions to get involved in corporate planning processes and to obtain control of economic activities. These problems might give rise to very interesting research work in the 1980s.

When developing theories and building models, it is often necessary to make abstractions and to introduce restrictive assumptions in order to use certain research methods and techniques. To test hypotheses and reach a high degree of generalization, statistical techniques are often used. In such tests quantitative information on various security market values, as well as annual reports, is preferred to internal information. This procedure has been questioned by Keenan [17]. Internal studies of investment and financial planning and decision making have also pointed out the importance of such factors as environment, structural context, impetus, commitment, "early warning" information systems, and financial mobility [4, 8]. When only market values and other kinds of external information on companies are used, all companies not quoted on stock or bond markets are excluded, and much information is lost.

Remarkable differences can be observed between theoretical assumptions and practical conditions for planning and decision making. There are a growing number of imperfections in all markets because of contracts, negotiations, agreements, and obligations with an enlarged number of business partners. Investment and financing alternatives are not always well defined, and their future consequences cannot be predicted for more than a few years. For large investment projects, such as acquisitions of other companies or investment in new factories, it is often impossible to separate the financing from the investment decision. They have to be solved simultaneously. The approval of loan proposals, the possibilities of issuing new shares, or the promises of loan guarantees from the government can be necessary conditions for carrying through large investment projects. Only for small, single investment projects can one avoid direct confrontation between investment and financing decisions and assume that the cost of capital problem is solved [19, p. 212].

What can be expected from the future? A short-term outlook can be made mainly from the horizon of Swedish companies [11]. Some recent articles in journals confirm these impressions [7, 9]. There will be continued rapid changes in the environment with great changes of ideologies, international relations, etc. For a small and highly industrialized country like Sweden, it is worth mentioning the rising competition from less-developed countries with rapidly growing industrialization. A high degree of internationalization and an extensive use of the international credit market make Swedish companies dependent on future fluctuations of the rates of foreign exchange. A further decrease in the rate of return on total capital will cause severe financing problems. For some years now there have been discussions on the creation of worker's funds with the control centralized to labor unions in order to increase their influence on corporate decision making. This is considered partly as a financing question, partly as a question of power and democracy.

What international research problems can be interesting for the future? At the aggregate level it would be interesting to compare the measures used in different countries to attract new industries. In Northern Ireland, for example, the British government offers many economic supports, tax deductions, advantageous depreciations rules, low rents for land, premises, etc. Such advantages are unique for industrialized countries and very difficult to compete with. Many Swedish companies have therefore located new factories in Northern Ireland. Another interesting subject is the total real effects on corporate investment and financial-policy decisions of measures used within countries to reach certain economic-political goals. Is there an unsolvable goal conflict between the government and the commercial and economic life in a "mixed" economy, such as the Swedish one? It would be of great interest to analyze in detail how the increasing number of governmental measures has affected real planning and decisions at the corporate level [10]. The increased size of companies due to acquisitions and mergers has been followed by decentralized decision making, except for investment and financing decisions. How is it possible to control and optimize these decisions from headquarters in more and more imperfect markets? Is there not a problem of information in multinational companies when it is difficult to be well informed about the environment in one country? It would also be interesting to analyze the difference in planning and decision making between growing and profitable companies, on the one hand, and unprofitable companies and companies in crisis, on the other. What is the situation in companies that are forced to liquidate? Is there a noticeable difference in the planning behavior or in the quality of the planning models? What improvements can be made?

CONCLUSIONS

The well-known formula for analyzing the effects of various debt/equity ratios on the rate of return on equity has been applied to annual report data from several companies quoted on the Swedish stock exchange. A few selected industrial companies have been scrutinized more carefully by means of internal interviews concerning their investment and financial behavior. Attention has been focused on changes in the financial environment and especially on the influence of governmental economic-political measures on corporate planning and decision making.

Over a period of ten years the debt/equity ratio has risen from 1.5 to approximately 4.0-5.0. The tendency toward higher fixed costs as a proportion of the total operating costs and rising depreciation and interest costs make the rate of return on total capital very sensitive to even small changes in the sales volume. In combination with high debt/equity ratios, these circumstances cause large fluctuations in the rate of return on equity. This is a serious problem for future planning. The financial development noticed is conditioned by general circumstances in various commercial markets and by an increasing interest from the government to control economic activities. Some restricting and stimulating measures, mostly directed to the industrial sector, have been classified as to their conceivable influence on corporate investment and financial and operative planning.

The real effects of the measures on corporate planning have been discussed. Measures seem to be accepted by companies up to a certain degree, but after having reached a situation like the Swedish one in 1975-1978, the role of many measures can be seriously questioned. Excessive government use of these measures and a very complicated pattern of all kinds of temporary measures are probably more disturbing than valuable for corporate planning. The real effects are limited and very difficult to measure afterward, even at an aggregate level.

The situation described is not unique for Swedish companies. Therefore some comments have been made as to interesting future research questions from a manager's point of view. There is a noticeable time delay between the appearance of many theoretical research results and their practical application. There are also great differences between theoretical assumptions and practical planning conditions. It would probably be fruitful to complete the purely theoretical research with more empirical information and to generate hypotheses from some observations made within companies.

APPENDIX TO FIGURE 3:
THE CLASSIFICATION METHOD

General or Selective Measures. This rough classification was originally derived by two Swedish economists, Lundberg and Wibble [22]. The first criterion was formal prescriptions or stipulations to use measures. Owing to this criterion, only changes of foreign exchange rates (devaluations or revaluations of the Swedish crown), changes of the official discount rate, and general corporate income taxes were looked upon as general measures. All kinds of regulations, special taxes, tax deductions, grants, special financial support, etc., were assigned to selective measures.

Industrial Measures as Stimulating or Restricting. In the next step, the study was limited to industrial measures only (not personal or private). As second and third criteria, I used the aim and the intended effects of measures to classify them as stimulating or restricting. All price regulations were regarded as restricting measures because they constitute a very serious interference in corporate planning. They are, of course, advantageous for companies buying other industrial products subject to price freezes.

Investment, Financing, and Operative Measures. This classification was made because of the effects of measures on various parts of a firm's long-range planning or short-term operative activities. Comments have been made under (a)-(c) and (A)-(H) in the text.

Financial support or other kinds of financial incentives are often used to stimulate investment activities. Under stimulating investment measures, I have, however, tried to distinguish between (A) release of investment funds (where appropriations to such funds had to be done during previous years from companies' income before appropriations and income taxes), (B) special tax deductions and grants for investments, (C) support for "excess" stocks, and (D) release of licenses and other measures for nonpriority building projects.

Identification and Information on Measures. The next step was to identify the measures and to gather information on them from the government and all departments and institutions involved in the realization of economic-political goals. In the beginning, this was a real problem for me and even for managers, especially those in small and medium-sized companies. We now have in Sweden a yearly special *Handbook of Support* [15], edited by the Federation of Swedish Industries. Such a catalog makes it somewhat easier to handle the problem. We also have a very good economic diary in *The Swedish Economy, Preliminary National Budget* [27].

Classification of Measures according to the Criteria. Each measure identified was then classified according to the criteria mentioned in the first three steps above. They were also visualized chronologically in Figure 3, together with an index of the economic situation. Very good indices for the whole Swedish industry or special branches are available in a quarterly journal, *Konjunkturbarometern* from the National Institute of Economic Research [18], or from surveys from several Swedish commercial banks [14, 25]. In Figure 3, I have used a business indicator where full capacity utilization and labor shortages are weighted against each other.

My intention was to illustrate the increasing turbulence in the environment when a government tries to fulfill all its economic-political goals, smooth out booms and recessions, and control business activities. Sometimes I had (and I still have) difficulties in interpreting the aim and intended effects of some measures.

Identification or Measurement of Real Effects. The last phase was to identify (eventually to measure) at various levels the real effects of the economic-political measures taken. This is a problem, since the effects of many single measures are interlaced with each other and with the effects of normal changes in corporate planning and operating activities. Statistics and other information may be used at the following levels:

1. The whole industry—indices of business activities, employment or unemployment figures, changes in the balance of payments, nominal tax rates compared to real tax rates after deductions, etc.
2. Special branches, small, medium-sized, and large firms—indices of business activities, the need for and the use of support, profitability figures, etc.
3. Regions—number of companies started or liquidated within the region or moved to the region, unemployment figures, etc.
4. Special measures—special studies of support to firms with "excess" stocks and support for training of employees under notice of layoff who are kept on by firms

5. Groups of companies or individual companies—analyses of their annual reports concerning profitability, investments and financial development, use of investment funds, the total amount of tax deductions, etc.
6. Specific projects—interviews concerning investment and financial calculations and decisions, the real effects of stimulating and restricting measures on decisions to accelerate or postpone investments, etc.
7. Operating level—changes of plans, building up of "excess" stocks instead of the laying off of employees, etc.

The government has initiated several investigations at the first four levels, often using extensive questionnaires with large samples of firms [6, 10, 26]. Even in other reports, measurements are made at these levels [13, 23]. I have made studies [11] at the last three levels in order to get supplementary information on planning behavior within firms (see also [24]).

REFERENCES

[1] Aharoni. Y. *The Foreign Investment Decision Process*. Boston: Harvard University, 1966.
[2] Ansoff, I. *Strategic Management*. London: Macmillan Publishing Company, 1978.
[3] Bertmar, L., and Molin, G. *Capital Growth, Capital Structure and Rates of Return—An Analysis of Swedish Industrial Companies* (in Swedish). Stockholm: Ekonomiska Forskningsinstitutet, 1977.
[4] Bower, J.L. *Managing the Resource Allocation Process: A Study of Corporate Planning and Investment*. Homewood, Ill.: Richard D. Irwin, 1972.
[5] Bower, J.L. "Planning within the Firm," *American Economic Review* 60, No. 2 (May 1970), pp. 186–194.
[6] *Cooperation for Regional Development* (in Swedish). Statens Offentliga Utredningar SOU, 1974:82.
[7] van Dam, A. "The Business Environment in the 1980s," *Long Range Planning* 10 (August 1977), pp. 8–12.
[8] Donaldson, G. *Strategy for Financial Mobility*. Boston: Harvard University, Graduate School of Business Administration, 1969.
[9] Edwards, J.P., and Harris, D.J. "Planning in a State of Turbulence," *Long Range Planning* 10 (June 1977), pp. 43–49.
[10] *Effects of Credit Policy—Swedish Survey Evidence 1969-1971*. Stockholm: Konjunkturinstitutet, 1973.
[11] Gandemo, B. *Corporate Finance—Results of Empirical Studies Compared to Theoretical Models and Changes in the Environment* (in Swedish). Skövde: Norstedts, 1976.
[12] Gershefski, G.W. *The Development and Application of a Corporate Financial Model*. Oxford, Ohio: Planning Executives Institute, 1968.

[13] Göransson, L. *Price Monitoring and Price Controls in Sweden.* Stockholm: National Swedish Price and Cartel Office, 1979.

[14] Götabanken Economic Survey, Gothenburg.

[15] *Handbook of Support 1977-78, A Review of Governmental Support to Industrial Companies* (in Swedish). Stockholm: Federation of Swedish Industries, 1977.

[16] Jönsson, S. "New Approaches in the Study of Corporate Investment Behaviour" (in Swedish), *Erhervsøkonomisk Tidskrift* (Denmark) 38 (1974), pp. 13-26.

[17] Keenan, M. "Models of Equity Valuation: The Great Serm Bubble," *Journal of Finance* 25, No. 2 (1970), pp. 243-273.

[18] *Konjunkturbarometern* (A quarterly journal with a summary in English). National Institute of Economic Research, Stockholm.

[19] Levy, H., and Sarnat, M. *Capital Investment and Financial Decisions.* London: Prentice-Hall International, 1978.

[20] Lindbeck, A. "Stabilization Policy in Open Economics with Endogenous Politicians," *American Economic Review, Papers and Proceedings* 66, No. 2 (May 1976), pp. 1-18.

[21] Lister, R.J. "Business Finance – An Evolving Field of Study," *Journal of Business Finance & Accounting* 5, No. 1 (1978), pp. 1-26.

[22] Lundberg, E., and Wibble, A. "New-Mercantilism and Selective Economic Policy" (in Swedish). In *Ekonomisk politik i förvandling.* Stockholm: SNS, 1970.

[23] Praski, S. "Experiences of the Support of Stocks" (in Swedish), *Ekonomisk Debatt* 5, No. 4 (1977), pp. 229-237.

[24] *Price Regulations – A Threat against the Legal Security – Interviews with 8 Managers* (in Swedish). Stockholm: Federation of Swedish Industries, 1978.

[25] *Skandinaviska Enskilda Banken* (quarterly review), 1968-1978.

[26] "Stock Support I – Preliminary Views on the Design of Support to Stock-Building in Industry" (in Swedish), Employment Department, DsA, 1975:6.

[27] *The Swedish Economy, Preliminary National Budget,* January 1979, Ministry of Economic Affairs and National Institute of Economic Research, Stockholm, 1979.

[28] Welter, P. "Financial Aspects of Company Planning," *Long Range Planning* 6, No. 1 (1973), pp. 36-41.

[29] Weston, J.F. "New Themes in Finance," *Journal of Finance* 29, No. 1 (1974), pp. 237-243.

3 THE INFLUENCE OF TAX INCENTIVES ON CAPITAL BUDGETING DECISIONS UNDER UNCERTAINTY

Dieter Schneider
Ruhr-Universität Bochum, West Germany

Tax incentives, especially tax-rate reductions or accelerated depreciation, are often recommended as a useful instrument to stimulate entrepreneurial investment and risk-taking. Quite the opposite conclusions, however, are drawn from portfolio selection models: In the papers by Domar and Musgrave [4], Mossin [11], Stiglitz [19], and others, it is shown that a risk-averse investor will increase risky investments when the income tax rate is increased (some restrictions omitted) and will decrease risky investments when the tax rate is reduced.

The aim of this paper is to prove that the effects of tax incentives on risk-taking are ambiguous, if the real conditions given by the tax law are taken into account. Additionally, it is argued that the portfolio models hitherto used for analyzing the interrelations between taxation and risk-taking considerably overrate the investor's ability to decide according to the expected utility theorem (or its simplifications, such as the mean-variance rule).

TAX INCENTIVES AND RISK-TAKING

Assumptions and Definitions

The main results of this paper will be derived under the assumption that tax incentives lead to nonmarginal income variations. This approach seems to be more realistic than the standard assumptions of portfolio theory, for it is applicable in the case of indivisible physical investments and does not necessarily require the differentiability of the utility function. Additionally, simple nonmarginal examples may be expedient for convincing not only economic theorists, but managers and tax experts as well.

Therefore I only investigate the choice between a riskless and a risky investment program when there are only two states of the world of equal probability. In one state of the world (the "good" one) the risky investment leads to a higher income than the riskless one, whereas in the other state (the "bad" one) the income from the risky investment will be lower than the riskless income. Both investments are assumed to be indivisible. Prior to a tax incentive, the investor is supposed to be indifferent to the choice between the riskless and the risky investment.

If expected utility maximization is postulated as in this section, the assumptions of only two states of the world and of equal probability are harmless. The results are also applicable to the choice between two risky investments, if we come to agree on the measurement of "more risk." The greater risk can be measured by the difference between the highest and the smallest income chance, their probabilities, and the number of states of the world. This will not be discussed here in detail.

Risk aversion is assumed throughout. Risk aversion implies diminishing marginal utility of income chances. It will be shown later why I refer to the expected utility of income "chances" and not to the commonly used expected utility of final wealth.

Diminishing marginal utility of income chances implies that the difference between the income of the risky investment in the "good" state of the world and the riskless income has to be greater than the difference between the riskless income and the income of the risky investment in the "bad" state of the world to make sure that the investor will be indifferent between the two investment opportunities. Such indifference is assumed here for the after-tax incomes of the risky and the riskless investments before a tax incentive is granted. The relation between the required income increment in the good state of the world and the given income diminution in the bad state of the world is called the *investor's relative risk premium.* From the preceding it follows that it has to be greater than one for any risk-averse investor. To determine the investor's relative risk premium exactly for any individual investor, it is necessary to have further information about the individual's expected utility function and, as nonmarginal income differences are considered here, about the absolute size of the riskless income and the income chances. For the moment, this information is taken as given so that the following example can illustrate the definition.

Example. An investor is supposed to be indifferent between the riskless income of 50 and the equally probable income chances of 40 and 70 from a risky investment; the investor's relative risk premium is then given by $(70 - 50)/(50 - 40) = 2$.

Whether the risky investment will be realized or not can generally be seen by comparing the investor's relative risk premium with the *relative risk premium of the risky investment,* which is just the relation between the positive and negative income difference that the risky investment grants compared to the riskless one. Only if both risk premiums coincide, as in the preceding example, will the investor be indifferent between the two investments. As long as the investor's relative risk premium is greater than the relative risk premium of the risky investment, the riskless investment will be preferred.

If the risky investment is described by two equally probable states of the world only, the *degree of risk* can be measured simply by the *percentage of income diminution,* i.e., the difference between the riskless income and the income in the "bad" state of the world relative to the riskless income (which is 20 percent in the example). The greater the percentage of income diminution, the greater the risk. Risk aversion (diminishing marginal utility of income chances) implies that the investor's relative risk premium must increase if the percentage of income diminution grows. If the investor is indifferent between the equally probable income chances of 40 and 70 and the riskless income of 50, he has to prefer 50 to the equally probable income chances of 30 and 90, although the relative risk premium of the risky investment is still 2, for the utility increment, when the income rises from 30 to 40, must be greater than the utility increment, when the income rises from 40 to 50, and so on, which means that in the example the investor's relative risk premium will be greater than 2 for an income diminution of 40 percent.

If a variation of the tax conditions does not change the riskless after-tax income, but leads to an increase in the percentage of income diminution and a constant (or diminished) relative risk premium of the risky investment, a risk-averse investor will always prefer the riskless investment. A decreased percentage of income diminution and a constant (or increased) relative risk premium of the risky investment will of course make risk-taking favorable for every risk-averter.

If a variation of the tax conditions changes the riskless after-tax income and leads to an increase in the percentage of income diminution, or if the variation of tax conditions leads to a higher relative risk premium of the risky investment but leaves the percentage of income diminution as it was, it is not certain that the risky investment will be preferred. The special form of the investor's risk aversion will determine whether he will choose the risky investment or the riskless one. There are three forms of risk aversion that have to be distinguished:

1. Constant relative risk aversion: The risk-averter wants the same relative risk premium if his net income grows, provided that the percentage of income diminution remains constant.
2. Increasing relative risk aversion: The risk-averter wants a higher relative risk premium if his net income grows, the percentage of income diminution being left as it was.
3. Decreasing relative risk aversion: The risk-averter wants a lower relative risk premium if his net income grows, again provided that the percentage of income diminution remains constant.

These three cases correspond to the constant, increasing, or decreasing elasticity of marginal utility of income chances and hence to the relative or proportional risk aversion as defined by Arrow [1] and Pratt [14].

This completes the preliminaries. Now we may ask which tax incentives will have an unambiguous influence on risk-taking. It turns out that only a small subset of all possible tax incentives yields this result.

Tax Incentives That Increase Risk-Taking for All Forms of Risk Aversion

Tax incentives will increase every risk-averter's risk-taking if, and only if, the percentage of income diminution decreases and the relative risk premium of the risky investment increases or remains constant, provided that the riskless after-tax income will not change. This will be achieved only by tax incentives that discriminate the riskless investment. The discrimination is present if only the after-tax income chances increase or else if only the safe after-tax income decreases.

Examples of tax incentives discriminating riskless investments are:

1. Improved tax deductibility of losses or expenditures for risky investments only

The effects on risk-taking due to a change from no (or partial) loss-offset to partial (or full) loss-offset have been well known since Domar and Musgrave [4].

The effect of an improved deductibility of expenditures is shown by the following case: An investor in West Germany must take into account that the deductibility of interest payments is partially restricted; apart from the personal or corporate income tax there is the so-called *Gewerbeertragsteuer*, which corresponds to some extent to a trade tax on income. For this, tax interest payments on long-term debts are not deductible. The investor may be indifferent at first between (1) borrowing a certain amount of money to realize a risky investment and (2) a riskless alternative, which in this case may be simply doing nothing. A variation of the tax conditions granting a tax deductibility of interest payments reduces the percentage of income diminution, full loss-offset provided. Now, every risk-averse investor will prefer the risky alternative.

2. Tax concessions to the risky investment alone

Tax concessions can be granted in various forms: Accelerated depreciation to the risky asset alone will result in a tax credit if the tax rate does not change in subsequent years and a full loss-offset is given. The valuation principle "cost or market, whichever is lower" and, in times of rising prices, the "lifo"-method grant a tax credit compared to other methods of stock valuation. The various occasions to defer taxes shall not be encountered.

Example. The investor has to choose between a riskless capital market investment (lending) with a pretax rate of return of $r = 10$ percent and a risky depreciable asset A_1. The payments of the depreciable asset are listed in Table 1,

Table 1

(a) *Risky Depreciable Asset A_1; No Taxation*					
d_0	d_1	d_2	d_3	d_4	d_5
$(p_a = 0.5)$					
−1000 +400	+360	+320	+280	+240	
+250	+240	+230	+220	+210	
$(p_b = 0.5)$					

Pretax rate of return (r):

$(p_a = 0.5)$ $r = 20$ percent   (Average annual income = 200)

$(p_b = 0.5)$ $r = 5$ percent   (Average annual income = 50)

(b) *Proportional Income Taxation (tax rate t = 50 percent) and Straight-Line Depreciation (depreciation rate 1/5 each year) for A_1*

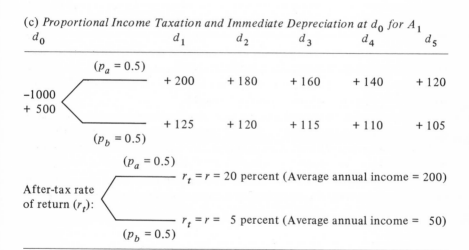

d_0		d_1	d_2	d_3	d_4	d_5
	$(p_a = 0.5)$					
−1000		+ 300	+ 280	+ 260	+ 240	+ 220
		+ 225	+ 220	+ 215	+ 210	+ 205
	$(p_b = 0.5)$					

After-tax rate of return (r_t):

$(p_a = 0.5)$ $r_t = 10$ percent (Average annual income = 100)

$t_t = 2.5$ percent (Average annual income = 25) $(p_b = 0.5)$

(c) *Proportional Income Taxation and Immediate Depreciation at d_0 for A_1*

d_0		d_1	d_2	d_3	d_4	d_5
	$(p_a = 0.5)$					
−1000 + 500		+ 200	+ 180	+ 160	+ 140	+ 120
		+ 125	+ 120	+ 115	+ 110	+ 105
	$(p_b = 0.5)$					

After-tax rate of return (r_t):

$(p_a = 0.5)$ $r_t = r = 20$ percent (Average annual income = 200)

$r_t = r = 5$ percent (Average annual income = 50) $(p_b = 0.5)$

where the probabilities of the states of the world a and b are denoted by p_a and p_b, and $d_0, d_1, \ldots, d_5$ indicate the dates of payment.

The pretax rates of return are 20 percent in state a and 5 percent in state b. Straight-line depreciation of 200 at each date (year) reduces the taxable income. For a proportional tax rate $t = 50$ percent, the tax payments will be in state a: 100 at d_1, 80 at d_2, and so on.

The after-tax payments of A_1 are easily calculated and also shown in Table 1. The after-tax rate of return will be 10 percent in state a and 2.5 percent in state b. In this example, straight-line depreciation is equal to economic depreciation, so that the after-tax rate of return differs from the pretax rate of return just by the product of the proportional tax rate and the pretax rate of return. Economic depreciation is defined by Preinreich [15] as payment at the end of a period less the product of the interest rate (here, rate of return) and the present value of future payments at the beginning of that period (here, prime cost or residual book value).

In deciding between the risky and the riskless investment, only the average annual incomes (rate of return in each state of the world multiplied by prime cost) are taken into account. For simplification, it is assumed that any amount needed to pay the average annual income can be borrowed at the rate of return and that any amount can be reinvested at this rate. Considerations based on a multiperiod utility function are not considered. The investor is supposed to be indifferent between the riskless after-tax income of 50 resulting from the riskless capital market investment and the two after-tax income chances of 25 and 100 offered by investing in the depreciable asset.

If immediate depreciation at the beginning of the first year is possible, the after-tax rate of return will be equal to the pretax rate of return, as long as a full loss-offset is allowed and no restrictions on reinvesting any amount at that rate of return are present. The after-tax income chances of the risky asset will increase to 200 in state a and 50 in state b; but the after-tax income of the riskless capital market investment will stay at 50. In this example, the risky asset will be chosen by everybody if immediate depreciation is possible.

In general, accelerated depreciation will unambiguously increase risk-taking if, and only if, an investor has to choose between a riskless nondepreciable asset and a risky depreciable asset after proportional income taxation with full loss-offset. This result is obtained because the accelerated depreciation only affects the risky investment. Just the average annual income chances of the risky asset increase, and therefore the percentage of income diminution becomes smaller.

Tax Incentives That Favor Risk-Taking Only for Single Utility Functions

We now turn to those tax incentives whose influence on risk-taking is ambiguous. They may be divided into two groups: First, there are tax incentives increasing risk-taking only for single forms of relative risk aversion (e.g., a general reduction of the proportional income tax rate). The second group consists of even less effective tax incentives, leading to a higher risk-taking only for single utility functions. For brevity we shall look at the second group only.

Accelerated Depreciation and the Choice between Depreciable Assets. If an investor has to choose between a risky depreciable investment and a riskless depreciable investment, and if he is indifferent between the two alternatives after taxation and regular depreciation, accelerated depreciation does not always give rise to a preference for the risky investment. Again the results for the choice between a risky and a riskless investment remain valid for the choice between any two risky assets or capital budgets.

Four cases have to be distinguished:

1. The present value of tax depreciation is equal to the present value of economic depreciation for both investments. The average annual incomes of the investment alternatives are given by multiplying the after-tax rate of return and the initial investment expenditure (the prime cost of the depreciable assets). It is always assumed that there are no restrictions on reinvesting or borrowing any amount at that rate of return.

If immediate depreciation is allowed, the rate of return will be the same before and after taxation, and the average annual income of the investment alternatives will be equal to the product of the pretax rate of return and the initial expenditure, so that only the riskless income increases, whereas the percentage of income diminution and the relative risk premium of the risky investment both remain constant.

Therefore an investor with decreasing relative risk-aversion will prefer the risky investment; an investor with increasing relative risk aversion will prefer the riskless investment. An investor with constant relative risk aversion will still be indifferent between the two alternatives. However, such a clear result can only be obtained in the case of immediate depreciation. For any other form of accelerated depreciation, the difference between the pretax and the after-tax rate of return will be less than the product of the pretax rate of return and the tax rate (full loss-offset provided). Additionally, the deviation of the rate of return after taxation from its pretax level will now depend on the corresponding amount of income before taxation. Hence it follows that if a tax incentive is granted in the form of an accelerated depreciation, the riskless income increases, whereas both the percentage of income diminution and the relative risk premium of the risky investment may decrease.

As an example, compare the risky investment A_1 with the riskless investment A_2, as described in Table 2. A_2 has a rate of return of 10 percent before taxation, so that after taxation at a rate of 50 percent and straight-line depreciation (which is equal to economic depreciation for this investment), the rate of return is 5 percent. The investor will be indifferent between A_1 and A_2 after taxation and straight-line depreciation.

Now consider the following accelerated depreciation for both alternatives: 400 at the end of the first year (at d_1), 150 in the remaining years (from d_2 to

d_5). The after-tax income chances of the risky investment A_1 (which are given by multiplying the rate of return with the initial investment expenditure, as already mentioned) will now be 27.23 and 108.41, whereas the riskless average annual income of A_2 will now be 54.37. The accelerated depreciation leads to a higher riskless income, but to a smaller percentage of income diminution and a smaller relative risk premium of the risky investment.

If the percentage of income diminution and the relative risk premium of the risky investment move in the same direction as in the example given above, the effect of a variation of the tax conditions on risk-taking cannot be predicted for any form of relative risk aversion, neither for constant nor decreasing nor increasing relative risk aversion: A smaller percentage of income diminution implies a smaller risk. But how much may the relative risk premium of the risky investment decrease for compensating the smaller risk in the case of an investor with constant or increasing relative risk aversion? Only if the behavior under uncertainty were specified more precisely, i.e., by a utility function up to a positive

Table 2

(a) *Riskless Depreciable Asset A_2*

d_0	d_1	d_2	d_3	d_4	d_5
-1000	+300	+280	+260	+240	+220

Rate of return before taxation:	10 percent
Rate of return after proportional taxation ($t = 50$ percent) and straight-line depreciation:	5 percent

(b) *Accelerated Depreciation for A_1 and A_2*

d_0	d_1	d_2	d_3	d_4	d_5
0	400	150	150	150	150

Average annual income chances of A_1: $p = 0.5$ — 27.23 ; $p = 0.5$ — 108.41

Average annual income of A_2: 54.37

Relative risk premium of A_1: $\dfrac{108.41 - 54.37}{54.37 - 27.23} = 1.9912$

linear transformation, could the effect of a variation of the tax conditions be calculated. Of course, this implies that *for any form of accelerated depreciation (except immediate depreciation with full loss-offset) risk-taking may decrease, as well as increase, if the investor is risk-averse!*

2. This result will be intensified, if the present value of tax depreciation exceeds the present value of economic depreciation for the riskless investment (discounted at the pretax rate of return), whereas the present value of tax depreciation is equal to the present value of economic depreciation for the risky investment. This will occur, if, for example, the riskless investment yields the same receipts in each year of its lifetime and the tax law permits only straight-line depreciation.

As an example, compare the risky investment A_1 with the riskless investment A_3, as described in Table 3. In the case of straight-line depreciation, the investor

Table 3

(a) *Riskless Depreciable Asset A_3*

d_0	d_1	d_2	d_3	d_4	d_5
− 1000	+ 261.95	+ 261.95	+ 261.95	+ 261.95	+ 261.95

Rate of return before taxation:	9.726 percent
Rate of return after immediate depreciation and proportional taxation with full loss-offset:	9.726 percent
Rate of return after proportional taxation ($t = 50$ percent) and straight-line depreciation:	5.000 percent

(b) *Straight-Line Depreciation for A_1 and A_2*

Relative risk premium of A_1: $\dfrac{100 - 50}{50 - 25} = 2$

(c) *Immediate depreciation for A_1 and A_3*

Relative risk premium of A_1: $\dfrac{200 - 97.26}{97.26 - 50} = 2.714$

may be indifferent between a riskless after-tax income of 50 and the after-tax income chances of 25 and 100. In the case of immediate depreciation, the investor is confronted with the riskless after-tax income of 97.26 and the after-tax income chances of 50 and 200. The riskless income increases; the percentage of income diminution decreases; the relative risk premium of the risky investment increases.

Therefore an investor with constant or decreasing relative risk aversion will favor risk-taking. For increasing relative risk aversion, the decision cannot be predicted.

The comparison between the results in Table 2 and Table 3 shows that more investors will prefer risky investments if immediate depreciation is allowed. The riskless investment in Table 2 has a "better" tax depreciation relative to its economic depreciation. Therefore immediate depreciation is a greater advantage for the risky investment.

But this result is restricted to the special case of immediate depreciation with full loss-offset. Any other form of accelerated depreciation can cause the percentage of income diminution and the relative risk premium of the risky investment to move in the same direction, so that the effect on risk-taking cannot be predicted as long as only the form of the investor's risk aversion is known.

3. Let us now turn to the situation opposite to that of Table 3. In the next example, the present value of tax depreciation exceeds the present value of economic depreciation for the risky investment, whereas now the present value of tax depreciation and economic depreciation are equal for the riskless investment.

The following will be the case if the alternatives are given by the riskless investment A_2 and the risky investment A_4, whose financial consequences are stated in Table 4.

In the case of straight-line depreciation, the investor may be indifferent between the riskless after-tax income of 50 from A_2 and the after-tax income chances of 100 and 25 from A_4.

In the case of immediate depreciation, the investor has to compare the riskless after-tax income of 100 from A_2 to the after-tax income chances of 190.74 and 49.24 from A_4. The riskless income and the percentage of income diminution are higher, whereas the relative risk premium of the risky investment is lower than before. Therefore an investor with constant or increasing relative risk aversion will prefer the riskless investment. But if he shows decreasing relative risk aversion, his decision cannot be predicted.

Comparing the results of Table 4 to those of Table 2, it follows that immediate depreciation will hinder more investors from risk-taking if the risky

Table 4

(a) *Risky Depreciable Asset A_4*

d_0	d_1	d_2	d_3	d_4	d_5
	$p = 0.5$				
	$+ 327.59$	$+ 327.59$	$+ 327.59$	$+ 327.59$	$+ 327.59$
-1000					
	$+ 230.49$	$+ 230.49$	$+ 230.49$	$+ 230.49$	$+ 230.49$
	$p = 0.5$				

Rate of return after immediate depreciation
and proportional taxation with full loss-offset:

$p = 0.5$ 19.074 percent

4.924 percent $p = 0.5$

Rate of return after proportional taxation
($t = 50$ percent) and straight-line depreciation:

$p = 0.5$ 10.000 percent

2.500 percent $p = 0.5$

(b) *Straight-Line Depreciation for A_2 and A_4*

Relative risk premium of A_4: $\dfrac{100 - 50}{50 - 25} = 2$

(c) *Immediate Depreciation for A_2 and A_4*

Relative risk premium of A_4: $\dfrac{190.74 - 100}{100 \quad - \quad 49.24} = 1.788$

investment has a "better" tax depreciation relative to economic depreciation. Immediate depreciation is now more favorable for the riskless investment.

But again this result only occurs if immediate depreciation and full loss-offset are allowed. For any other form of accelerated depreciation, the percentage of income diminution and the relative risk premium of the risky investment can move in the same direction, so that the decision cannot be predicted as long as only the form of risk aversion is known.

4. The last cases to consider are those in which the present value of tax depreciation is either higher or lower than the present value of economic depreciation for the risky investment, as well as for the riskless investment. If immediate depreciation is allowed, the riskless income increases, whereas the percentage of income diminution and the relative risk premium of the risky investment decrease. The decision is not predictable as long as only the form of relative risk aversion is known. Even for investors with the same form of risk aversion, immediate depreciation can either favor or hinder risk-taking! Two examples are given in Table 5.

An investor with constant relative risk aversion may have a logarithmic utility function. Therefore he will be indifferent between the riskless investment A_3 and the risky investment A_4 if straight-line depreciation is allowed. In the case of immediate depreciation and full loss-offset, this investor will prefer the riskless investment A_3.

Another investor with constant relative risk aversion knows his utility function as given by (b) in Table 5. He will be indifferent between the risky investment A_4 and the riskless investment A_5 given by d_0: $-$ 1.000; d_1 to d_5: $+$ 249.254. This riskless investment has a rate of return of $r = 7.818$ percent before taxation, which reduces to $r_t = 4$ percent for a proportional tax rate of $t = 50$ percent and straight-line depreciation. But if immediate depreciation and full loss-offset are allowed, he will prefer the risky investment.

Table 5

(a) *Utility Function $U(y) = \log y$;*
    Investment Alternatives A_3 and A_4

$U(50) = 0.5U(100) + 0.5U(25);\ \ U(97.26) > 0.5U(190.74) + 0.5U(49.24)$

(b) *Utility Function $U(y) = a - by^{-1} (a > b > 0)$;*
    Investment Alternatives A_4 and A_5 (-1000 at d_0; $+249.254$ at $d_1, \ldots, d_5$)

$U(40) = 0.5U(100) + 0.5U(25);\ \ U(78.18) < 0.5U(190.74) + 0.5(49.24)$

Whether accelerated depreciation has a positive or negative influence on risk-taking always depends on:

1. The time structure of the net payments of the risky and the riskless invest-ment (which determines economic income and economic depreciation)
2. The time structure of tax depreciation
3. The individual utility function; only in some special cases there is a unique solution for constant, decreasing, or increasing relative risk aversion.

Since there is no unique relation between the time structure of net payments and the time structure of tax depreciation, and since there is no single utility function for all investors in a country, an improvement of depreciation allowances can have a positive, as well as a negative, influence on risk-taking. Accelerated depreciation cannot be recommended as a useful instrument for encouraging risky investments.

The Combined Effects of Profit and Loss Discriminations and Tax Concessions in Reality. Every personal or corporate income tax law in the world shows profit and loss discriminations, as well as tax concessions: Nowhere is a full loss-offset allowed. In general, the taxable profit of firms is realized at the time when products are sold, but economic income is realized only in the period when active debts will be paid. Apart from these simple forms of profit and loss dis-criminations, there are simple "tax concessions," such as the devaluation of doubtful debts, the principle of "cost or market, whichever is lower," and many other accounting specialities; depreciation will now be omitted. The combined effects of profit and loss discriminations and tax concessions given by the tax law and accounting conventions will be that, because of the differences between taxable income and economic income, the tax payments are generally a nonpro-portional function of economic income in each state of the world.

If the relation between the amount of profit and loss discriminations or the amount of tax concessions and the economic income before taxation is greater for the risky investment in only one state of the world (respectively, only some states), but smaller in the other state (respectively, some other states), any non-discriminatory tax incentive (a reduction of tax rates, tax credits) can induce the percentage of income diminution and the relative risk premium of the risky investment to move in the same direction, so that the effect of the tax incentive on risk-taking cannot be predicted. A reduction, as well as an increase, of risk-taking is possible. Therefore the ambiguous conclusions for accelerated deprecia-tion, as discussed in the previous section, carry over to a large set of possible tax incentives.

This indeterminacy will be enlarged when we compare not only single investments but also alternative capital budgets for a firm as a whole. But "rational"
decisions under uncertainty require that we consider the financial situation of a
firm or a person as a whole. Therefore it may be concluded that, taking into
account the conditions given by the tax law and actual accounting conventions,
the effects of nondiscriminatory tax incentives, especially tax-rate reductions,
cannot be predicted if only the special forms of relative risk aversion are known
and not the utility function itself. But in reality we can only assume that most
investors are risk-averse; we seldom know the form of their relative risk aversion,
and we hardly ever know more for all (or most) investors in a country.

Direct Progressive Taxation.   Direct progressive taxation is defined by increasing
marginal tax rates. Of course, as no unequivocal results can be obtained about
the effects of tax incentives on risk-taking, if proportional taxation prevails, the
results in the case of direct progressive taxation will be ambiguous too. Nevertheless, as long as taxable income is equal to economic income, the effects of tax
incentives can be described for proportional and indirect progressive (degressive)
taxation. But if direct progressive taxation takes place, the effects of tax incentives can no longer be described even under the simplifying assumption that taxable income does not differ from economic income. This has been shown in [17].

CAN THE EFFECTS OF TAX INCENTIVES ON RISK-TAKING BE JUDGED BY MAXIMIZING THE EXPECTED UTILITY OF INCOME CHANCES?

Expected Utility as a Function of Final Wealth or of Income Chances

The above conclusions are based on the hypothesis of expected utility maximization of income chances. The first objection against this approach may be that
when judging the effects of tax incentives on risk-taking, actual and not rational
behavior has to be considered.

If we look at actual investment behavior, we may suspect taxation to be
quite irrelevant to risk-taking. Recent empirical investigations [7, 8, 16] have
shown that:

1. Many firms do not consider taxation in their investment decisions.
2. The majority of all firms do not pay explicit attention to alternative
    states of the world when planning investments.

If taxation is not taken into consideration in the decision process, it cannot be of any influence to risk-taking. If there is no planning with explicit regard to uncertainty, even those firms considering taxation in their capital budgeting decisions cannot be influenced in their risk-taking. Of course, tax incentives can result in better financial capabilities. But more tax credits or retained earnings do not necessarily lead to more investments and more risk-taking. Repayment of debts or increased cash balances may also seem expedient, especially in times of depression.

Furthermore, the answers to interviews will often be biased by the desire to get tax advantages. The results of empirical investigations therefore do not permit us to conclude whether tax incentives favor (or hinder) risk-taking. Consequently, the better way to predict economic behavior is to determine the decisions of a rational person with "realistic" goals in a "realistic" environment—i.e., to construct "realistic" models of rational behavior. An attempt to approximate the investor's real environment was made in the previous section, where profit and loss discriminations and tax concessions were included. But may the maximization of expected utility of income chances be regarded as "realistic" behavior of a rational person under uncertainty?

The choice problem investigated here consists of the decision between riskless and risky actions. To solve this problem, we need a measure of the preference for more or less risk. It must be emphasized that the preference for risk is not independent of the measure of any goal. Maximization of expected utility of wealth chances describes another behavior under uncertainty than the one described by maximization of expected utility of income (or of money or of consumption).

It is easy to see that constant (increasing, decreasing) relative risk aversion with respect to income chances implies another behavior under uncertainty and therefore other reactions to tax incentives than constant (increasing, decreasing) relative risk aversion with respect to final wealth. In the first case, marginal "utility" diminishes, for example, by 1 percent, if an income chance increases by 1 percent; in the second case, marginal "utility" diminishes by, say, 1 percent, if a final wealth chance increases by 1 percent.

There are four arguments to measure the expected utility of income chances rather than the expected utility of final wealth chances:

1. If expected utility of income chances is chosen, the interrelations between *income* taxation and risk-taking can be described in a simple, pedagogically favorable way. However, this may be a weak argument for a pure theorist.

2. Only for timeless decision problems, and not for temporal decision problems, does there always exist an expected utility function for final wealth describing the preferences on probability distributions, as Mossin [12, 13] has shown. Theoretically, an intertemporal utility function for multi-

period consumption would be necessary for temporal (or multiperiod) decision problems. Since such functions cannot be determined practically today, we must look for an approximate solution. Working with the utility of average annual income chances may serve as an approximation, for this preserves the multiperiod nature of the decision problem by introducing standardized withdrawals for consumption as the argument of the utility function.

3. The expected utility hypothesis requires a set of behavior postulates. Arrow [2, p. 48] considers the assumption of (monotone) continuity "to be the harmless simplification almost inevitable in the formalization of any real-life problem." This is wrong. Monotone continuity implies substitution of more risk and more wealth for less risk and less wealth over all ranges of wealth, from the regions of bankruptcy up to billions of dollars. But people (especially the directors of corporations) will not always take more and more risk if only wealth chances increase sufficiently. In reality there is an upper bound to risk-taking where the continuous utility function converts into a lexicographic one. I cannot see why such behavior should be irrational.

4. The strongest argument for measuring risk aversion by expected utilities of income chances and not of wealth chances may be the following: Expected utility related to wealth is not empirically testable, even under ideal circumstances; expected utility related to income chances is testable. Income is defined here as a flow of money in a time period, the excess of receipts over expenditures, summed up to the end of that period. But what is the "wealth" of a "going concern" (a firm or a "gainfully employed person") at that date? Arrow [2, p. 92] proposes to take "for simplicity . . . wealth to be a single commodity and disregard the difficulties of aggregation over many commodities. For most purposes [wealth] is taken to be the money value of commodity holdings . . . at market prices. There is no loss in generality under perfect competition so long as prices remain constant." But in reality there is no investment decision under perfect competition, and prices scarcely remain constant. The wealth of any going concern is equal to the sum of the market prices of its commodities only by chance, even if market prices for all its (used) commodities exist. The only way to measure the wealth of a going concern is to define wealth as a discounted value of future income streams. But under uncertainty this valuation model leads to insoluble difficulties: (a) We do not know the appropriate discount factor, because in reality there is no perfect capital market, granting that any sum of money can be invested or borrowed at the same interest rate.
(b) Each preference (utility) index must correspond to one, and only one,

value of final wealth. But how shall initial wealth (i.e., the wealth before deciding between an additional risky and an additional riskless investment) be measured unanimously so that one cardinal utility index is related to one, and only one, value of final wealth, if wealth has to be defined as the value of uncertain future income streams discounted at a rate not exogenously given by a perfect capital market?

Can Personal Probabilities Be Quantified in Reality?

It is well known that the application of the expected utility theorem requires the existence of quantitative personal probabilities. The same set of axioms may be used to define expected utility and personal probabilities [6]. Quantitative personal probabilities are interpreted as rational betting quotients, and de Finetti [5] and others have proposed to derive these betting quotients from a coherent betting system by constructing additional bets. A coherent betting system is given if a sure loss, a so-called Dutch-book, is ruled out. However, in the last years many objections have been raised against this method and the Dutch-book argument it implies [3,18,20]. I will not repeat these objections, but will give you two arguments indicating that it seems to be practically impossible to quantify personal probabilities in a reasonable way so that the expected utility theorem can be applied.

The first objection is that no axiomatization of expected utility and quantitative personal probabilities can avoid an infinite number of bets to become necessary for determining the betting quotients (see [9, p. 208] for details). But this means that the betting approach is not "constructive" at all.

The second objection is that weak axioms of measurability for personal probabilities no longer allow us to think of the expected utility theorem as the only rational decision rule. If quantitative measurement of probabilities is no longer postulated, other concepts than the expected utility theorem may no longer be rejected as irrational. The interesting work of Levi [10] in this area cannot be discussed here in detail.

Since every human being has only a limited capacity to collect and evaluate information, it is practically impossible to determine a closed set of states of the world. But the closed-set assumption is a fundamental axiom of probability theory. This axiom missing, the rules of probability calculus cannot be applied, because the mathematical concept of probability implies that the states of the world are mutually exclusive and exhaustive. This independence and completeness of the states of the world can only be granted if one of the states is defined by "not the other states" and if it is empirically true that the probability is zero for those states of the world, which are not explicitly enumerated. For economic decisions, this can be granted seldom, if at all.

Let us consider a small example: Someone suggests that you play dice with him. The rules of the game are rather simple: One of the dice is thrown, and if a six appears, you win a certain amount of money; otherwise, you lose. Obviously, you think of two states of the world — "six appears" and "six does not appear." Now the probabilities of these two states have to be calculated.

Under the assumption that the dice are fair, most people would conclude that the probabilities are 1/6 and 5/6, respectively. But the second state of the world "six does not appear" also includes the event that no side of the die appears or that it cannot be observed which side appears (perhaps a dog catches the die or the die disappears in the sewer). Of course, when playing dice, such cases could be ruled out by agreements among the players to repeat the throw. But economic, as well as political, decisions cannot be fully organized by contracts and agreements so that all those elements of the set called "not the explicitly defined states of the world" can be enumerated.

This inevitably makes simplifications necessary for practical decision making under uncertainty, especially for complex capital budgeting decisions. The states of the world that could be distinguished practically are always incompletely specified. All or some of the them contain an indeterminate number of possible future events whose consequences are not precisely reflected in the formulation of the decision problem.

But if these simplifications are made, no coherent betting system can be constructed by the decision maker, for those future events not incorporated in the states-of-the-world formulation may create a loss, which allows a Dutch-book to be made against the decision maker. Thus we have to conclude that the necessary simplifications in economic decision making under uncertainty at the same time destroy the quantification of personal degrees of belief.

In general, we have to distinguish six classes of decision problems according to the different degrees of measurability for personal probabilities:

1. *Decisions with quantitative probabilities,* where personal probabilities are at least measurable on an interval scale. This is the only case where the expected utility theorem guarantees rational decisions (and is sometimes referred to as the situation of "decisions under risk").

2. *Decisions with quantitative probability ranges,* where personal probabilities are measurable on a hyperordinal scale; i.e., if the differences of the degrees of belief for the alternative states of the world can be ordered (i.e., the difference between the degrees of belief for state A and B is greater than the difference between the degrees of belief for state A and C, and so on).

3. *Decisions with ordinal probabilities,* where personal probabilities can be measured only on an ordinal scale; i.e., if only the degrees of belief for the states can be ordered (i.e., the occurrence of state A is more probable than the occurrence of state B, and so on).
4. *Decisions with partially ordinal probabilities,* where only for some states of the world can an ordering for their degrees of belief be established.
5. *Decisions with nominal probabilities,* where personal probabilities can be measured only on a nominal scale; i.e., if only the set of alternative states of the world can be described completely, but no ordering of probabilities is possible. (This is sometimes referred to as the situation of "decisions under uncertainty" in the sense of Frank H. Knight.)
6. *Decisions with partially nominal probabilities,* where there is not even a closed set of alternative states of the world.

In the present state of the art, rational decision rules are only known for the first, partly for the second, and, with additional assumptions, the fifth case [10,18].

This disappointing status of the theory of rational decisions may constitute an objection against my paper: What remains valid of an investigation of the influence of tax incentives on capital budgeting decisions under uncertainty that presumes the expected utility theorem, if one of this theorem's key assumptions, the existence of quantitative probabilities, cannot be assured? My answer is that we have to use this approach at the moment, despite the objections, because it is the best that economic theory can offer at the moment for analyzing entrepreneurial decisions under uncertainty. But the objections against the expected utility hypotheses will reinforce my former conclusion that the effects of tax incentives on capital budgeting decisions under uncertainty will be ambiguous if realistic tax conditions (progressive taxation, profit and loss discriminations, tax concessions) are taken into account.

CONCLUSIONS

The main results may be stated as follows:

1. Tax incentives do not decrease (i.e., increase or do not influence) the risk-taking of a risk-averse investor if, and only if, riskless or less risky investment opportunities are discriminated.
2. The effects of nondiscriminatory tax incentives, such as a general reduction of the income tax rate or the substitution of straight-line depreciation by accelerated depreciation, are ambiguous and critically depend on

the time structure of payments resulting from a capital budget in the alternative states of the world, on the deviations of taxable income from economic income, and on the investor's utility function.

3. Maximization of the expected utility of final wealth may neither describe the actual decision-making behavior in the real world nor may it be an applicable rule for rational decision making. The quantitative measurement of personal probabilities, which is a necessary condition for the expected utility theorem to hold, will be feasible only under a very restrictive and unrealistic set of assumptions. As soon as the quantification of personal probabilities becomes impossible, "rational" decision making can no longer be defined unambiguously at the current state of the art. In this case, the indeterminateness of the effects of tax incentives on risk-taking will be enlarged substantially, and the results of capital budgeting theory and portfolio models depending on the expected utility theorem or on the mean-variance rule seem to be questionable.

REFERENCES

[1] Arrow, Kenneth J. *Aspects of the Theory of Risk Bearing.* Helsinki: Yrjö Jahnsoonin Säätiö, 1965.

[2] Arrow, Kenneth J. *Essays in the Theory of Risk-Bearing.* Amsterdam: North-Holland Publishing Company, 1970.

[3] Baillie, Patricia. "Confirmation and the Dutch Book Argument," *British Journal for the Philosophy of Science* 24 (1973), pp. 393–397.

[4] Domar, Evsey D., and Musgrave, Richard A. "Proportional Income Taxation and Risk-Taking," *Quarterly Journal of Economics* 58 (May 1944), pp. 388–422.

[5] Finetti, Bruno de. *Theory oj Probability,* Vol. 1. New York: John Wiley & Sons, 1974.

[6] Fishburn, Peter C. "A General Theory of Subjective Probabilities and Expected Utilities," *Annals of Mathematical Statistics* 40 (August 1969), pp. 1419–1429.

[7] Grabbe, Hans Wilhelm. *Investitionsrechnungen in der Praxis – Ergebnisse einer Unternehmensbefragung.* Cologne: Deutscher Instituts-Verlag, 1976.

[8] Honko, Jaakko, and Virtanen, Kalervo. *The Investment Process in Finnish Industrial Enterprises.* Helsinki: The Helsinki School of Economics, 1976.

[9] Krantz, David H.; Luce, R. Duncan; Suppes, Patrick; and Tversky, Amos. *Foundations of Measurement,* Vol. 1. New York: Academic Press, 1971.

[10] Levi, Isaac, "On Indeterminate Probabilities," *Journal of Philosophy* 71 (July 1974), pp. 391–418.

[11] Mossin, Jan. "Taxation and Risk-Taking: An Expected Utility Approach," *Economica* 35 (February 1968), pp. 74–82.

[12]   Mossin, Jan. "A Note on Uncertainty and Preferences in a Temporal Context," *American Economic Review* 59 (1969), pp. 172–174.

[13]   Mossin, Jan. *Theory of Financial Markets.* Englewood Cliffs, N.J.: Prentice-Hall, 1973

[14]   Pratt, John W. "Risk Aversion in the Small and in the Large," *Econometrica* 32 (January–April 1964), pp. 122–136.

[15]   Preinreich, Gabriel A.D. "Annual Survey of Economic Theory: The Theory of Depreciation," *Econometrica* 6 (1938), pp. 219–241.

[16]   Rockley, Lawrence Edwin. *Investment for Profitability: An Analysis of the Policies and Practices of UK and International Companies.* London: Business Books, 1973.

[17]   Schneider, Dieter. "Gewinnbesteuerung und Risikobereitschaft: Zur Bewaehrung quantitativer Ansaetze in der Entscheidungstheorie," *Zeitschrift fuer betriebswirtschaftliche Forschung* 29 (October 1977), pp. 633–666.

[18]   Schneider, Dieter. "Messbarkeitsstufen subjektiver Wahrscheinlichkeiten als Erscheinungsformen der Ungewissheit," *Zeitschrift fuer betriebswirtschaftliche Forschung* 31 (February 1979), pp. 89–122.

[19]   Stiglitz, Joseph E. "The Effects of Income, Wealth, and Capital Gains Taxation on Risk-Taking," *Quarterly Journal of Economics* 83 (May 1969), pp. 263–283.

[20]   Winkler, Robert L. "The Quantification of Judgement: Some Methodological Suggestions," in James S. Bicksler and Paul A. Samuelson, eds. *Investment Portfolio Decision-Making.* Lexington, Mass.: D.C. Heath, 1974.

II INVESTMENT ISSUES IN COMPLEX ENVIRONMENTS

4 THE IMPACT OF STOCHASTIC PROJECT LIVES ON CAPITAL BUDGETING DECISIONS

Roger P. Bey
University of Missouri-Columbia

The concept of evaluating capital budgeting projects on the basis of a discounted cash-flow analysis is well established in both the academicians' and the practitioners' worlds [4, 9, 13]. However, for purposes of simplification the suggested procedures often are based on a set of unrealistic assumptions. For example, a project's life (N) often is assumed to be a constant, that is, known with certainty, whereas in reality it is stochastic. The stochastic nature of a project's life may be due to competitive technological advances, changes in consumer tastes and preferences, and the impact of complementary projects. The consequences of incorrectly assuming that N is a constant are unknown. However, as shown in the following section, the mean and variance of the net present value (NPV) distribution are biased if N is assumed to be a constant when in fact it is stochastic.

A number of researchers have addressed some of the statistical considerations necessary to incorporate a stochastic project's life into the calculation of the means and variances of the NPVs. However, no one has determined either the magnitude of the errors that financial managers may be unknowingly including in their analysis by incorrectly assuming that N is a constant or provided an

63

operational procedure to allow financial managers to consider N stochastic. The purpose of this research is to determine the impact on NPV capital budgeting decisions of incorrectly assuming that a project's life is a constant and to provide an operational procedure that allows N to be stochastic in NPV capital budgeting models.

Hertz [3], Wagle [14], Greer [2], and Van Horne [12] have considered the problem of evaluating capital budgeting projects with stochastic lives. Hertz allowed N to be stochastic in a simulation model, but provided neither a statistical framework for allowing N to be stochastic nor an analysis of the impact of a stochastic N on capital budgeting decisions. Wagle developed the necessary statistical formulas for calculating the expected NPV and variance of NPVs when N is stochastic. However, Wagle did not provide an operational framework for including a stochastic N in a capital budgeting analysis. Greer studied the desirable distributional characteristics of N and suggested a beta distribution. Although the required estimates of the beta distribution are simple, computation of the distribution's parameters is fairly complex, and computing the necessary discrete probabilities when N is stochastic from the beta distribution is quite tedious. Van Horne suggested a probability tree approach in which N is stochastic and the cash flows are temporally dependent. His methodology allowed for the correct calculation of the mean and variance of the NPVs, but the number of estimates required hinders implementation. For example, a three-state, ten-year project required more than 150,000 estimates.

Young and Contreras [16], Perrakis and Henin [7], Perrakis and Sakin [8], and Rosenthal [10] have addressed the related problem of discounting cash flows that occur randomly. Young and Contreras developed the necessary discount factors for the expected NPV when N is distributed in accordance with various probability distributions and (1) a project consists of a single cash flow that occurs at some random point in time and (2) a project consists of a uniform cash flow with an uncertain termination point. Rosenthal built on Young and Contreras' work and developed the set of discount factors for the variance of the NPVs when N is stochastic and the characteristics of N and the cash flows are the same as for Young and Contreras. Unfortunately, neither of these studies adequately describes a realistic capital budgeting situation. Perrakis and Sakin assume that the sequence of cash flows follows a renewal process in which the cash flows occur at random points and terminate after a fixed interval. However, the resulting analytical solution is complex and the necessary input estimates are difficult for a financial manager to secure.

The remainder of this paper is organized in four sections. The necessary statistical framework is contained in the next section, after which the research methodology is described. The results are given in the following section. The final section presents a summary and conclusions.

STATISTICAL BACKGROUND

If a mean-variance capital budgeting decision rule is used, it is necessary to estimate the mean and variance of the project's return distribution. Therefore the
potential error that may be introduced by assuming N is constant when N is
stochastic can be analyzed by comparing the calculations of the mean and variance of the sum of N variables when N is certain and when N is stochastic. Let

$$Y = X_1 + X_2 + \cdots + X_n,$$

where $X_1, X_2, \ldots$ are independent and identically distributed stochastic variables. If N is constant, the associated mean and variance are

$$E[Y] = E\left[\sum_{i=1}^{n} X_i\right] = nE[X] \qquad (1)$$

$$\sigma^2(Y) = \sigma^2\left(\sum_{i=1}^{n} X_i\right) = n\sigma^2(X). \qquad (2)$$

However, if N is a nonnegative integer-valued stochastic variable independent of
the Xs, the associated mean and variance, as given by Ross [11] and Parzen
[6], are

$$E[Y] = E\left[\sum_{i=1}^{N} X_i\right] = E[N]E[X] \qquad (3)$$

and

$$\sigma^2(Y) = \sigma^2\left(\sum_{i=1}^{N} X_i\right) = E[N]\sigma^2(X) + E[X]^2\sigma^2(N). \qquad (4)$$

If $E[N] = n$, the $E[Y]$ is the same when N is a constant and when N is stochastic. However, a comparison of equations (2) and (4) indicates that $\sigma^2(Y)$
is biased downward by a factor of $E[X]^2\sigma^2(N)$ if N is assumed to be constant
when N is stochastic. The magnitude of the bias may be considerable and is illustrated in the following simple example: Let $E[X] = 100$, $\sigma^2(X) = 200$, $E[N]$
$= 10$, and $\sigma^2(N) = 5$, where in a capital budgeting framework X corresponds to a
project's cash flow, Y to the NPV, and N the project life. Assuming a zero discount rate and $E[N] = n$, equation (2) yields

$$\sigma^2(\text{NPV}) = 10(200) = 2000.$$

The correct analysis based on equation (4) is

$$\sigma^2(\text{NPV}) = 10(200) + (100)^2(5) = 52{,}000.$$

There seems to be little doubt that failure to include the stochastic nature of project lives in the calculation of $\sigma^2(\text{NPV})$ can substantially alter the magnitude of the estimate of $\sigma^2(\text{NPV})$ and may influence the firm's decision to accept or reject the project.

Since a project's cash flows typically are nonindependent and nonidentically distributed, it is necessary to rewrite equations (3) and (4) under more general conditions. Following Ross but allowing the random variables to be independent and nonidentically distributed, the variance of the sum of the random variables is

$$\sigma^2\left(\sum_{i=1}^{N} X_i\right) = E\left[\left(\sum_{i=1}^{N} X_i\right)^2\right] - \left(E\left[\sum_{i=1}^{N} X_i\right]\right)^2, \tag{5}$$

which can be rewritten as

$$\sigma^2\left(\sum_{i=1}^{N} X_i\right) = \sum_{i=1}^{n} P_i E\left[\left(\sum_{j=1}^{i} X_j\right)^2\right] - \left(\sum_{i=1}^{n} P_i E \sum_{j=1}^{i} X_j\right)^2, \tag{6}$$

where

P_i = probability of the project terminating in period i, and
n = realization of N.

Define

$$Z_i = \sum_{j=1}^{i} X_j,$$

and from the definition of the variance,

$$E[Z_i^2] = \sigma^2(Z_i) + (E[Z_i])^2. \tag{7}$$

Substitution of Z_i into equation (7) yields

$$E[Z_i^2] = E\left[\left(\sum_{j=1}^{i} X_j\right)^2\right] = \sum_{j=1}^{i} \sigma^2(X_j) + \left(\sum_{j=1}^{i} E[X_j]\right)^2. \tag{8}$$

The expected value of equation (8) is

$$E[Z^2] = \sum_{i=1}^{n} P_i E\left[\left(\sum_{j=1}^{i} X_j\right)^2\right] = \sum_{i=1}^{n} P_i \left(\sum_{j=1}^{i} \sigma^2(X_j) + (E[X_j])^2\right), \tag{9}$$

which is substituted into equation (6) to yield

$$\sigma^2\left(\sum_{i=1}^{N} X_i\right) = \sum_{i=1}^{n} P_i\left(\sum_{j=1}^{i} \sigma^2(X_j) + \left(\sum_{j=1}^{i} E[X_j]\right)^2\right)$$

$$-\left(\sum_{i=1}^{n} P_i \sum_{j=1}^{i} E[X_j]\right)^2. \tag{10}$$

If the independence assumption is relaxed, we obtain[1]

$$\sigma^2\left(\sum_{i=1}^{N} X_i\right) = \sum_{i=1}^{n} P_i\left(\sum_{j=1}^{i} \sigma^2(X_j) + 2 \sum_{j=1}^{i-1} \sum_{k=j+1}^{i} \text{cov}(X_j, X_k)\right.$$

$$\left.+\left(\sum_{j=1}^{i} E[X_j]\right)^2\right) - \left(\sum_{i=1}^{n} P_i \sum_{j=1}^{i} E[X_j]\right)^2. \tag{11}$$

The $E\left[\sum_{i=1}^{N} X_i\right]$ for nonidentically distributed random variables is

$$E\left[\sum_{i=1}^{N} X_i\right] = \sum_{i=1}^{n} P_i \sum_{j=1}^{i} E(X_j), \tag{12}$$

which holds for both independent and dependent Xs.

All the above can be cast in a discounting framework by assuming X_j is the jth-period cash flow (CF_j) and r is the discount rate. Then

$$X_j = CF_j/(1+r)^j,$$

$$\sigma^2(X_j) = \sigma^2(CF_j)/(1+r)^{2j},$$

$$\text{cov}(X_j, X_k) = \text{cov}(CF_j, CF_k)/(1+r)^{j+k},$$

$$\sigma^2\left(\sum_{i=1}^{N} X_i\right) = \sigma^2(NPV),$$

and

$$E\left[\sum_{i=1}^{N} X_i\right] = E[\text{NPV}].$$

An interesting and simplifying condition in all of the above is that the $E[\text{NPV}]$ and $\sigma^2(\text{NPV})$ remain functions of the means, variances, and covariances of the cash flows. The only additional information required to calculate $E[\text{NPV}]$ and $\sigma^2(\text{NPV})$ when N is stochastic is the probability distribution of N.

RESEARCH METHODS

Determination of the impact on capital budgeting decisions of incorrectly assuming that N is constant requires specification of an evaluation procedure and a controlled data set. The evaluation was performed by measuring the change in the $E[\text{NPV}]$ and $\sigma^2(\text{NPV})$ for both individual capital budgeting projects with independent cash flows and portfolios of capital budgeting projects with temporally independent and autocorrelated cash flows. The consistency of the portfolio efficient sets also was studied.

Two sets of cash flows for a firm plus nine projects with wide-ranging values were studied. The marginal probability distributions of the cash flows were assumed to be triangular. This assumption allowed the cash flows to be stochastic and yet completely specified by three estimates: the pessimistic (A), modal (B), and optimistic (C) cash flows. The cash-flow distributions were symmetric and nonsymmetric and changed in shape over time. The triangular distribution allowed the characteristics of many other distributions to be approximated by altering the estimates of A, B, and C. Furthermore, the mean of a triangular distribution is

$$\mu = \tfrac{1}{3}(A + B + C),$$

and the variance is

$$\sigma^2 = \tfrac{1}{18}[(C - A)^2 + (B - A)(B - C)].$$

Therefore, for independent cash flows, $E[\text{NPV}]$ and $\sigma^2(\text{NPV})$ can be calculated simply by knowing A, B, and C. The cash flows were assumed to occur at one-year intervals.

The distribution of N was assumed to be triangular. The discrete probabilities required for equations (10), (11), and (12) were estimated by integrating the triangular pdf. The linearity of the triangular pdf makes the integration very simple; that is, the cumulative probability for any value T is given as

$$(T - A)^2/(B - A)(C - A) \quad \text{for } A \leqslant T \leqslant B$$
$$1 - (C - T)^2/(C - B)(C - A) \quad \text{for } B \leqslant T \leqslant C.$$

P_i for $i > A$ is defined as $T_i - T_{i-1}$ or simply as the area under the triangular distribution between i and $i - 1$. If $i \leqslant A$, P_i equals zero.

Three project-life distributions, as listed in Table 1, were used with each set of cash flows. N and CF were assumed to be independent.

Application of a mean-variance $(E - V)$ portfolio approach followed Weingartner [15] and is

$$\text{max:} \quad \mu - \lambda\sigma^2 = \sum_{i=1}^{M} \mu_i X_i - \lambda \sum_{i=1}^{M} \sum_{j=1}^{M} X_i X_j \sigma_{ij}$$

$$\text{subject to:} \quad X_i = 0, 1 \quad i = 2, 3, \ldots, M$$

$$X_1 = 1$$

where μ and σ^2 are the mean and variance of the NPV of the portfolio of projects and λ is a risk-aversion parameter. The existing firm is X_1.

The required data for the $E - V$ formulation are the joint NPV distributions for all possible combinations of projects. The data were estimated in accordance with the economic state and simulation procedure developed by Bey and Singleton [1].[2] The essence of this procedure for independent cash flows with a con-

Table 1. Project-Life Probability Distributions for Cash-Flow Data Sets

| | | Cash-Flow Set 1 | | | | | Cash-Flow Set 2 | | | |
| | | B | | | | | B | | | |
Project	A	1	2	3	C	A	1	2	3	C
1[a]	25	25	25	25	25	25	25	25	25	25
2	0	2	6	10	12	0	3	10	17	20
3	0	4	10	18	20	0	2	9	16	18
4	0	3	8	14	16	0	2	5	8	10
5	0	3	9	16	18	0	1	4	6	8
6	0	2	6	10	12	0	2	5	8	10
7	0	1	3	5	6	0	3	6	10	12
8	0	4	10	18	20	0	3	7	12	14
9	0	2	6	10	12	0	3	8	14	16
10	0	4	12	22	24	0	4	12	21	25

[a]The existing firm

stant N is as follows: First, separate the cash-flow distributions into a set of economic states where each economic state corresponds to a level of economic activity and the economic states are assumed to be distributed normally. Second, generate a set (200 in this study) of economic state sequences where each state sequence consists of one economic state for each period. Third, for each project a series of cash flows is selected in accordance with each state sequence. (It should be noted that for a given project, a given economic state in a given period does not imply a fixed cash flow; the cash flows are a function of the economic state and are stochastic.) Fourth, each cash-flow series is discounted, and the collection of the project NPVs is the project sample NPV distribution. The identical set of economic state sequences is used for every project since all projects coexist in the same planning horizon; that is, the cash flows of all projects in a given time period are a function of the same economic factors.

The joint NPV distributions are formed as follows: Let X and Y represent vectors of NPVs for projects X and Y, and let x_i and y_i correspond to the NPV for project X and Y associated with state sequence i. Since projects X and Y are physically independent, the joint NPV of X and Y is $x_i + y_i$. The same condition holds for all project combinations and state sequences; that is, the joint NPV distribution for any combination of projects is the sum of the associated project NPV vectors.

Autocorrelation was included in the analysis through the economic state and simulation procedure by assuming that the economic states followed a Gaussian first-order Markov process. The marginal probability of each of the economic states was assumed to be 0.2, and the degree of autocorrelation varied from −1.0 to 1.0.

Simulation of the project NPVs also was carried out for a stochastic N. When N was stochastic, the length of each cash-flow sequence was a function of the distribution of N. However, the simulation was carried out in such a manner that the cash flows for the years that were common to both the constant and stochastic N sequences were identical. The foregoing was done to ensure that any observed differences were due to the impact of whether N was constant or stochastic and were not due to sampling error.

RESULTS

The objective of this study was to determine the impact on capital budgeting decisions of assuming that N is constant when N is stochastic. Therefore the results of this study are reported primarily in terms of the differences in the means and variances of individual projects and portfolios and the consistency of the composition of the $E - V$ efficient sets. The standard of comparison was the result obtained when N was stochastic.

Individual Projects

The means and variances of NPVs for individual projects with independent cash flows, a constant N, and a stochastic N are reported in Tables 2 and 3.

An examination of Tables 2 and 3 reveals a considerable difference in the magnitudes of the means and variances of the NPVs when N was assumed to be constant or stochastic. Since Tables 2 and 3 are based on equations (10) and (12) and did not involve simulation, the differences cannot be contributed to sampling error but are related directly to whether N is constant or stochastic. As previously stated, it is unrealistic to assume that a project's life is known with certainty; therefore we conclude the observed differences are errors introduced into the NPV analysis by incorrectly assuming that N is a constant.

Table 4 lists the percent error in the means and variances of each project and data set. The percent error was defined as

$$\text{percent error} = \frac{\begin{array}{c}\text{mean (variance) for} \\ \text{constant } N\end{array} - \begin{array}{c}\text{mean (variance) for} \\ \text{stochastic } N\end{array}}{\text{mean (variance for stochastic } N)}.$$

The percent error in the mean NPVs was both positive and negative, although usually positive, and varied with both the set of cash flows and the distribution of N. The largest errors in the mean NPVs occurred when N was highly positively skewed. The direction of the error, positive or negative, was a function of both the project-life distribution and the pattern of cash flows and ranged from –192 to 157 percent. The mean of the absolute value of the errors of the mean NPVs ranged from 9 to 50 percent.

Since the variance cannot be less than zero and since a project's variance of NPVs when N is constant may be greater than, equal to, or less than the variance of NPVs when N is stochastic, the possible range of the percent error in the variance of NPVs is from –100 to ∞ percent. In this study, all of the project variances had negative percent errors. That is, assuming that N is constant underestimated the project variance. The range of the variance errors was –28 to –95 percent. The mean of the absolute value of the variance errors ranged from 55 to 69 percent. Hence, on average the variance was underestimated by more than 50 percent of the maximum possible amount.

Although the absolute mean percent error in the mean NPVs is substantially less than the absolute mean percent error for the variance of NPVs, both are of

Table 2. Means of NPVs by Project and Data Set

Project	Stochastic N Data Sets[a]						Constant N Data Sets					
	11	12	13	21	22	23	11	12	13	21	22	23
1[b]	2326	2326	2326	3749	3749	3749	2326	2326	2326	3749	3749	3749
2	15	32	44	70	86	91	20	37	50	84	96	101
3	14	28	41	56	78	94	22	34	46	61	83	100
4	26	50	71	-73	-44	-17	40	56	75	-78	-41	-9
5	47	60	70	12	32	43	48	63	76	15	36	48
6	9	32	53	32	51	64	5	33	61	40	59	72
7	12	23	32	31	48	64	15	25	35	40	57	73
8	34	83	129	40	53	64	64	105	129	52	57	65
9	62	88	111	-72	-24	14	48	89	122	-50	-4	36
10	49	79	105	-123	-62	-12	60	87	115	-100	-41	11

[a] Data set IJ refers to cash-flow set I, project-life set J.
[b] The existing firm

Table 3. Variances of NPVs by Project and Data Set

Project	Stochastic N Data Set[a]						Constant N Data Set					
	11	12	13	21	22	23	11	12	13	21	22	23
1[b]	6402	6402	6402	12186	12186	12186	6402	6402	6402	12186	12186	12186
2	1170	950	939	1349	1037	941	152	199	244	542	614	662
3	1021	785	732	1683	1368	1369	123	143	164	403	453	480
4	5109	4778	4939	5370	5275	5490	3002	3236	3402	1741	1933	2073
5	1016	891	937	1794	1594	1608	424	475	538	615	701	743
6	5049	5455	5911	1958	1624	1533	3419	3889	4264	424	474	520
7	869	816	845	2353	2059	1939	409	466	512	666	705	735
8	13366	11004	11099	1175	984	987	3091	3387	3785	365	428	476
9	4833	4813	5003	15193	13210	12577	2496	2701	2853	6206	6534	6767
10	3462	2566	2463	19879	16335	16494	175	206	236	5583	5736	5848

[a]Data set IJ refers to cash-flow set I, project-life set J.
[b]The existing firm

73

Table 4. Percent Error in Means and Variances by Project and Data Set

Project	Data Set Means[a]						Data Set Variances					
	11	12	13	21	22	23	11	12	13	21	22	23
1[b]	0	0	0	0	0	0	0	0	0	0	0	0
2	30	15	13	20	12	11	-87	-79	-74	-60	-41	-30
3	53	20	14	9	6	6	-88	-82	-78	-76	-67	-65
4	53	13	6	7	-7	-47	-41	-32	-31	-68	-63	-62
5	3	6	9	25	13	12	-58	-47	-43	-66	-56	-54
6	-50	4	14	25	16	13	-32	-29	-28	-78	-71	-66
7	24	10	10	29	19	14	-53	-43	-39	-72	-66	-62
8	86	27	0	30	8	2	-77	-69	-66	-69	-57	-52
9	-23	2	10	-31	-83	157	-48	-44	-43	-59	-51	-46
10	23	11	9	-19	-34	-192	-95	-92	-90	-72	-65	-62
Absolute mean[c]	38	12	9	22	22	50	64	57	55	69	60	55

[a]Data set *IJ* refers to cash-flow set *I*, project-life set *J*.
[b]The existing firm
[c]The mean of the absolute value of the errors excluding project 1

such a magnitude that decision errors could be made by assuming that N is constant. If a firm faced capital rationing and selected projects on the basis of the project NPVs, different ranking and different projects may be accepted due to assumptions about N. For example, for data set 11, the project rank order is 9, 10, 5, 8, 4, 2, 3, 7, 6 when N is stochastic and 8, 10, 5, 9, 4, 3, 2, 7, 6 when N is constant. A similar situation holds if the project variances are rank ordered. In either case the relative and absolute desirability of the projects may be distorted by incorrectly assuming that the project life is known with certainty. Given the foregoing, we conclude that Lewellen and Long's [5] untested conclusion that consideration of project lives as a random variable will have a small impact on expected NPVs and that the gain from considering uncertain project lives will be modest must be rejected. In contrast, although the financial consequences associated with failing to consider the stochastic nature of project lives cannot be specified and is a function of the projects considered, we conclude that it is critical to consider the uncertainty of the randomness associated with project lives for a proper analysis of both the expected NPVs and variances of NPVs for individual capital budgeting projects.

Portfolios of Projects

A summary of the NPV means and variances of the portfolio efficient combinations for data set 11 and three levels of autocorrelation (i.e., ρ equal to –0.5, 0.0, and 0.5) are given in Table 5.[3]

A comparison of the mean NPVs indicates that, as expected, the portfolio means usually are slightly larger when N is assumed constant. However, since in this study the firm is much larger than the projects considered—a typical real-world situation—and the firm was assumed not to fail, the percentage difference between the portfolio mean NPVs when N is constant or stochastic is quite small.

The impact on the portfolio variance by assuming that N is constant varies as a function of the cash flows, the distribution of N, and ρ. A summary of the average error in the portfolio variance is listed in Table 6.

The average error in the variance was smaller than what would be expected by examining Table 3 and simply combining the project variances without considering the interproject covariances. Examination of the variance-covariance matrix revealed that the covariances between projects were almost always positive. Also, when N was constant, projects had larger covariances than when N was stochastic. The differences in the interproject covariances increased as the degree of autocorrelation increased. In fact, when ρ equaled 0.5, the interproject covariances for projects with a constant N had increased enough not only to offset the underestimated project variances, but also to cause the portfolio variances to be

Table 5. Portfolio Means and Variances of NPVs for Data Set 11

Efficient Combination	Stochastic N				Constant N			
	Mean	Variance ρ			Mean	Variance ρ		
		−0.5	0.0	0.5		−0.5	0.0	0.5
1	2330	3125	7605	19358	2330	3125	7605	19358
5	2376	5088	10907		2386	3896	9744	24744
10	2377		16555	25090	2429	5338	13399	34141
42	2423			32234	2450	6205	15619	39905
104	2437	9039						
105	2437	18540						
127	2489			54891	2470	7213	18335	46671
190		15346						
237								
238	2503		30258		2483		20808	
292					2530	13315		
313								
344	2516		34182					
360	2503	17416						
418	2530	21228	39838	78212				
423					2544	21203	38292	95074
441					2580	23297	57249	
488					2593			
499	2556	30165						
507	2593	48021	91415		2629	34564	84638	208164
512	2604	60311	118848	228676	2637	50231	119841	

Table 6. Average Error in Portfolio Variances Due to Assuming a Constant Project Life

Data Set	ρ		
	-0.5	0.0	0.5
11	-25	-9	2
12	-21	-2	14
13	-28	-8	5
21	-26	13	27
22	-1	6	6
23	-17	1	14

Note: Table based on those combinations that were common to both efficient sets

overestimated by about 2 to 27 percent. The critical point is that although the objective of this research was not to determine the importance of considering autocorrelation in capital budgeting decisions, it is evident that relaxing two common capital budgeting assumptions creates an interaction effect that may substantially influence capital budgeting decisions.

The commonality of the efficient sets between projects with a constant and stochastic N is given in Table 7. The denominator of each fraction listed is the number of efficient combinations in a given data set when N is stochastic. The numerator is the number of efficient combinations contained in the union of the efficient sets when N is constant and N is stochastic. No definitive relationship is apparent between the commonality of the efficient sets and distribution of N. The overlap in the two sets ranged from 44 to 100 percent. The mean

Table 7. Fraction of the Stochastic N Efficient Combinations Common to the Constant N Efficient Combinations

Data Set	ρ		
	-0.5	0.0	0.5
11	4/9	4/9	3/6
12	8/10	6/9	5/8
13	7/13	7/10	6/9
21	7/7	5/7	4/7
22	5/7	4/7	5/7
23	7/9	7/8	7/8

overlap was 67 percent. That is, for the data tested, if a financial manager assumed N was constant when N was stochastic, on average about two-thirds of the correct efficient combinations were contained in the realized efficient set.

CONCLUSIONS

The empirical results of this study indicate that incorporating the uncertainty associated with the life of capital budgeting projects into a capital budgeting decision analysis has a substantial impact on the risk and return characteristics, when measured as the mean and variance of NPVs, of individual capital budgeting projects. Likewise, when a portfolio approach to capital budgeting was taken, the large errors in the estimates of the individual project variances associated with assuming constant project lives were reduced because of the smaller interproject covariances associated with projects when N is stochastic than when N is constant.

The portfolio variance also was influenced by the degree of autocorrelation. When ρ was zero or negative, the portfolio variance was less when N was constant than when N was stochastic. However, when ρ was positive, the difference in the portfolio variance when N was constant and N was stochastic declined as ρ increased. When ρ equaled 0.5, the portfolio variance when N was constant exceeded the portfolio variance when N was stochastic. The reason for this condition was an interaction effect between the nature of project life and the degree of autocorrelation on the NPV distributions. That is, when N was stochastic, the interproject covariances decreased more rapidly than when N was constant. This interaction was unexpected and emphasizes the difficulty and limitations associated with studying capital budgeting decision rules by relaxing one constraint at a time.

Approximately two-thirds of the correct efficient combinations were contained in the constant project-life efficient set. Likewise, a number of combinations not in the stochastic project-life efficient set were contained in the constant project-life efficient set. Therefore, a financial manager who incorrectly assumes that project life is constant has a considerable chance of selecting a nonoptimal combination of projects.

The lack of consistency between efficient sets when N is constant and N is stochastic, the bias in the estimates of $E[\text{NPV}]$ and $\sigma^2(\text{NPV})$, and the impact on the interproject covariances owing to the interaction between the nature of N and the degree of autocorrelation leads us to conclude that for a good capital budgeting analysis, it is critical to consider project life as stochastic and the cash flows as intertemporally dependent. Substantial improvements in the capital budgeting decision process may be gained by relaxing the assumption that the lives of capital budgeting projects are known with certainty and cash flows are temporally independent. Therefore, it is recommended that the economic state and simulation methodology used in this study be adopted by financial managers. In contrast to other suggested procedures, the foregoing methodology is operational, easily understood, easily conveyed, and requires a minimal number of estimates.

NOTES

1. Derivation of equation (11) is similar to equation (10) except that

$$\sigma^2(X_i) = \sum_{j=1}^{i} \sigma^2(X_j) + 2 \sum_{j=1}^{i-1} \sum_{k=j+1}^{i} \text{cov}(X_j, X_k).$$

2. A detailed explanation of the economic state and simulation procedure is given in Bey and Singleton [1].

3. The results from the other five data sets tested are similar and are not reported because of space considerations.

REFERENCES

[1]   Bey, Roger P., and Singleton, J. Clay. "Autocorrelated Cash Flows and the Selection of a Portfolio of Capital Assets," *Decision Sciences* (October 1978), pp. 640–657.

[2]   Greer, Willis R., Jr. "Capital Budgeting Analysis with the Timing Events Uncertain," *Accounting Review* 6 (January 1970), pp. 103–14.

[3]   Hertz, David B. "Risk Analysis in Capital Investment," *Harvard Business Review* (January–February 1964), pp. 95–106.

[4]   Klammer, Thomas. "Empirical Evidence of the Adoption of Sophisticated Capital Budgeting Techniques," *Journal of Business* 40 (July 1972), pp. 387–397.

[5]   Lewellen, Wilbur G., and Long, Michael S. "Simulation versus Single Value Estimates in Capital Expenditures Analysis," *Decision Sciences* 3 (October 1972), pp. 19–34.

[6]   Parzen, Emanuel. *Stochastic Processes.* San Francisco: Holden-Day, 1962.

[7]   Perrakis, Stylianos, and Henin, Claude. "The Evaluation of Risky Investment with Random Timing of Cash Returns," *Management Science* 21 (September 1974), pp. 79–86.

[8]   Perrakis, Stylianos, and Sabin, Izzet. "On Risky Investments with Random Timing of Cash Returns and Fixed Planning Horizon," *Management Science* 24 (March 1976), pp. 799–809.

[9] Petty, J. William; Scott, David F.; and Bird, Monroe M. "The Capital Expenditure Decision-Making Process of Large Corporations," *Engineering Economist* 20 (Spring 1975), pp. 159–172.

[10] Rosenthal, Richard E. "The Variance of Present Worth of Cash Flows under Uncertain Timing," *Engineering Economist* 23 (Spring 1978), pp. 163–170.

[11] Ross, Sheldon M. *Introduction to Probability Models.* New York: Academic Press, 1972.

[12] Van Horne, James C. "Capital Budgeting under Conditions of Uncertainty as to Project Life," *Engineering Economist* 17 (Spring 1972), pp. 189–199.

[13] Van Horne, James C. *Financial Management and Policy,* 4th ed., Englewood Cliffs, N.J.: Prentice-Hall, 1977.

[14] Wagle, B. "A Statistical Analysis of Risk in Capital Investment Projects," *Operational Research Quarterly* 18 (March 1967), pp. 13–33.

[15] Weingartner, H. Martin. "Capital Budgeting of Interrelated Projects: Survey and Synthesis," *Management Science* 12 (March 1966), pp. 485–516.

[16] Young, Donovan, and Contreras, Luis E. "Expected Present Worths of Cash Flows under Uncertain Timing," *Engineering Economist* 20 (Summer 1975), pp. 257–268.

5 CAPITAL BUDGETING UNDER QUALITATIVE DATA INFORMATION

Wolfgang Bühler
University of Dortmund, West Germany

Approaches to the capital budgeting problem can roughly be classified as being concerned with:

- The selection of technically and economically independent or interrelated projects
- Decisions under certainty or decisions under uncertainty
- The development of valuation criteria (economics-finance approach) or efficient solution techniques (engineering–management science approach)[1]

This paper deals with the accept-reject decision for a *single* project under *uncertainty* from the engineering–management science point of view. The approach used differs from the well-known methods of evaluating risky single-investment projects in the assumptions concerning the available information about future uncertain data.

The known procedures to analyze single investment projects with uncertain data can be divided into two main groups: the structure–oriented and the decision-oriented methods.[2]

Structure-Oriented Methods

The immediate goal in applying a structure-oriented method is to find out how the evaluation criterion (e.g., the internal rate of return) depends on the uncertain data. The analysis results, therefore, not in a recommendation to accept or reject a certain project, but in a better insight into the structure of the problem, which possibly improves the final decision. Within the group of structure-oriented methods, one may differentiate between two principal types of approach depending on the information available about uncertain data.

An application of an approach of the *first type* requires the *knowledge* of the *distribution functions* of the uncertain data. Based on these distribution functions, it is possible, at least in principle, to calculate the distribution function of such *evaluation criteria* as the present value [2, 16, 35, 41, 43, p. 24, 44, 45, 66, 67, 68, 94], the *internal rate of return* [20, 39, 42, 70], or the *payback period* [62].[3] Analytical and simulation techniques have been proposed for computing the distribution function of the evaluation criterion. It should be noted, however, that both techniques have their specific deficiencies: Analytical methods are applicable only under very restrictive assumptions regarding the stochastic dependencies or the types of distribution functions of the random data; an application of the central limit theorem is problematic because of the discounting procedure [28, 43, p. 26], and the simulation procedure converges rather slowly if the random data are correlated.

If it is not possible to specify the distribution functions of the uncertain data, then valuable insights into the stability of a capital budgeting decision can be gained if the sensitivity of the corresponding evaluation criterion relative to changes of the uncertain data could be determined. The study of the effect of variations in uncertain data without knowing their distribution functions represents the goal of approaches of the *second type*. The methods proposed include local sensitivity analysis [10, 48, 95] based on differential calculus and global sensitivity analysis including break-even analysis [34, p. 97].

Decision-Oriented Methods

The application of a decision-oriented method provides the basis for either accepting or rejecting a risky investment project. Most of these methods require a knowledge of the distribution functions of the uncertain data. They differ insofar as some authors use the Von Neumann–Morgenstern utility theory directly in order to elicit the risk-utility function of the decision maker(s) [30, pp. 294, 86] and to compute the expected utility of the risky project (based on the distribution function of the evaluation criterion), whereas others reduce the mean value of the *evaluation criterion* or of the *random data* by an amount that depends on the risk of the project or of the individual data (certainty equivalent methods). Assuming a quadratic utility function, the risk reduction depends on the variance of the evaluation criterion or on the variance of the random data [1]. Some authors suggest risk reductions that are determined by the probability of loss [33], the standard deviation [56], or the semivariance [59, 60]. These suggestions are not necessarily consistent with the expected utility model. The same is true for the perhaps most widely used model in both theory and practice, the risk-adjusted discount method [76, p. 284, 65, p. 328]. An essential part of the group of decision-oriented methods, which require the knowledge of the distribution functions of all uncertain data, constitute the economics-finance approaches based on the single-period Sharpe-Lintner-Mossin CAPM [80, 54, 64] and its multiperiod extensions [61]. The mean-variance capital budgeting models proposed by Biermann and Hass [9], Bogue and Roll [11], Hamada [32], Rubinstein [71], and Stapleton [87] are based mainly on the single-period CAPM and are equivalent in terms of their decision criteria, on which the accept-reject decision for a single risky investment is based.[4] Recently, considerable effort has been made to attack the multiperiod capital budgeting problem within the framework of a multiperiod CAPM [7, 8, 65].[5]

Most decision-oriented methods are based on the assumption that the distribution functions of the uncertain data are known. Exceptions are provided by the papers of Bennion [6] and Singhvi [82], who adopt a game-theoretic approach.

Critique and Outline of the Paper

The short survey of the state of the art given above shows that most of the proposals for selecting risky investment projects require either *complete* knowledge or assume that no knowledge exists about the distribution functions of uncertain data. The second assumption seems to be not very realistic, since experience and some vague feelings about the development of the economy in general and the firm in particular will make it possible for the management to classify at least some of the future values of the uncertain data as more probable than others.[6] The first assumption, however, demands a more detailed consideration. To judge this assumption, it has to be made clear which interpretation of probability is used to solve capital budgeting problems.

Essentially, three foundations of probabilities exist: the view based on relative frequencies and the logical and subjective views.[7]

- The concept of frequency applies meaningfully only to repetitive events.[8] Since most capital budgeting decisions typically are made only once and have to be performed in a nonstationary, increasingly dynamic and changing business environment, an estimation of probability distributions by means of statistical techniques is in most cases impossible. The assumption of normally distributed random data should especially be brought to doubt.[9]

- The *logical* concept suffers from its lack of applicability. As long as it is not known how to determine probabilities that are independent of the individual, this concept is of no use for risky capital budgeting decisions.

- Most of the proposals on how to select risky investment projects assume implicitly or explicitly that the required probabilities should be estimated subjectively by the investor. This assumption takes into account the once-only character of most of the capital budgeting decisions. Usually, however, the discussion does not enter into the central problem of every theory of subjective probabilities. This problem is one of consistently estimating probabilities so that they satisfy the axioms of Kolmogoroff and so that they can be handled as in traditional probability theory. Therefore, the practicability of the concept of subjective probabilities depends crucially on the ability of the investor to quantify his subjective ideas about the probabilities of future events in such a way that these probabilities can be accepted as mathematical probabilities. The experimental psychological literature investigates this problem by dividing it into two subproblems:

Within the *first subproblem,* it is assumed that the individual is basically able to estimate probabilities and to handle these as elementary calculus of probability indicates. The purpose of the experiments is to check which elicitation techniques are most suitable and how accurate estimates of probabilities are. The results are not too encouraging since they show that the estimates depend strongly on the elicitation techniques used [18] and that the expense of obtaining estimates is rather high.[10]

More interest in our context is deserved in the *second subproblem* of whether individuals are able to consistently estimate probabilities at all. This problem immediately raises the question of to which extent the intuitive-comparative [29, 51] or the decision-oriented [75, 88] axioms of subjective probabilities have positive-descriptive character. A great number of experiments have been performed to resolve this question by testing single axioms (especially the sure-thing principle [75, p. 21, 77, p. 79, 57, p. 10, 84]) as well as complete systems of axioms for subjective probabilities and the closely related subjective expected utility theories [57, 92]. The results can be summarized as follows:

The descriptive power of the various axioms varies [57]. Whereas individuals immediately correct violations of comparatively simple axioms (e.g., the transitivity axiom), if their inconsistencies are pointed out to them [57], they refuse to change their decision if relatively complicated axioms (e.g., the sure-thing principle) are violated [84].

The spirit of decision analysis to decompose a complex problem into simpler hypothetical problems that management is *forced* to solve (possibly without having thought about these problems before) may lead to management's not accepting the solution of the complex problem [86].

Probability judgments by individuals violate "rational" axioms of subjective probability theory by a number of biases [83], which leads Tversky [92] to the critical comment that it is a still unsettled question whether the axioms of subjective decision theory are suitable to describe individual behavior under uncertainty.

This paper tries to develop an approach selecting single risky capital budgeting projects under the assumption that management has some qualitative ideas about the future development of the business environment (affecting the investment decision), but it is not assumed that these ideas can be quantified by a probability distribution.[11] The following three examples should serve as an intuitive introduction to the main concept:

- The economic life of a project depends heavily on technological progress. An estimation of the probability distribution of a project's economic life is most likely to be impossible. Management, however, might be able to make branch-conditioned ordinal estimates stating that, for example, a six-year economic life is more probable than a ten-year one.
- The wages paid in the next years depend on future union contracts. The rate of increase of wages lies between 5 percent and 10 percent with certainty. In addition, because of the general economic climate and the specific situation in the line of business, it is more probable that the union contract leads to an increase of wages between 6.5 percent and 7 percent than between 8 percent and 9 percent, which again is more probable than a rate of increase between 5 percent and 6 percent.
- Future sales opportunities are of central importance for a capital budgeting decision. Expectations on sales volume in a future period will depend on the sales volumes in previous periods. In general, an estimation of the stochastic process of future sales volumes will not be possible. All the

same, it might be possible to make a judgment of the following kind: "If in period t the sales volume results in an amount between 200,000 and 220,000 units, then it is more probable that in period $t + 1$ the sales volume ranges between 210,000 and 230,000 than between 260,000 and 280,000 units, considering business environment and the individual advertising expenditures."

Information that allows subjective judgments as described in the examples above is called *qualitative*. In the first example there exists qualitative information on a *discrete* quantity (economic life), in the second the qualitative information refers to *intervals* that may contain possible values of the uncertain increase of wages, whereas the third example serves as a demonstration that qualitative information may lead to qualitative-conditional judgments of probability.

The paper is organized as follows: The next section gives a rigorous definition of the concept of qualitative information and presents a solution procedure for a general decision problem under qualitative information. A generalization of the terminal value method in the case of qualitative information follows. Then it is shown that the conceptual analysis of the previous section can be applied to real-world problems by splitting future cash flows into their components. Finally, the limits of this concept are discussed.

THE GENERAL DECISION PROBLEM UNDER QUALITATIVE INFORMATION

Definition of a Decision Problem under Qualitative Information

The normal form of a decision problem is defined by a set A of alternatives, a set S of states of nature, and an outcome function O defined on $A \times S$. It is assumed that $A := \{a_1, \ldots, a_m\}$ is finite, and, for the time being, that $S := \{s_1, \ldots, s_n\}$ is also finite. Following Fishburn [23, p. 187, 24] and Fourgeaud, Lenclud, and Sentis [26], the vague ideas of the decision maker about the uncertain future states of nature, which have been formulated in an intuitive manner above, are characterized by three conditions:[12]

   i. At least two states of nature s, $t \in S$ exist so that the decision maker is able to specify whether:

     • s is not less probable than t or
     • t is not less probable than s.

ii. If $r \in S$ is not less probable than $s \in S$, and s is not less probable than $t \in S$, then it holds that r is not less probable than t.

iii. s is not less probable than s for all $s \in S$.

It is therefore assumed that the information available to the management about future development of uncertain data can be represented by a weak partial order "not less probable than" defined in the set $S \times S$ of states of nature. In analogy to the term of qualitative probability, introduced by Savage [75, p. 32], this type of information is called qualitative and will be denoted by the symbol $\geqslant$. The first condition stated above simply excludes the case that management has no intuitive feeling at all about the probability of future events. It should be noted, however, that this condition does not imply the completeness of $\geqslant$; i.e., it is not required that two states of nature are always comparable with respect to $\geqslant$. The number of states of nature by which management represents the future and also the number of probability relations between these states depend on the experience acquired by management; knowledge about the development of business's environment; and the amount of energy that management is willing to spend in order to specify intuitive judgments. The second condition ensures the transitivity of the relation $\geqslant$ and is assumed to be basic for "rational" behavior, although experiments show that sometimes individuals even violate this axiom [92, p. 32]. The third condition makes $\geqslant$ reflexive and is stated for technical reasons only.

It is well known that every partial order can be represented equivalently by a directed graph Γ, the nodes of which are identified with the states of nature. Two nodes $s_j, s_k \in S \, (s_j \neq s_k)$ are connected by a directed arc $(s_j, s_k) \, (j,k = 1, \ldots, n)$ if, and only if, the relation $s_j \geqslant s_k$ holds and if there exists no node $s_l \in S$ with the property $s_j \geqslant s_l \geqslant s_k$. This last condition guarantees a minimal representation of the graph Γ.

Summing up, a decision problem under qualitative information is characterized by a set A of acts, a set S of states of nature, an outcome function O, and qualitative information $\geqslant$ on $S \times S$.

An arbitrary propability distribution $p = (p_1, \ldots, p_n)$ defined on s^{13} is said to be consistent with qualitative information $\geqslant$ if, and only if,

$$s_j \geqslant s_k \quad \text{implies } p_j \geqslant p_k \quad \text{for all } s_j, s_k \in S.$$

The set of all probability distributions that are consistent with qualitative information is denoted by P. Every element of P can be represented by an n-dimensional vector $p \in \mathfrak{R}^n$, satisfying the following two conditions:

i. $\displaystyle\sum_{j=1}^{n} p_j = 1; \quad p_j \geqslant 0, \quad j = 1, \ldots, n.$

ii. From $s_j \geqslant s_k$ follows $p_j \geqslant p_k$ $(j,k = 1, \ldots, n)$.

Equation (1) represents a linear inequality system that defines a compact polyhedron in $\mathcal{R}^n$. In addition, there exists always at least one probability distribution that is consistent with the qualitative information of management, since, for example, the uniform probability distribution $p = 1/n(1, \ldots, 1)$ satisfies (1). Hence qualitative information is never self-contradictory.[14]

Example 1. An investment project is acquiring a limited partnership interest in a limited partnership. The object of this company entails carrying out tax-privileged projects. The success of participation for the special partner depends on three circumstances:

1. Does the company achieve the tax-privileged object within the legal time span?
2. Does the company become insolvent before the special partner is able to cancel the partnership?
3. Will there be a change of the tax laws within the next two years so that the possibility of negative capital accounts for special partners are abrogated?

There exist eight states of nature, s_j, each of which consists of three components. Each component may have the value "yes" (y) or "no" (n).
Let

$$s_1 = (y,y,y), \quad s_2 = (y,y,n), \quad s_3 = (y,n,y), \quad s_4 = (n,n,y),$$
$$s_5 = (y,n,n), \quad s_6 = (n,y,n), \quad s_7 = (n,n,y), \quad s_8 = (n,n,n).$$

The available information enables the investor to make the following qualitative judgments:

$$s_5 \geqslant s_7; \quad s_8 \geqslant s_7; \quad s_7 \geqslant s_4; \quad s_2 \geqslant s_6; \quad s_2 \geqslant s_1.$$

Figure 1 corresponds to this qualitative information. The set P of probability distributions that are consistent with the qualitative information of the investor is defined by the linear inequality system:

i. $\displaystyle\sum_{j=1}^{8} p_j = 1; \quad p_j \geqslant 0 \quad (j = 1, \ldots, 8).$

ii. $p_5 \geqslant p_7; \quad p_8 \geqslant p_7; \quad p_7 \geqslant p_4; \quad p_2 \geqslant p_6; \quad p_2 \geqslant p_1.$

For example, the probability distribution $(1/5, 2/5, 0, 0, 1/5, 0, 0, 1/5)$ is consistent with $\geqslant$, whereas $(0, 1/4, 1/2, 1/4, \ldots, 0)$ is not.

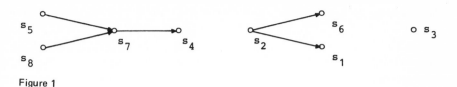

Figure 1

Solution of the General Decision Problem under Qualitative Information

The suggestion of how to solve a decision problem under qualitative information will be divided into three steps. The first two steps refer to a decision-theoretic foundation of the solution of a decision problem under qualitative information. The detailed description of the axiomatic two-stage approach used, although far from being without problems, is out of the scope of this paper.[15] The third step deals with a simple method for determining an optimal solution for a decision problem under qualitative information. This method exploits the special structure of the set P of probability distributions consistent with $\geqslant$ and will be discussed in detail.

Step 1: Transformation of Outcomes to Utilities. For the time being, it is assumed that the individual considers a fixed probability distribution $p \in P$. In that case, he faces a decision problem with known probability distribution, and it is possible, at least in principle, to apply expected utility theory (in a very general sense) to describe the behavior of this individual in risky situations. However, it has to be made very clear that it would be contradictory to assume on the one hand that the individual satisfies the Von Neumann–Morgenstern (or some related) axioms, and that on the other hand he is not able to specify subjective probabilities. This contradiction results from the fact that only very simple additional requirements are needed to construct subjective probabilities if the Von Neumann–Morgenstern axioms are satisfied,[16] and vice versa.[17] In addition, it can be shown that the hypothetical decision situations used to determine Von Neumann–Morgenstern utilities by means of the continuity axiom can be used to determine subjective probabilities.[18] Therefore an expected utility theory with a weakened continuity axiom has been developed. In the end, this weakening of the continuity axiom leads to intransitivities of indifferences with respect to outcomes and therefore to a theory similar to that developed by Aumann [4, 5]. The results of the first step are utilities u_{ij} of outcomes $o_{ij} = O(a_i, s_j)$ and the possibility to value each act a_i for fixed probability distribution $p \in P$ by expected utility

$$U(a_i,p) = \sum_{j=1}^{n} u_{ij}p_j \qquad (a_i \in A, \ p \in P).$$

Step 2: Transformation of a Decision Problem under Qualitative Information about S to a Decision Problem with Complete Ignorance with Respect to P. All the available information about future uncertain data is represented by the set P of all probability distributions consistent with $\geqslant$. So it is reasonable to adopt the argument that it cannot be decided which of two elements of P is more likely to represent the "true," but unknown, probability distribution of the states of nature. Hence the decision problem under qualitative information $(A, S, O, \geqslant)$ is transformed to a decision problem (A, P, U) with complete ignorance with respect to P. In the second step, Milnor's [63] axioms for decision problems without any probability knowledge are generalized to the case of an infinite number of states of nature.

This axiomatic two-stage procedure leads, finally, to the result that a max min solution of (A, P, U) is accepted as a solution of the corresponding decision problem $(A, S, O, \geqslant)$ under qualitative information; ie., every optimal solution $\bar{a} \in A$ satisfies the equation

$$U(\bar{a}, \bar{p}(\bar{a})) = \max_{i=1,\ldots,m} \ \min_{p \in P} \sum_{j=1}^{n} u_{ij}p_j. \tag{2}$$

Critique of Steps 1 and 2. The two-stage procedure described above can be criticized for several reasons. The most important might be:

i. The assumption that the utilities u_{ij} are determined *independently* from the qualitative information
ii. The application of the max min principle

Of course, it will not be possible to weaken this critique completely. However, an intuitive justification of the procedure developed might be helpful:

i. The most desirable approach to a decision problem under qualitative information from a decision theoretic point of view would be to develop an integrated expected utility theory for this type of vague information. The literature provides essentially two proposals to treat decision problems with partially known probabilities.[19] The first one incorporates the partial information into the probabilities by slanting them in a systematic way. The utility function, however, is assumed to be of general validity. Fellner [21] and the two-stage procedure above are examples of this approach. The second proposal does not slant probabilities, but incorporates partial information into the utility function [27, 85]. Both approaches therefore implicitly or explicitly separate the determination of utilities and probabilities, which, in the end, is a consequence of independence of beliefs and tastes, the central assumption of subjective expected utility theory. So in relaxing assumption (i), one is leaving the realm of subjective expected utility theory.

ii. The individual axioms on which the max min principle can be based, as well as the whole principle, have often been criticized [54, p. 294]. One argument often advanced is that the max min principle contradicts the Bernoulli principle (Von Neumann–Morgenstern axioms) [77, p. 106].

Implicitly this argument assumes that the probabilities of the states of nature are known. Exactly this condition is not true in a decision problem under qualitative information. In addition, there is some empirical evidence that individuals base their decisions under uncertainty to a large extent on the worst possible case [82, p. 794]. The investigation of Greer [31] especially shows that the worst possible result of a capital budgeting decision heavily influences the final decision.

Step 3: Solution Method for a Decision Problem under Qualitative Information.
To determine an optimal act of a decision problem under qualitative information requires the solution of m linear programming problems.

$$U_i = \min_{p \in P} \sum_{j=1}^{n} u_{ij} p_j \qquad i = 1, \ldots, m. \qquad (3)$$

In the following, an elementary solution procedure for the linear programs, (3) will be presented by characterizing the extreme points of P. This procedure permits the solution of decision problems under qualitative information of realistic size "by hand."

Recall the definition (1) of the set P of all probability distributions consistent with $\geqslant$ and the representation of qualitative information by a directed graph Γ. Then the following result holds:

A probability distribution $p \in P$ of the states of nature is an *extreme point* of P if, and only if, it satisfies the following two conditions:[20]

i. $p_j \geqslant 0$ and $p_k > 0$ implies $p_j = p_k$.
ii. If p_j and p_k are positive, then there exists an undirected path in Γ that connects the nodes s_j and s_k, and every node on this path has positive probability (with respect to p).

This result states that every extreme point of P (and hence at least one worst *a priori* probability $\bar{p}$) is a generalized uniform distribution, defined on a subset of S. However, it should not be concluded from this result that there are any connections between the solution of decision problems under qualitative information and the solution of decision problems under uncertainty using the principle of insufficient reason or the principle of maximal entropy.

From i and ii, it follows that a subset T of S is the *support*[21] of an extreme point of P if, and only if,

   i. $s_k \in T$, $s_j \geqslant s_k$ implies $s_j \in T$ (i.e., if s_k has positive probability, and if s_j is not less probable than s_k, then s_j must have positive probability), and

   ii. s_j, $s_k \in T$ implies that there exists an undirected path in Γ that connects the nodes s_j and s_k, and every node on this path is an element of T.

A support T with properties i and ii is termed feasible and connected. Based on the properties i and ii of the supports of extreme probability distributions, the linear programming problems (3) can be solved by the following simple device:

1. Construct all feasible and connected supports $T_k \leqslant S$ ($k = 1, \ldots, K \leqslant 2^n$) by inspection of the graph Γ. The extreme point (probability distribution) p^k corresponding to T_k is

$$p_j^k = \begin{cases} 1/|T| & \text{if } s_j \in T \\ 0 & \text{if } s_j \notin T \end{cases} \quad j = 1, \ldots, n,$$

where $|T|$ denotes the number of elements of T.

2. The expected utility of act a_i with respect to p^k (or T_k) comes to

$$U(a_i, p^k) = 1/|T_k| \cdot \sum_{s_j \in T_k} u_{ij} \quad k = 1, \ldots, K. \tag{4}$$

Let $\bar{k}$ be the index for which $U(a_i, p^k)$ is minimal with respect to k. Then $p^{\bar{k}}$ is an optimal solution of the ith linear programming problem in (3), and $U(a_i, p^{\bar{k}})$ equals U_i.

3. The solution of the max min problem (2) is obtained by maximizing U_i with respect to i ($i = 1, \ldots, m$).

Example 2. Consider the problem introduced in example 1. The investor is assumed to have two alternatives:

  a_1: Participation in the limited partnership with an amount of 100,000 DM

  a_2: Purchase or risk-free bonds of the same amount

The planning period considered corresponds with the minimum duration of the partnership before it can be canceled for the first time. The utilities of the net present values of the cash flows (after taxes) discounted by the risk-free interest rates (after taxes) are given in the matrix below:

	s_1	s_2	s_3	s_4	s_5	s_6	s_7	s_8
a_1	10	50	25	0	100	5	0	25
a_2	20	20	20	20	20	20	20	20

There are nine feasible and connected supports:

$$T_1 = \{s_5\}, \quad T_2 = \{s_8\}, \quad T_3 = \{s_5,s_7,s_8\}, \quad T_4 = \{s_4,s_5,s_7,s_8\}, \quad T_5 = \{s_2\},$$

$$T_6 = \{s_2,s_6\}, \quad T_7 = \{s_1,s_2\}, \quad T_8 = \{s_1,s_2,s_6\}, \quad T_9 = \{s_3\}.$$

The associated expected utilities for the two acts are as follows:

	T_1	T_2	T_3	T_4	T_5	T_6	T_7	T_8	T_9
a_1	100	25	125/3	125/4	50	55/2	30	65/3	25
a_2	20	20	20	20	20	20	20	20	20

From this table it can be concluded that even in the worst possible case this participation is slightly better than the risk-free investment.

SELECTION OF AN INVESTMENT PROJECT UNDER QUALITATIVE INFORMATION

The concept of qualitative information as it was introduced in the preceding section can be generalized to cover the following cases of uncertainty:[22]

- The set S of states of nature is infinite since some of the uncertain data (e.g., prices, sales volumes) should be considered as being continuous random variables.
- Qualitative information refers to nonsimple events (e.g., it is not less probable that the economic life of an investment project amounts to seven or eight years rather than nine years or more).
- Qualitative information refers to dependent uncertain data (e.g., prices *and* sales volumes) of the same period.
- Qualitative information refers to dependent uncertain data of different periods.

In this section a generalized concept of qualitative information is applied to the problem of selecting a single investment project.

It is assumed that a stream of incremental cash flows $d_0, d_1, \ldots, d_T$ can be attributed to the proposed project. T denotes the fixed economic life of the investment. The project will be evaluated on the basis of its terminal value (future value at the end of year T). The interest rate will be denoted by r, the compound rate by $q = 1 + r$.

It is natural to assume further that the cash flows d_t ($t = 0, \ldots, T$) are continuous random variables and that the information about d_t depends on the actual values of former cash flows. Therefore the first and the fourth possibilities, described above, will be considered in this section to generalize the concept of qualitative information.

Terminal Value of an Investment under Qualitative-Conditional Information

Experience, knowledge about the development of the business environment, and the internal conditions of the business generally will lead to the following *basic* information of the investor about the cash flows:

i. The cash flow d_t lies between a lower bound L_t and an upper bound U_t ($L_t \leqslant U_t; t = 0, \ldots, T$).

ii. The possible range $[L_t, U_t]$ of d_t can be divided into n_t left-handed closed and nonoverlapping subintervals s_{tj} ($j = 1, \ldots, n_t$) containing the actual cash flows ($t = 0, \ldots, T$). These intervals are the basis for the qualitative-conditional information available to the investor which will be defined below.

iii. The subjective judgments with respect to the initial outlay d_0 can be represented by qualitative information.

The judgment of which two possible values of d_t are more probable will generally depend on the actual cash flows up to period t. If, for example, the cash flows are influenced mainly by the success of a new product, then comparatively high cash flows in the first periods will give management an idea that the new-product introduction has been successful and that a high cash flow in period t is more probable than a low one.

In general, an individual will not be able to realize the complete history of cash flows when ranking the possible values of d_t with respect to their probabilities. In the most simple case, he will take into account only the cash flow d_{t-1} of the immediately preceding period. This case will be treated here.

To formalize the qualitative-conditional information that the investor is assumed to have, the end of year $t - 1$ and year t will be considered. According to ii, the possible cash flows generated in $t - 1$ and t are elements of the sub-intervals $s_{t-1,k}$ ($k = 1, \ldots, n_{t-1}$) or s_{tj} ($j = 1, \ldots, n_t$), respectively. If the actual value of d_{t-1} lies in $s_{t-1,k}$, then, in general, the cash flow d_t will be limited to some of the invervals $s_{t,j}$. The set of all intervals s_{tj} ($j = 1, \ldots, n_t$), which may contain d_t, if d_{t-1}, is an element of $s_{t-1,k}$, which will be denoted by S_{tk}. Graphically, the information on cash flows of succeeding years and their compatibility can be represented by transition lines, as shown in Figure 2.

Given a cash flow $d_{t-1} \in s_{t-1,k}$, the investor will be able to rank some of the intervals $s_{tj} \in S_{tk}$ as to whether the probability that d_t lies in interval s_{tj} is not less than the probability that d_t lies in interval s_{tl}. This order of elements of S_{tk} will be denoted by $\geqslant^{t,k}$. Summing up, it is assumed that the information available to the investor can be characterized by the three basic conditions i, ii, and iii stated above and the following two additional conditions:

iv. For every interval $s_{t-1,k}$ the investor is able to specify the set S_{tk} of intervals so that the cash flows d_{t-1} and d_t are compatible in the following sense: Whenever d_{t-1} is an element of $s_{t-1,k}$ then it is possible according

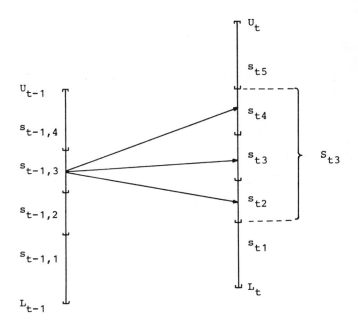

Figure 2

to the available information that d_t is an element of s_{tj} for every $s_{tj} \in S_{tk}$ $(j = 1, \ldots, n_t; k = 1, \ldots, n_{t-1}; t = 1, \ldots, T)$.

v. S_{tk} can be ordered by a weak partial order $\geqslant^{t,k}$ satisfying the conditions i, ii, and iii by which qualitative information was defined earlier $(k = 1, \ldots, n_{t-1}: t = 1, \ldots, T)$.

Information of this type is called *qualitative-conditional*. It consists of one partial order on $\{s_{01}, s_{02}, \ldots, s_{0n_0}\}$ and $n_0 + n_1 + \cdots + n_{T-1}$ conditional partial orders on S_{tk} $(k = 1, \ldots, n_{t-1}; t = 1, \ldots, T)$.

As in the case of qualitative information, the possible range $U_t - L_t$ of cash flows, the number of subintervals into which $[L_t, U_t]$ can be divided, the degree of dependence between succeeding cash flows, measured by the number of elements S_{tk} contains, and the number of probability relations between ranges of cash flows depend on experience, knowledge about the development of business's environment, and on the effort the investors are willing to take to specify their qualitative-conditional information. The quality of qualitative-conditional information increases as $U_t - L_t$ decreases and as n_t and the number of probability relations increase.

The question arises again of which probability distributions are consistent with qualitative-conditional information about the cash flows of an investment. Let p be the probability law of a Markovian process with values in $S = [L_0, U_0] \times [L_1, U_1] \times \cdots \times [L_T, U_T]$. p^0 denotes the associated marginal probability distribution in $t = 0$, and p^t $(t = 1, \ldots, T)$ denotes the associated conditional distributions.

Because of the Markovian property, the equation

$$p^t(I_t | I_{t-1}, \ldots, I_0) = p^t(I_t | I_{t-1})$$

holds for every sequence of subintervals $I_t \leqslant [L_t, U_t]$. An arbitrary Markovian process with values in S is said to be consistent with qualitative-conditional information if, and only if, the following three conditions are satisfied:

i. $s_{0j} \geqslant s_{0l}$ implies $p^0(s_{0j}) \geqslant p^0(s_{0l})$ $(j,l = 1, \ldots, n_0)$; $\Sigma_{j=1}^{n_0} p^0(s_{0j}) = 1$; $p^0(s_{0j}) \geqslant 0$ $(j = 1, \ldots, n_0)$.

ii. From $s_{tj} \notin S_{tk}$ follows $p^t(s_{tj} | s_{t-1,k}) = 0$ $(k = 1, \ldots, n_{t-1}; j = 1, \ldots, n_t;$ $t = 1, \ldots, T)$.

iii. From $s_{tj} \geqslant^{t,k} s_{tl}$ follows $p^t(s_{tj} | s_{t-1,k}) \geqslant p^t(s_{t,l} | s_{t-1,k})$; $\Sigma_{j=1}^{n_t} p^t(s_{tj} | s_{t-1,k})$ $= 1$, $p^t(s_{tj} | s_{t-1,k}) \geqslant 0$ $(k = 1, \ldots, n_{t-1}; j = 1, \ldots, n_t; t = 1, \ldots, T)$.

These conditions are simply a transformation of probability judgments $\geqslant$, $\geqslant^{t,k}$ to the usual order $\geqslant$ of real numbers. The set of all Markovian processes p that are consistent with qualitative-conditional information is denoted by $\bar{P}$. For any

$p \in \bar{P}$, the expected terminal value of an investment project with uncertain cash flows d_t $(t = 0, \ldots, T)$ is[23]

$$TV(p) = E_p \left(\sum_{t=0}^{T} d_t q^{T-t} \right). \tag{5}$$

Applying the worst-case concept of the previous section, the investment project with qualitative-conditionally known cash flows is valued according to the following principle:

$$TV = \min_{p \in \bar{P}} E_p \left(\sum_{t=0}^{T} d_t q^{T-t} \right). \tag{6}$$

If TV is positive, the project will be accepted; if TV is negative, it will be rejected.

The computation of the terminal value TV seems to be impossible because of the "indeterminable" set of Markovian processes satisfying the conditions i, ii, and iii above. However, it will be shown below that the terminal value TV and a worst *a priori* Markovian process exist (this is not obvious) and that the terminal value TV can be computed in an elementary way.

Computation of the Terminal Value of an Investment Project under Qualitative Information

In this subsection, a technical digression will be made in order to demonstrate that the value (terminal value or net present value) of an investment project whose cash flows are known only qualitative-conditionally can be computed very easily "by hand."[24] This question, whether a proposed evaluation criterion for investment projects can actually be computed, is, from management science's point of view, a central one. It can be shown that for every Markovian process p, a Markovian chain $M(p)$ exists with the following properties:

- $M(p)$ is consistent with qualitative-conditional information; i.e., $M(p) \in \bar{P}$.
- At the utmost, the smallest cash flow of each interval s_{tj} (left-hand end of the interval) occurs with positive probability with respect to $M(p)$ $(j = 1, \ldots, n_t; t = 0, \ldots, T)$.
- $E_p (\Sigma_{t=0}^{T} d_t q^{T-t}) \geqslant E_{M(p)} (\Sigma_{t=0}^{T} d_t q^{T-t})$; i.e., the terminal value $TV(p)$ is not smaller than the terminal value $TV(M(p))$ of the project.

From these results it follows that the minimization process in (6) can be restricted to discrete Markovian chains. Each of these Markovian chains M is defined by an initial distribution $M_0' = (p_1^0, \ldots, p_{n_0}^0)$ and T transition matrices.

$$
M_t = \begin{pmatrix}
p_{11}^t & \cdots p_{1n_t}^t \\
\cdot & \cdot \\
\cdot & \cdot \\
\cdot & \cdot \\
p_{n_{t-1},1}^t & \cdots p_{n_{t-1},n_t}^t
\end{pmatrix} \quad t = 1, \ldots, T.
$$

p_{kj}^t denotes the probability that in period t the actual value of cash flow d_t equals d_{tj}, given the cash flow $d_{t-1,k}$ in period $t-1$. d_{tj} and $d_{t-1,k}$ denote the smallest cash flow lying in the intervals s_{tj} and $s_{t-1,k}$, respectively. These transition probabilities are not known exactly.

The set p_t ($t = 1, \ldots, T$) of all transition matrices M_t, consistent with qualitative-conditional information, satisfies the following conditions:

i.   From $s_{tj} \notin S_{tk}$ follows $p_{kj}^t = 0$. That is, if a cash flow in period t of amount d_{tj} is impossible, given a cash flow in period $t-1$ of amount $d_{t-1,k}$, then $p_{kj}^t = 0$).

ii. From $s_{tj} \geqslant^{t,k} s_{tl}$ follows $p_{kj}^t \geqslant p_{kl}^t$.

$$
\Sigma_{j=1}^{n_t} p_{kj}^t = 1, \quad p_{kj}^t \geqslant 0 \quad (k = 1, \ldots, n_{t-1}; j = 1, \ldots, n_t; \qquad (7)
$$
$$
t = 1, \ldots, T).
$$

The set P_0 of all discrete initial distributions M_0 consistent with the qualitative information with respect to d_0 is defined analogous to that in the previous section.

It is well known that the probability distribution of the possible values $(d_{t1}, d_{t2}, \ldots, d_{t,n_t}) =: D_t$ of d_t with respect to the Markovian chain M is given by the following product of the initial distribution M_0 and the transition matrices M_τ ($\tau = 1, \ldots, t$):

$$
M_0' M_1 M_2 \cdots M_t.
$$

Hence the expected value of d_t with respect to M equals

$$
M_0' M_1 M_2 \cdots M_t D_t,
$$

and (6) can be reduced to the following nonlinear optimization problem in M_0, $M_1, \ldots, M_T$:

$$
\text{TV} = \min (M_0' D_0 q^T + M_0' M_1 D_1 q^{T-1} + \cdots + M_0' M_1 M_2 \cdots M_T D_T) \qquad (8)
$$
$$
M_t \in P_t \ (t = 0, \ldots, T).
$$

Equation (8) has an optimal solution (worst *a priori* Markovian chain), since the objective function is continuous with respect to M_t ($t = 0, \ldots, T$), and the set of Markovian chains, consistent with qualitative-conditional information, is compact and nonempty. The value TV of an investment project under qualitative-conditional information can be determined, as will be shown, "by hand" in an elementary way. For this reason, the following facts are used:

- Every transition matrix M_t consists of n_{t-1} conditional probability distributions $p_k^t = (p_{k1}^t, \ldots, p_{kn_t}^t)$ ($k = 1, \ldots, n_{t-1}$). p_k^t describes the transition behavior of the cash flows in period $t - 1$ and t, given that d_{t-1} equals $d_{t-1,k}$.

$$M_t = \begin{pmatrix} p_1^t \\ \cdot \\ \cdot \\ \cdot \\ p_{n_{t-1}}^t \end{pmatrix} \qquad t = 1, \ldots, T.$$

- From (7), it follows that qualitative-conditional information leads to inequalities between components p_{kj}^t of the same conditional probability distribution p_k^t. So the minimization with respect to M_t can be decomposed into n_{t-1} minimization processes with respect to p_k^t ($k = 1, \ldots, n_{t-1}$), which are independent of each other.
- From (7) and from the results obtained in the previous section, it can be concluded that the extreme conditional probability distributions consistent with the available information are generalized uniform distributions.
- Since the transition matrix M_t occurs in the last $T - t + 1$ terms of the objective function (8) only, and since the product $M_0' M_1 \cdots M_{t-1}$ is nonnegative, the worst transition matrix $\bar{M}_t$ does not depend on $M_0, M_1, \ldots, M_{t-1}$. Hence the minimization with respect to M_t can be performed independently of the information about $d_0, \ldots, d_{t-1}$.

These observations lead to the following rollback procedure for computing TV:

In the *first* step, the worst transition matrix $\bar{M}_T$ is determined by solving the n_{T-1} linear programming problems

$$\min \{p_k^T D_T | p_k^T \in P_{Tk}\} \qquad (k = 1, \ldots, n_{T-1}), \tag{9}$$

where P_{Tk} denotes the set of all conditional probability distributions p_k^T consistent with $\geqslant^{T,k}$. The optimal solutions $\bar{p}_k^T$ of (9) are generalized uniform distributions, which can be easily computed by using the results of the previous section. By means of the conditional probability distributions $\bar{p}_k^T$, the worst possible behavior of cash flow d_T is given by

$$\bar{M}_T = \begin{pmatrix} \bar{p}_1^T \\ \cdot \\ \cdot \\ \cdot \\ \bar{p}_{n_{T-1}}^T \end{pmatrix}.$$

In the *second* step, $\bar{M}_{T-1}$ is determined by solving the n_{T-2} linear programming problems

$$\min \{p_k^{T-1}(D_{T-1}q + \bar{M}_T D_T)|p_k^{T-1} \in P_{T-1,k}\} \qquad (k = 1, \ldots, n_{T-2}).$$

In step $T-1$, the n_0 linear optimization problems

$$\min \{p_k^1(D_1 q^{T-1} + \bar{M}_2 D_2 q^{T-2} + \cdots + \bar{M}_T D_T)|p_k^1 \in P_{0,k}\} \qquad (k = 1, \ldots, n_0)$$

have to be solved. The results $\bar{p}_k^1$ yield the worst probability behavior $\bar{M}_1$ of d_1.

In the last step, the worst initial distribution M_0 is determined by solving one linear programming problem. The optimal value of this last linear programming problem equals the terminal value TV of the investment project. This procedure of determining the terminal value of an investment project with qualitative-conditional knowledge of cash flows will be demonstrated by a detailed example in the Appendix.

The objective of this section was to show that the concept of qualitative information can be generalized in such a manner that it covers in many cases the information available to investors in a very natural way. The next section generalizes this analysis in two respects. First, the cash flows d_t will be divided into their principal components, each of which is known only qualitatively. Second, it will be shown that the concept of qualitative information can be applied to a number of problems within the capital budgeting context.

GENERALIZATIONS

Selection of Single Investment Projects

Qualitative Information with Respect to Components of the Cash Flows. In general, the available information about the development of the economy, the branch, and the business in particular will not lead to a global estimation of cash flows, but to an estimate of the principal components of d_t ($t = 0, \ldots, T$). These are, for example, ($t = 0, \ldots, T$):[25]

$x_t \geqslant 0$ number of units produced *and* sold in period t ($x_0 = 0$)

$\alpha_t \leqslant 0$ initial outlays, including disbursements to procure and install the project, and cash outflows caused by additional investments that are necessary to utilize the project (for example, an increase of stocks)

$\beta_t \leq 0$ cash outflows that are independent of the production volume

$\gamma_t \leq 0$ cash outflows per unit produced

$\pi_t \geq 0$ selling price per unit

With these components of the cash flows d_t, the uncertain terminal value of the investment is given by

$$\sum_{t=1}^{T} [(\pi_t + \gamma_t)x_t + \beta_t]q^{T-t} + \sum_{t=0}^{T} \alpha_t q^{T-t}. \tag{10}$$

In analogy to the preceding section, it may be realistic to assume that the investor has qualitative-conditional information with respect to production volumes x_t, primary investment outlays α_t, and production-independent cash outflows β_t, whereas the sum of selling price π_t and cash outflows γ_t per unit is only known qualitatively. Then, applying the same argument as before, it can be shown that the accept-reject decision can be based on the following evaluation criterion:

$$\text{TV} = \min \left\{ \sum_{t=1}^{T} \left[p^t G_t \left(\prod_{\tau=1}^{t} M_\tau^x \right) X_t + \left(\prod_{\tau=1}^{t} M_\tau^\beta \right) B_t \right] q^{T-t} + \sum_{t=0}^{T} \left(\prod_{\tau=0}^{t} M_\tau^\alpha \right) A_t \right\}$$

$$M_t^\beta \in P_t^\beta; \quad M_t^x \in P_t^x; \quad p^t \in P_t \quad t = 1, \ldots, T \tag{11}$$

$$M_t^\alpha \in P_t^\alpha \qquad\qquad\qquad t = 0, \ldots, T.$$

The meaning of the symbols in this evaluation criterion is as follows:

A_t, B_t, G_t, X_t: The components of these vectors are the left-hand end of the intervals that may contain the actual values of α_t, β_t, $\pi_t + \gamma_t$, and x_t. These vectors correspond to the vectors D_t in the previous section.

$M_t^\alpha, M_t^\beta, M_t^x$:   Markovian transition matrices, which are consistent with the information on α_t, β_t, and x_t.

p^t: Probability distributions consistent with the knowledge of $\pi_t + \gamma_t$.

$P_t^\alpha, P_t^\beta, P_t^x$:   The sets of all transition matrices consistent with the knowledge of α_t, β_t, and x_t.

P_t: The set of all probability distributions consistent with the available information of $\pi_t + \gamma_t$.

From these notations, it follows that, for example, $p^t G_t$ and

$$\left(\prod_{\tau=1}^{t} M_\tau^x\right) X_t$$

equal the expected value of the cash-relevant contribution margin per unit $\pi_t + \gamma_t$ and of the production volume x_t, evaluated with respect to $p^t \in P_t$ and $M_\tau \in P_\tau^{px}$ ($\tau = 1, \ldots, t$). The product of these two terms represents the expected contribution margin. Here it is assumed that the information $\pi_t + \gamma_t$ is independent from the information on the production volume in period t.

The computation of TV can be performed very easily by using the results of the preceding section, which can be carried over immediately.

Stationary Information with Respect to the Components of the Cash Flows. Sometimes the available information is not sufficient to make time-dependent estimates of the cash flows; i.e., the investor assumes implicitly that the investment project generates the following sequence of cash flows:

$$(\alpha_0, (\pi + \gamma)x + \beta, (\pi + \gamma)x + \beta, \ldots, (\pi + \gamma)x + \beta).$$

In this case (10) can be reduced to

$$[(\pi + \gamma)x + \beta] \cdot s_{\overline{T}|r} + \alpha_0 q^T,$$

where $s_{\overline{T}|r}$ denotes the future value of an annuity of 1 DM per year for T years. The evaluation criterion can be reduced to

$$\left. \begin{aligned} \text{TV} = \min \ [pG \cdot p^x X + p^\beta B] \cdot s_{\overline{T}|r} + p^\alpha A q^T \\ p \in P; p^x \in P^x; p^\alpha \in P^\alpha; p^\beta \in P^\beta, \end{aligned} \right\} \quad (12)$$

where P, P^x, P^α, P^β are the sets of all probability distributions that are consistent with the "stationary" qualitative information about $\pi + \gamma, x, \alpha_0,$ and β.

If α_0 is known precisely, $\pi + \gamma$ and β with sufficiently high precision, (12) can be reduced to

$$\left. \begin{aligned} \text{TV} = (\pi + \gamma) \cdot s_{\overline{T}|r} \cdot \min p^x X + \alpha_0 \\ p^x \in P^x. \end{aligned} \right\} \quad (13)$$

In this case the investor only needs to specify the lower and upper bounds for future production volumes x, some typical ranges of x within these limits, and his feelings about whether one range of x is not less probable than another.

The payback criterion is one of the most popular investment criteria used in practice [76]. Neglecting the interest effect, included in (13) by $s_{\overline{T}|r}$, the worst possible payback period comes to

$$PBP = \frac{|\alpha_0|}{\pi + \gamma} \cdot \min_{p^x \in P^x} \sum_{j=1}^{n_x} \frac{1}{x_j} \cdot p_j^x. \tag{14}$$

$x_j \geq 0$ and p_j^x denote the components of X and p^x, n_x the number of subintervals into which the possible range of future production volumes is divided. Thus the payback period under qualitative information can be easily determined by means of the solution method described earlier.

Qualitative Knowledge of the Economic Life of the Investment Project. To simplify notation, it is assumed for the subsequent discussion that the qualitative conditional information refers directly to the cash flows. The results, however, can be carried over directly to the case that d_t is separated into its components.

For a number of reasons, financial management usually faces the problem of not knowing the exact economic life of a project. Changes of the business environment in general and especially technical progress, changing market behavior, and possible legal regulations may lead to qualitative information on the economic life of the project.

If $\bar{t}, \bar{t} + 1, \ldots, T$ are the possible economic lives, the expected terminal value of the project with respect to any Markovian chain, consistent with the information about the cash flows, is given by

$$\sum_{t=0}^{l} \left(\prod_{\tau=0}^{t} M_\tau \right) D_t q^{T-t} \quad l = \bar{t}, \ldots, T.$$

According to the evaluation criterion of the preceding section, the terminal value of a project whose economic life is known qualitatively only comes to

$$TV = \min \left\{ \sum_{t=0}^{\bar{t}-1} \left(\prod_{\tau=0}^{t} M_\tau \right) D_t q^{T-t} + \sum_{l=t}^{T} \left[\sum_{t=\bar{t}}^{l} \left(\prod_{\tau=0}^{t} M_\tau \right) D_t q^{T-t} \right] p_l \right\}$$

$$M_t \in P^t \quad (t = 0, \ldots, T); \quad p \in P_L.$$

P_L denotes the set of all probability distributions $p = (p_{\bar{t}}, \ldots, p_T)$ consistent with the qualitative information on economic life of the project. Again, TV can be computed easily by exploiting the results of the preceding section. It should be pointed out, however, that the worst transition behavior of cash flows, described by $\bar{M}_0, \ldots, \bar{M}_T$, and the worst *a priori* probability distribution of economic life are interrelated and have to be computed simultaneously.

Incomplete Capital Market. In the preceding analysis, cash inflows and cash outflows have been compounded with the same interest rate r. If, however, debit rate r_s and credit rate r_h differ ($r_s > r_h$), if cash outflows $d_t < 0$ are covered by a credit at an interest rate r_s p.a. and maturity T, and if analogically cash inflows $d_t > 0$ are invested for $T - t$ periods at an interest rate r_h p.a., then the uncertain terminal value of an investment project is given by

$$\sum_{t=0}^{T} [d_t^+ (1 + r_h)^{T-t} - d_t^- (1 + r_s)^{T-t}].$$

d_t^+ and d_t^- correspond to the positive and negative part of d_t, respectively (i.e., $d_t^+ - d_t^- = d_t; d_t^+ \cdot d_t^- = 0; d_t^+, d_t^- \geq 0$). Assuming that the cash flows are known qualitative-conditionally, the terminal value of the project is given by

$$TV(r_h, r_s) = \min \sum_{t=0}^{T} \left[\left(\prod_{\tau=0}^{t} M_\tau \right) \cdot (D_t^+(1 + r_h)^{T-t} - D_t^- (1 + r_s)^{T-t}) \right]$$

$$M_t \in P_t \quad (t = 0, \ldots, T). \tag{15}$$

D_t^+ and D_t^- are defined analogously to d_t^+ and d_t^-:

$$D_t^+ - D_t^- = D_t; \quad D_t^+ \cdot D_t^- = 0; \quad D_t^+, \quad D_t^- \geq O_{n_t}.$$

The computation of TV (r_h, r_s) on which the accept-reject decision may be based is performed in the same way as described earlier. In generalizing a result of Henke [37], it can be shown that (under very weak assumptions with respect to the transition behavior of cash flows) for every credit rate r_h, a "critical" debit rate $\bar{r}_s \geq -1$ exists so that

$$\left. \begin{array}{ll} TV (r_h, r_s) \geq 0 & \text{for all } r_s \leq \bar{r}_s, \text{ and} \\ TV (r_h, r_s) \leq 0 & \text{for all } r_s \geq \bar{r}_s. \end{array} \right\} \tag{16}$$

The "critical" debit rate $\bar{r}_s$ (which depends on r_h) satisfies the equation TV $(r_h, \bar{r}_s) = 0$ and therefore can be interpreted as a generalized internal rate of return under qualitative-conditional information. If r_h reflects the required rate of return of funds used within the firm, (16) means that the project should be accepted only if the actual debit rate r_s is lower than the "critical" debit rate $\bar{r}_s$.[26]

If the stream of uncertain cash flows d_t has the special structure $d_0 \leq 0$, $d_t \geq 0$ ($t = 1, \ldots, T$) for all possible values (i.e., $U_0 \leq 0, L_t \geq 0; t = 1, \ldots, T$), then r_s can be computed explicitly as

$$\bar{r}_s = \sqrt[T]{\left| \sum_{t=1}^{T} \left(\prod_{\tau=0}^{t} \bar{M}_\tau \right) D_t (1 + r_h)^{T-t} \middle/ \left(\prod_{\tau=0}^{T} \bar{M}_\tau \right) D_0 \right|} - 1.$$

This representation of the "critical" debit rate $\bar{r}_s$ under qualitative-conditional information generalizes a proposal by Baldwin for the assessment of investment projects.

Selection of Interrelated Investment Projects

The analysis performed in the preceding sections can be carried over immediately to select a number of projects out of a set of contingent and mutually exclusive projects. In this situation, one way to pick the best portfolios is to rank properly defined combined projects according to their terminal value TV and to accept them in the order of their ranking until some scarce resource (e.g., the capital budget in $t = 0$) is exhausted. Management faces much more difficult problems, however, if additional dependencies are introduced into the capital budgeting process by limited future resources, the actual availability of which depends on uncertain, possibly unforeseeable environmental events. In addition, the situation will be complicated further if future uncertain investment and financing opportunities are integrated into the analysis. The treatment of these broader types of interrelationships in a financial planning procedure, which might support the strategic capital budgeting process, depends strongly on the extent to which improbable and very unfavorable events ("killer variables")[27] are considered. If a corporation's resilience to unfavorable events is rather high, and if these events are judged as highly improbable, it can be reasonable to exclude them from the analysis. This approach implicitly assumes that the corporation is always able to react on neglected unfavorable developments without taking a significant bankruptcy risk. The transfer of this concept to formal planning methods leads to the chance-constraint approach. An application of the concept of qualitative information to the simultaneous determination of interrelated short-term investment and financing alternatives has been performed in [15].[28]

The second possibility consists of taking highly improbable and unfavorable events into account in order to develop plans for early actions in cases of emergency. Within the formal planning methods, this approach has been discussed as multistage programming (programming with recourse). An approach to multistage investment and financial planning under qualitative information has been described in [13, pp. 423–474]. Its application to real-world problems, however, seems not to be possible yet.

CONCLUSIONS

Most approaches to capital budgeting under uncertainty assume that probability distributions of the uncertain data are available. In many cases, however, such environmental dynamics as technical progress, changing market behavior, increasing variability of exchange rates and prices of raw materials, and increasing legal regulations prevent a quantitative specification of the probability distributions of important environmental variables. This aspect has been taken into account in this paper by making much weaker assumptions on the available information about future events. The only supposition is that management is able to state the possible values (or ranges) of the most important environmental variables and to rank them partially according to its judgment of which value (range) is more probable than another. This type of information will be available in many realistic situations.

It has been shown that, based on this concept of qualitative information, an evaluation of single risky projects by means of their terminal value is possible. However, any other evaluation criterion could have been used. In addition, it has been pointed out that the concept of qualitative information can be applied to most problems in the financial field.

From the management-science point of view, it is essential to note that the actual determination of the "best" project is very easy to perform and that rules of thumb, widely used in practice, can easily be adapted to this information concept.

An application of the qualitative information concept may be limited for several reasons:

First, management must be able to specify the possible future values of the most important environmental variables. This task is far from easy. However, this specification will be indispensable for every "rational" decision because a selection of risky investment projects taking unforseeable future events into account is a contradiction in terms.

Second, the number of possible values (ranges) of future uncertain data and the number of probability relations between these values depend strongly on the cognitive capacity of the individuals involved in the decision process. About five to eight possible values for every important environmental variable seem to be the maximum number for an individual to process simultaneously. Typically, these values are often ranked according to Figure 3; i.e., individuals look for a "most probable" (reference) value and rank the other values with respect to this. It should be noted that the concept of qualitative information leads to an evaluation of projects, other than the usual max min principle, depending on the type and number of probability relations.

Third, the comprehension of complicated dependencies between environmental variables will in some cases be possible only in a limited way. The specification of qualitative-conditional probability relations is generally restricted to events in the near future.

Fourth, an undifferentiated and inflexible application of the max min concept may not be accepted by the individuals involved in the decision process,

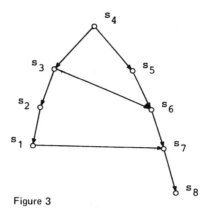

Figure 3

since it does not clarify the influence of some environmental variables on the final decision. Hence the concept of qualitative information should be combined with a sensitivity analysis concerning the probability relations stated and the possible values of uncertain data considered.

APPENDIX

Example 3. This example serves to illustrate the approach developed in the third section of this paper: how to select an investment project with qualitative-conditionally known cash flows.

The information about the lower and upper bounds of cash flows d_t and the subintervals s_{tj} are presented in Table 1 and Table 2.

Table 1. Lower and Upper Bounds of Cash Flows

t	0	1	2	3
L_t	-90	-10	20	50
O_t	-90	20	50	80

Table 2. Information about Subintervals

s_{tj} t	s_{t1}	s_{t2}	s_{t3}	s_{t4}	s_{t5}	n_t	
1	[-10, 0)	[0, 10)	[10, 15)	[15, 20]	—	4	
2	[20, 30)	[30, 35)	[35, 40)	[40, 50]	—	4	$n_0 = 1$
3	[50, 60)	[60, 65)	[65, 70)	[70, 75]	[75, 80]	5	

The specific cash flow vectors D_t thus read

$$D_0 = (-90), D_1 = (-10, 0, 10, 15), D_2 = (20, 30, 35, 40),$$
$$D_3 = (50, 60, 65, 70, 75).$$

The compound rate q is assumed to be 1 in order to increase the clarity of the argument.

The transition structure of cash flows is described in Figure 4. Since the initial outlay d_0 is known with certainty, M_0 degenerates to a one-point distribution, and M_1 is a vector with four components. The conditional partial orders $\geqslant^{t,k}$ are represented by the directed graphs in Figure 5. For example, the sets of conditional probability distributions, consistent with $\geqslant^{1,1}$, $\geqslant^{2,2}$, and $\geqslant^{3,4}$, are given by

$$P_{11} = \left\{ p_1^1 \in \mathfrak{R}^4 : p_{13}^1 \geqslant p_{12}^1 \geqslant p_{11}^1 \geqslant 0; \quad p_{13}^1 \geqslant p_{14}^1 \geqslant p_{11}^1 \geqslant 0; \quad \sum_{j=1}^4 p_{1j}^1 = 1 \right\},$$

$$P_{22} = \left\{ p_2^2 \in \mathfrak{R}^4 : p_{23}^2 \geqslant p_{22}^2 \geqslant 0; \quad p_{23}^2 \geqslant p_{24}^2 \geqslant 0; \quad p_{21}^2 = 0; \quad \sum_{j=1}^4 p_{2j}^2 = 1 \right\},$$

$$P_{34} = \left\{ p_4^3 \in \mathfrak{R}^5 : p_{45}^3 \geqslant p_{44}^3 \geqslant 0; \quad p_{41}^3 = p_{42}^3 = p_{43}^3 = 0; \quad \sum_{j=1}^5 p_{4j}^3 = 1 \right\}.$$

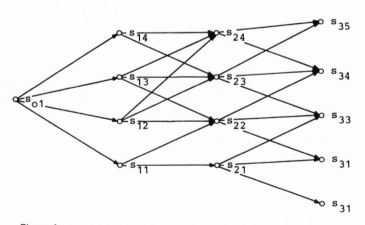

Figure 4

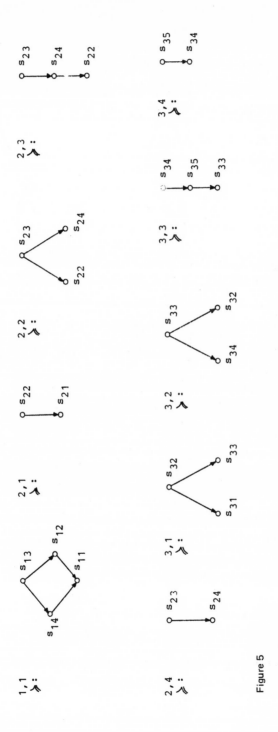

Figure 5

109

First solution step $[D_3 = (50; 60; 65; 70; 75)]$:

$$
\begin{pmatrix}
\min\{p_1^3 D_3 | p_3^3 \in P_{31}\} \\
\min\{p_2^3 D_3 | p_2^3 \in P_{32}\} \\
\min\{p_3^3 D_3 | p_3^3 \in P_{33}\} \\
\min\{p_4^3 D_3 | p_4^3 \in P_{34}\}
\end{pmatrix}
=
\begin{pmatrix}
\min\{60; 55; 62, 5; 175/3\} \\
\min\{65; 67, 5; 62, 5; 65\} \\
\min\{70; 72, 5; 70\} \\
\min\{75; 72, 5\}
\end{pmatrix}
=
\begin{pmatrix}
55 \\
62, 5 \\
70 \\
72, 5
\end{pmatrix}.
$$

Worst *a priori* transition matrix $\bar{M}_3$:

$$
\bar{M}_3 =
\begin{pmatrix}
\frac{1}{2} & \frac{1}{2} & 0 & 0 & 0 \\
0 & \frac{1}{2} & \frac{1}{2} & 0 & 0 \\
0 & 0 & 1 & 0 & 0 \\
0 & 0 & 0 & \frac{1}{2} & \frac{1}{2}
\end{pmatrix}.
$$

Second solution step $[\bar{D}_2 = D_2 + \bar{M}_3 D_3 = (75; 92, 5; 105; 112, 5)]$:

$$
\begin{pmatrix}
\min\{p_1^2 \bar{D}_2 | p_1^2 \in P_{21}\} \\
\min\{p_2^2 \bar{D}_2 | p_2^2 \in P_{22}\} \\
\min\{p_3^2 \bar{D}_3 | p_3^2 \in P_{23}\} \\
\min\{p_4^2 \bar{D}_4 | p_4^2 \in P_{24}\}
\end{pmatrix}
=
\begin{pmatrix}
\min\{92, 5; 83, 75\} \\
\min\{105; 98, 75; 108, 75; 103, 33\} \\
\min\{105; 108, 75; 103, 33\} \\
\min\{105; 108, 75\}
\end{pmatrix}
=
\begin{pmatrix}
83, 75 \\
98, 75 \\
103, 33 \\
105
\end{pmatrix}.
$$

Worst *a priori* transition matrix $\bar{M}_2$:

$$
\bar{M}_2 =
\begin{pmatrix}
\frac{1}{2} & \frac{1}{2} & 0 & 0 \\
0 & \frac{1}{2} & \frac{1}{2} & 0 \\
0 & \frac{1}{3} & \frac{1}{3} & \frac{1}{3} \\
0 & 0 & 1 & 0
\end{pmatrix}.
$$

Last solution step $[\bar{D}_1 = D_1 + \bar{M}_2 D_2 + \bar{M}_3 D_3 = (73, 75; 98, 75; 113, 33; 120)]$:

$$\min\{p_1^1 \bar{D}_1 | p_1^1 \in P_{11}\} = \min\{113, 33; 116, 66; 106, 04; 110, 69; 101, 46\}.$$

The worst transition matrix $\bar{M}_1$ is

$$\bar{M}_1 = (\tfrac{1}{4}, \tfrac{1}{4}, \tfrac{1}{4}, \tfrac{1}{4}),$$

and the terminal value of the project comes to

$$TV = -90 + 101, 46 = 11, 46 \geqslant 0.$$

Hence, as far as the decision is based on this criterion, the project should be accepted.

NOTES

1. See Thompson [91, p. 125].
2. The methods to solve general capital budgeting problems under uncertainty can be classified in the same way.
3. An analysis of interrelated projects by structure-oriented methods based on random input data has been performed, for example, by Jacob [46], Hespos and Strassmann [40], and Salazar and Sen [72].
4. For details, see Senbet and Thompson [80].
5. In addition, the efforts are directed toward an integration of the engineering-management science and the economics-finance point of view. See, for example, Ben-Shahar and Werner [7] and Thompson [91].
6. It should be noted that a sensitivity analysis is performed in which the ultimate goal is to make a decision by comparing the investor's subjective expectations about the "most probable" values of the uncertain data with the result of the sensitivity analysis.
7. A critical summary of the different concepts of probability can be found, for example, in Fine [22], Fishburn [23, p. 131], Raiffa [69, p. 278], and Savage [73, p. 575].
8. See Savage [75], pp. 4 and 61.
9. For a more detailed discussion, see Schneider [78].
10. See Chesley [17, 18], Krantz et al. [53, p. 400], Savage [74], and Winkler [96].
11. For two related concepts, see Hellwig and Hülsmann [36] and Jacob and Karrenberg [47].
12. Compare, in addition, Kofler [50] and Henry-Larbordère and Zerhouni [38].
13. More exactly, on the power set of S.
14. This is not necessarily true if qualitative information refers to nonsimple probability events (elements of the power set of S). See, for example, Kraft, Pratt, and Seidenberg [52] and Scott [79].
15. For details, see Bühler [13], p. 124.
16. See, for example, Anscombe and Aumann [3]. They show that a twofold application of the Von Neumann-Morgenstern axiom, one to "roulette lotteries" and one to "horse lotteries," results in subjective probabilities.
17. See, for example, Savage [75, p. 37, theorem 3].
18. For details, see Bühler [13, p. 126].
19. See Franke [27, p. 269].
20. For generalizations of this result, see Bühler [12, 13, p. 91].
21. The support of a discrete probability distribution is the set of all simple events that have positive probability with respect to p.
22. See Bühler [13, pp. 91–123].
23. A utility-theoretic formulation will be disregarded here.
24. This subsection can be omitted by a reader not interested in the technical details of computing TV.
25. See, for example, Kilger [49].
26. Similar results can be obtained when the credits to cover cash outflows and the additional investment of cash inflows have maturities of one period. These results are generalizations of a proposal given by Teichroew, Robichek, and Montalbano [89, 90].
27. See Derkinderen and Crum [19].
28. For an application of the concept of qualitative information to portfolio theory, see [14].

REFERENCES

[1] Adelson, R.M. "Criteria for Capital Investment: An Approach through Decision Theory," *Operational Research Quarterly* 16 (1965), pp. 19-50.

[2] Albach, H., and Schüler, W. "On a Method of Capital Budgeting under Uncertainty," *Journal of Mathematical and Physical Sciences* 4 (1970), pp. 208-226.

[3] Anscombe, F.J., and Aumann, R.J. "A Definition of Subjective Probability," *Annals of Mathematical Statistics* 34 (1963), pp. 199-205.

[4] Aumann, R.J. "Utility Theory without the Completeness Axiom," *Econometrica* 30 (1962), pp. 445-462.

[5] Aumann, R.J. "Utility Theory without the Completeness Axiom, A Correction," *Econometrica* 32 (1964), pp. 210-212.

[6] Bennion, E.G. "Capital Budgeting and Game Theory," *Harvard Business Review* 34 (1956), pp. 115-123, citing: "Capital Investment Decision," reprints from *Harvard Business Review*, pp. 120-128.

[7] Ben-Shahar, H., and Werner, F. "Multiperiod Capital Budgeting under Uncertainty: A Suggested Application," *Journal of Financial and Quantitative Analysis* 12 (1977), pp. 859-877.

[8] Bhattacharya, S. "Project Valuation with Mean-Reverting Cash Flow Streams," *Journal of Finance* 33 (1978), pp. 1317-1331.

[9] Biermann, H., and Hass, J.E. "Capital Budgeting under Uncertainty: A Reformulation," *Journal of Finance* 28 (1973), pp. 119-129.

[10] Bloech, J. "Untersuchung der Aussagefähigkeit mathematisch formulierter Investitions-Modelle mit Hilfe einer Fehlerrechnung," dissertation, Göttingen, 1966.

[11] Bogue, M.C., and Roll, R. "Capital Budgeting of Risky Projects with 'Imperfect' Markets for Physical Capital," *Journal of Finance* 29 (1974), pp. 601-613.

[12] Bühler, W. "Characterization of the Extreme Points of a Class of Special Polyhedra," *Zeitschrift für Operations Research* 19 (1975), pp. 131-137.

[13] Bühler, W. "Investitions- und Finanzplanung bei qualitativer Information," unpublished Habilitationsschrift, Aachen, 1976.

[14] Bühler, W. "Portefeuilleplanung bei unvollkommen bekannten Mittelwerten und Varianzen," in K. Brockhoff *et al.*, *Proceedings in Operations Research* 7 (1977), pp. 158-167.

[15] Bühler, W., and Gehring, H. "Short Term Financial Planning with Uncertain Receipts and Disbursements," *European Journal of Operations Research* 2 (1978), pp. 313-326.

[16] Canada, J.R., and Wadsworth, H.M. "Methods for Quantifying Risk in Economic Analysis of Capital Projects," *Industrial Engineering* 19 (1968), pp. 32-37.

[17] Chesley, G.R. "Elicitation of Subjective Probabilities: A Review," *Accounting Review* 50 (1975), pp. 325-337.

[18] Chesley, G.R. "Subjective Probability Elicitation Techniques: A Performance Comparison," *Journal of Accounting Research* 16 (1978), pp. 225-241.

[19] Derkinderen, F.G.J., and Crum, Roy L. "Strategic Management of the Financial Resource Allocation Process," paper presented at the eighth annual meeting of the Financial Management Association, Minneapolis, October 1978.

[20] Fairley, W., and Jacoby, H. "Investment Analysis Using the Probability Distribution of the Internal Rate of Return," *Management Science* 21 (1975), pp. 1428-1437.

[21] Fellner, W. *Probability and Profit*. Homewood, Ill.: Richard D. Irwin, 1965.

[22] Fine, T.L. *Theories of Probabilities*. New York: Academic Press, 1973.

[23] Fishburn, P.C. *Decision and Value Theory*. New York: John Wiley & Sons, 1964.

[24] Fishburn, P.C. "Analysis of Decisions with Incomplete Knowledge of Probabilities," *Operations Research* 13 (1965), pp. 217-237.

[25] Fishburn, P.C. "Weak Qualitative Probability on Finite Sets," *Annals of Mathematical Statistics* 40 (1969), pp. 2118-2126.

[26] Fourgeaud, Lenclud, and Sentis. "Critère de choix en avenir partiellement incertain, revue Française d'automatique," *Informatique et Recherche Opérationelle* 2 (1968), pp. 9-20.

[27] Franke, G. "Expected Utility with Ambiguous Probabilities and 'Irrational' Parameters," *Theory and Decision* 9 (1978), pp. 267-283.

[28] Gerber, H.U. "The Discounted Central Limit Theorem and Its Berry-Esséen Analogue," *Annals of Mathematical Statistics* 42 (1971), pp. 389-392.

[29] Good, I.J. *Probability and the Weighing of Evidence*. London: Macmillan Publishing Company, 1950.

[30] Grayson, C.J. *Decisions under Uncertainty: Drilling Decisions by Oil and Gas Operations*. Cambridge, Mass.: Harvard University Press, 1960.

[31] Greer, W.R. "Theory versus Practice in Risk Analysis: An Empirical Study," *Accounting Review* 49 (1974), pp. 496-505.

[32] Hamada, R.S. "Portfolio Analysis, Market Equilibrium and Corporation Finance," *Journal of Finance* 24 (1969), pp. 13-31.

[33] Hanssmann, F. "Probability of Survival as an Investment Criterion," *Management Science* 15 (1968/69), pp. 33-48.

[34] Hax, H. *Investitionstheorie*, 2nd ed. Würzburg: Physica, 1972.

[35] Heider, M. "Simulationsmodell zur Risikoanalyse für Investitionsplanungen," dissertation, Bonn, 1969.

[36] Hellwig, K., and Hülsmann, J. "Über ein Modell der Investitionsprogrammplanung unter Unsicherheit," *Operations Research Verfahren* 18 (1974), pp. 141-146.

[37] Henke, M. "Vermögensrentabilität – ein einfaches Investitionskalkül," *Zeitschrift für Betriebswirtschaft* 43 (1973), pp. 177-198.

[38] Henry-Labordère, A.L., and Zerhouni, C.M. "Décision Bayésienne avec information incomplète," *Metra* 11 (1972), pp. 669–685.

[39] Hertz, D.B. "Risk Analysis in Capital Investment," *Harvard Business Review* 42 (January–February 1964), pp. 95–106.

[40] Hespos, R.F., and Strassmann, P.A. "Stochastic Decision Trees for the Analysis of Investment Decisions," *Management Science* 11 (1964/65), pp. B244–259.

[41] Hillier, F.S. "The Derivation of Probabilistic Information for the Evaluation of Risky Investments," *Management Science* 9 (1962/63), pp. 443–457.

[42] Hillier, F.S. "Supplement to 'The Derivation of Probabilistic Information for the Evaluation of Risky Investments,'" *Management Science* 11 (1964/65), pp. 485–487.

[43] Hillier, F.S. *The Evaluation of Risky Interrelated Investments.* Amsterdam: North-Holland Publishing Company, 1969.

[44] Hillier, F.S., and Heebink, D.V. "Evaluating Risky Capital Investments," *California Management Review* 7 (1965), pp. 71–80.

[45] Horne, J. van. "Capital Budgeting Decisions Involving Combinations of Risky Investments," *Management Science* 13 (1966/67), pp. B84–92.

[46] Jacob, H. "Zum Problem der Unsicherheit bei Investitionsentscheidungen," *Zeitschrift für Betriebswirtschaft* 37 (1967), pp. 153–187.

[47] Jacob, H., and Karrenberg, R. "Die Bedeutung von Wahrscheinlichkeitsintervallen für die Planung bei Unsicherheit," *Zeitschrift für Betriebswirtschaft* 47 (1977), pp. 673–696.

[48] Joy, M.R., and Bradley, I.O. "A Note on Sensitivity Analysis of Rates of Return," *Journal of Finance* 28 (1973), pp. 1255–1261.

[49] Kilger, W. "Kritische Werte in der Investitions- und Wirtschaftlichkeitsrechnung," *Zeitschrift für Betriebswirtschaft* 35 (1965), pp. 338–353.

[50] Kofler, E. "Entscheidungen bei teilweise bekannter Verteilung der Zustände," *Zeitschrift für Operations Research* 18 (1974), pp. 141–157.

[51] Koopmann, B.O. "The Axioms and Algebra of Intuitive Probability," *Annals of Mathematics* 41 (1940), pp. 269–292.

[52] Kraft, C.H.; Pratt, J.W.; and Seidenberg, A. "Intuitive Probability on Finite Sets," *Annals of Mathematical Statistics* 30 (1959), pp. 408–419.

[53] Krantz, D.H.; Luce, R.D.; Suppes, P.; and Tversky, A. *Foundations of Measurement,* Vol. I. New York: Academic Press, 1971.

[54] Lintner, J. "The Valuation of Risk Assets and the Selection of Risky Investments in Stock Portfolios and Capital Budgets," *Review of Economics and Statistics* 47 (1965), pp. 13–37.

[55] Luce, R.D., and Raiffa, H. *Games and Decisions.* New York: John Wiley & Sons, 1957.

[56] Lutz, F., and Lutz, V. *The Theory of Investment of the Firm.* Princeton, N.J.: Princeton University Press, 1951.

[57] MacCrimmon, K.R. "Descriptive and Normative Implications of the

Decision-Theory Postulates," in K. Borch and J. Mossin, eds., *Risk and Uncertainty*. New York: Macmillan Publishing Company, 1968.

[58]   Mao, J.C. *Quantitative Analysis of Financial Decisions*. London: Macmillan Publishing Company, 1969.

[59]   Mao, J.C. "Models of Capital Budgeting, E-V VS E-S," *Journal of Financial and Quantitative Analysis* 4 (1970), pp. 657–675.

[60]   Mao, J.C., and Brewster, J.F. "An E-S_h Model of Capital Budgeting," *Engineering Economist* 15 (1970), pp. 103–121.

[61]   Merton, R.C. "An Intertemporal Capital Asset Pricing Model," *Econometrica* 41 (1973), pp. 867–887.

[62]   Miller, V.V.; Anderson, L.P.; and Josephs, S.S. "Abstract: A Probability Distribution of Discounted Payback for Evaluating Investment Decisions," *Journal of Financial and Quantitative Analysis* 7 (1972), pp. 1439–1442.

[63]   Milnor, J. "Games against Nature," in R.M. Thrall, C.H. Coombs, and R.L. Davis, eds., *Decision Processes*. New York, 1954, pp. 49–59.

[64]   Mossin, J. "Equilibrium in a Capital Asset Market," *Econometrica* 34 (1966), pp. 768–783.

[65]   Myers, S.C., and Turnbull, S.M. "Capital Budgeting and the Capital Asset Pricing Model: Good News and Bad News," *Journal of Finance* 32 (1977), pp. 321–333.

[66]   Ostergaard, S.D. "Stochastic Investment Models and Decision Criteria," *Swedish Journal of Economics* 73 (1971), pp. 157–183.

[67]   Perrakis, S., and Henin, C. "The Evaluation of Risky Investments with Random Timing of Cash Returns," *Management Science* 21 (1974/75), pp. 79–86.

[68]   Perrakis, S., and Sahin, I. "On Risky Investments with Random Timing of Cash Returns and Fixed Planning Horizon," *Management Science* 22 (1976), pp. 799–809.

[69]   Raiffa, H. *Decision Analysis*. Reading, Mass.: Addison-Wesley Publishing Company, 1970.

[70]   Robichek, A.A. "Interpreting the Results of Risk Analysis," *Journal of Finance* 30 (1975), pp. 1384–1386.

[71]   Rubinstein, M.E. "A Mean Variance Synthesis of Corporate Financial Theory," *Journal of Finance* 28 (1973), pp. 167–181.

[72]   Salazar, R.C., and Sen, S.K. "A Simulation Model of Capital Budgeting under Uncertainty," *Management Science* 15 (1968/69), pp. B161–179.

[73]   Savage, L.J. "The Foundations of Statistics Reconsidered," in J. Neyman, ed., *Proceedings of the 4th Berkeley Symposium on Mathematical Statistics and Probability*, Vol. 1. Berkeley, Calif., 1961, pp. 575–586.

[74]   Savage, L.J. "Elicitation of Personal Probabilities and Expectations," *Journal of the American Statistical Association* 66 (1971), pp. 783–801.

[75]   Savage, L.J. *The Foundations of Statistics*, 2nd ed. New York: Dover, 1972.

[76]   Schall, L.D.; Sundem, G.L.; and Geijsenbeek, W.R. "Survey and Analysis

of Capital Budgeting Methods," *Journal of Finance* 33 (1978), pp. 281–287.

[77] Schneeweiss, H. *Entscheidungskriterien bei Risiko.* Berlin: Springer-Verlag, 1967.

[78] Schneider, D. "Messbarkeitsstufen subjektiver Wahrscheinlichkeiten als Erscheinungsformen der Ungewissheit," *Zeitschrift für betriebswirtschaftliche Forschung* 31 (1979), pp. 89–122.

[79] Scott, D. "Measurement Structures and Linear Inequalities," *Journal of Mathematical Psychology* 1 (1964), pp. 233–247.

[80] Senbet, L.W., and Thompson, H.E. "The Equivalence of Alternative Mean-Variance Capital Budgeting Models," *Journal of Finance* 33 (1978), pp. 395–401.

[81] Sharpe, W. "Capital Asset Prices: A Theory of Market Equilibrium under Condition of Risk," *Journal of Finance* 19 (1964), pp. 425–442.

[82] Singhvi, S.S. "Game Theory Technique in Investment Planning," *Long Range Planning* 7 (1974), pp. 59–61.

[83] Slovic, P. "Psychological Study of Human Judgment: Implications for Investment Decision Making," *Journal of Finance* 27 (1972), pp. 779–799.

[84] Slovic, P., and Tversky, A. "Who Accepts Savage's Axiom?" *Behavioral Science* 19 (1974), pp. 368–373.

[85] Smith, V.L. "Measuring Non-Monetary Utilities in Uncertain Choices: The Ellsberg Urn," *Quarterly Journal of Economics* 83 (1969), pp. 324–329.

[86] Spetzler, C.S. "The Development of a Corporate Risk Policy for Capital Investment Decisions," *IEEE Transactions on Systems Science and Cybernetics* 4 (1968), pp. 279–300.

[87] Stapleton, R.C. "Portfolio Analysis, Stock Valuation and Capital Budgeting Decision Rules for Risky Projects," *Journal of Finance* 26 (1971), pp. 95–117.

[88] Suppes, P., and Winet, M. "An Axiomatization of Utility Based on the Notion of Utility Differences," *Management Science* 1 (1955), pp. 259–270.

[89] Teichroew, D.A.; Robichek, A.; and Montalbano, M. "Mathematical Analysis of Rates of Return under Certainty," *Management Science* 11 (1964/65a), pp. 395–403.

[90] Teichroew, D.A.; Robichek, A.; and Montalbano, M. "An Analysis of Criteria for Investment and Financing Decisions under Certainty," *Management Science* 12 (1965/66b), pp. 151–179.

[91] Thompson, H.E. "Mathematical Programming, the Capital Asset Pricing Model and Capital Budgeting of Interrelated Projects," *Journal of Finance* 31 (1976), pp. 125–131.

[92] Tversky, A. "Additivity, Utility, and Subjective Probability," *Journal of Mathematical Psychology* 4 (1967), pp. 175–201.

[93] Tversky, A. "Intransitivity of Preferences," *Psychological Review* 76 (1969), pp. 31–48.

[94] Wagle, B. "A Statistical Analysis of Risk in Capital Investment Projects," *Operational Research Quarterly* 15 (1967), pp. 13–33.

[95] Whisler, W.D. "Sensitivity Analysis of Rates of Return," *Journal of Finance* 31 (1976).

[96] Winkler, R.L. "The Assessment of the Prior Distribution in Bayesian Analysis," *Journal of the American Statistical Association* 62 (1967), pp. 776–800.

6 EVALUATING INTERNATIONAL PROJECTS:

An Adjusted Present Value Approach

Donald R. Lessard
Massachusetts Institute of Technology

In evaluating projects that cut across national boundaries, firms must deal with a variety of issues seldom encountered within a single country that affect the distribution of net operating cash flows available to the parent, as well as the valuation of these cash flows.[1] Factors influencing the statistical distribution of net operating cash flows, in addition to differences in fundamental economic and political conditions in various countries, include differing rates of inflation and volatile exchange rates that may or may not cancel each other, differences in tax rules and tax rates, and restrictions or taxes on cross-border financial transactions. Factors that may influence the valuation of operating cash flows with a

An earlier version of this paper was published in D. R. Lessard, ed., *International Financial Management* (New York: Warren, Gorham, & Lamont, 1979). I am grateful to a large number of persons who have commented on the earlier versions of this paper, including Fischer Black, Gene Carter, Rich Cohn, Gunter Franke, Christine Hekman, Stewart Myers, Joel Ornstein, Jim Paddock, Alan Shapiro, and Kirit Vora. All remaining errors and arbitrary choices are, of course, my responsibility.

118

given statistical distribution include incomplete and often segmented capital markets that result from controls on financial transactions both within and among countries; the dependence of net of tax cash flows available to the parent on the firm's overall tax and cash-flow position in various countries; the availability of project-specific concessional finance—loans, guarantees, or insurance against commercial or political risks; and, on occasion, requirements to issue securities—especially equity—within markets partially or totally isolated by barriers to internal or cross-border financial transactions. Further, the available cash flows and their value to the firm often depend on the specific financing of the project, not only because of concessional financing opportunities, but also because the costs or limits on cross-border transfers often depend on the nature of the financial transaction involved, e.g., interest or principal, fees, dividends, or payment for goods.

As a result of these various factors, it is often necessary to distinguish project and parent cash flows, to recognize interactions between the financing and valuation of a project, to take into account dependencies between project valuation and the corporation's overall tax and cash-flow situation, and to incorporate in the valuation criterion the perspectives of multiple investors not sharing a common capital market. Thus traditional weighted-average cost of capital rules that implicitly separate investment and financing decisions often are inapplicable or misleading,[2] as well as exceedingly complex. [3] A variety of alternative approaches has been put forward,[4] some involving multiple investment criteria,[5] others requiring the consideration of the "full-system" effects of the project in question,[6] and others providing relatively complex criteria reflecting the existence of multiple investors based in less than fully integrated capital markets.[7]

This paper seeks to show that an adjusted present value approach (APV), based on the value additivity principle (VAP) that holds for independent projects in complete capital markets, provides a relatively simple framework for evaluating most international projects consistent with state-of-the-art financial practice. It is restricted to projects wholly owned by the parent or whose equity is shared by investors having access to the same relatively complete capital markets. It does not address the valuation of projects by joint ventures in which equity is shared by investors based in markets segmented by barriers[8] or the relative valuation of particular projects by firms based in countries with relatively complete markets and by local firms operating in a more restricted capital market— a potential motivation for direct foreign investment.[9]

Special attention is given to the valuation of operating cash flows that are not denominated in any specific currency but that reflect the interaction of inflation rates and exchange rates and of nominal cash flows, such as depreciation tax shields and debt service that are contractually denominated in a specified currency.

The paper is organized in six sections. The second section describes the APV approach and discusses the circumstances under which it is applicable. The third section discusses the valuation of operating and contractual cash flows. The fourth section presents a general APV formula for foreign projects that distinguishes between operating and contractual cash flows and takes into account the effects of differing tax systems, exchange and credit restrictions, and concessional financing opportunities, together with their interactions with the structure of the project's cross-border interaffiliate financing, as well as with the local subsidiary and parent firm's external financing. The fifth section discusses briefly the risk premiums applicable to the various cash flows, and the last section discusses the implementation of the APV approach, especially with regard to approaches involving multiple cash-flow estimates and simulation.

THE ADJUSTED PRESENT VALUE APPROACH

As a result of the "cost of capital revolution" of the 1960s, the dominant approach to project evaluation is to discount expected after-tax project cash flows by a weighted-average cost of capital,

$$\text{NPV} = \sum_{t=0}^{T} \frac{\overline{\text{CF}}_t}{(1 + \rho^*)^t}, \tag{1}$$

where NPV is net present value, $\overline{\text{CF}}_t$ is the expected total after-tax project cash flow in period t, and ρ^* is the weighted-average cost of capital. ρ^* in turn is usually defined as

$$\rho^* = (1 - \lambda)\rho^E + \lambda r(1 - \tau), \tag{2}$$

where λ is the weight of debt in the total capital structure, r is the pretax interest rate on debt, τ is the corporate tax rate, and ρ^E is the required rate of return on equity.

The advantage of the traditional approach is its simplicity. It imbeds in a single discount rate all financing considerations, thus enabling planners to focus on the project's investment characteristics. However, different discount rates are required for projects that differ from a firm's typical project in terms of either business risk or contribution to debt capacity, and equation (2) provides little guidance since ρ^E will be changed by an unspecified amount. Both conditions are the rule rather than the exception for foreign projects. Further, when the financing complications of foreign projects are introduced, the weighted-average approach becomes complex and cumbersome, removing its major advantage. In fact, when financing sources for foreign projects include limited amounts of restricted funds or project-specific concessionary credit, there will be different weighted-average costs for projects that differ only in scale. With capital structures that vary over time—which is typical of projects financed independently of the parent to minimize taxes, to take advantage of project-specific financing subsidies, or to minimize political risks—a different weighted average will be required in different years of the project's life.

Differences in project debt capacity can be incorporated via the alternative weighted-average formula developed by Modigliani and Miller:

$$\rho^* = \rho[1 - \tau\lambda], \tag{3}$$

where ρ is the "all-equity" required rate of return reflecting the project's business risk. Further, it can be generalized to situations where business risk differs as well. The *project* required rate of return, ρ_j^*, is given by

$$\rho_j^* = [r + \beta_j(\rho_m - r)] \, [1 - \tau\lambda], \tag{4}$$

where β_j is the project's beta coefficient (adjusted to remove the effect of leverage) and $(\rho_m - r)$ is the risk premium on the market portfolio.

As noted by Myers [16], however, formulas (2) and (4) are exactly correct only if the cash flows are perpetual and λ is constant over time. In many cases where projects are financed from a common corporate pool, the errors are not serious. However, if the financial structures of specific foreign projects differ from those of the parent firm or vary over the project lives because of the availability of concessional finance, tax considerations, or efforts to reduce political or currency risks, even the generalized formula (4) is likely to be misleading.

To deal with the problem, Myers [16] suggests a return to the basic Modigliani-Miller equation underlying (3). Rather than implicitly incorporating financial factors in ρ^*, the approach values them explicitly in an adjusted present value equation:

$$\text{APV} = \sum_{t=0}^{T} \frac{\overline{\text{CF}}_t}{(1 + \rho_j)^t} + \sum_{t=0}^{T} \frac{TS_t}{(1 + r)^t}, \tag{5}$$

where the first term is the present value of the total expected operating cash flows discounted by ρ_j, the "all-equity" discount rate reflecting the project's business risk, and the second term is the present value of the tax shields arising from debt, discounted at the before-tax cost of debt, r. This is a direct application of the value additivity principle (VAP)—that in equilibrium the market value of any set of "risk-independent" cash flows available for distribution to security holders (after corporate taxes) is equal to the sum of the values of the individual components.[10]

Applicability of VAP to International Projects

Value additivity is a robust concept. Haley and Schall [11, pp. 230–237] show that it applies without exception for securities (claims to income streams) issued in complete, competitive capital markets with neutral personal taxes. Further, they argue that because of clientele effects, VAP will hold in general for individual firms even if personal taxes are not neutral in their treatment of interest, dividend, and capital gain income. Most importantly, they point out that even if markets are not complete (i.e., that there is no perfect substitute for one or more of the income streams provided by the firm or project), the potential for investor arbitrage will generally maintain value additivity. It breaks down when certain transactions are restricted or costly, and as a result the potential for investor arbitrage is impaired.

At first glance, this latter condition appears to rule out VAP for projects with income streams subject to cross-border costs or restrictions or to projects in countries with capital markets isolated by such barriers. However, VAP requires only that investors can engage in arbitrage among the various income streams available for distribution by the parent firm after corporate taxes. Thus any restrictions or taxes on cross-border transfers to the parent must be reflected in the income stream components, but will not affect the ability to combine or divide these remittable, net of corporate tax streams for valuation.

The fact that local capital markets are not competitive because of internal controls or lack of the necessary institutional infrastructure or are isolated from other markets by barriers to cross-border transactions is irrelevant in the valuation of projects by wholly owned ventures in such countries by firms based in countries with relatively open, competitive capital markets. These conditions may change the investment opportunity set facing the firm through their impact on the competition for projects resulting from differences in project valuation by local and international firms, but the appropriate context for the valuation of these flows is the base country capital market. Even in the case of joint ventures, these conditions will have no effect on the valuation of a given set of income streams by the international firm, although they may lead to different valuation criteria for the local firm and hence to lack of agreement between the participants regarding investment and financing decisions.[11]

RECOGNITION OF INFLATION AND EXCHANGE RATE CHANGES

An individual international project may involve cash flows in several different currencies, some proportion of which will be contractually denominated in those currencies and the remainder of which will be determined by the interactions of future business conditions and changes in relative prices, price levels, and exchange rates. These flows can be viewed from four different perspectives as illustrated in Table 1: either in the base currency or the local currency and either in current or constant terms. The only critical requirement for correct valuation is that the discount rates used are consistent with the way the cash flows are stated—i.e., if current values are used, the discount rates must incorporate the relevant inflation premiums; if constant, the discount rates should not include inflation premiums.

Table 1.   Alternative Cash-Flow Perspectives

| Currency | Treatment of Inflation | |
	Constant	Current
Local	I	II
Base	III	IV

Common practice in estimating and evaluating cash flows can be characterized as follows: Firms first project expected revenues and expenses in constant terms, linking present unit costs and revenues with future unit sales projections. These flows are transformed into current terms by inflating them at the anticipated general rate of inflation. If the flows are not already stated in the base currency, they then are translated into current base currency units using projected exchange rates. This process involves moving from quadrant I in Table 1 to quadrant II and then to quadrant IV. Although there is nothing necessarily incorrect with this approach, it often is applied inconsistently, and important interdependencies between inflation and exchange rates and their impacts on operating and contractual cash flows are often overlooked. Further, it is difficult to extend this approach to accommodate a range of operating cash-flow estimates consistent with various economic scenarios or to cash-flow estimates generated by simulation. Each scenario must incorporate explicit assumptions regarding inflation rates, exchange rates, and cash flows, while a simulation requires the joint distribution of the three sets of variables.

The basis for a simpler, yet more transparent approach is provided by the set of equilibrium relationships between interest rates, rates of inflation, and changes in exchange rates that (tend to) hold in efficient markets—purchasing power parity and the (domestic and international) Fisher effect.[12] Even when these relationships do not hold precisely, they serve to highlight the impact on cash flows of the interactions between inflation and exchange rates and to provide insights regarding the valuation of these flows.

It is useful to separate cash flows into two groups: (1) operating cash flows that are not contractually denominated in nominal terms and whose value in constant terms is relatively independent of inflation, and (2) contractual flows denominated in a particular currency whose value in current terms is relatively independent of inflation. A different treatment is appropriate for each of the two classes of flows.

Operating Cash Flows

The home currency value of operating cash flows in another currency is given by

$$V = \sum_{t=1}^{T} \frac{\overline{CF}\,(\text{current})_t * \overline{S}_t}{(1+\rho)^t} = \sum_{t=1}^{T} \frac{\overline{CF}\,(\text{constant})_t\,(1+\overline{I})^t * \overline{S}_t}{(1+\rho)^t}, \tag{6}$$

where $\overline{CF}$ (current) are expected cash flows in current local terms and $\overline{CF}$ (constant) are the expected flows in constant terms, and ρ is the all-equity rate appropriate for flows in the home currency with the project's risk.

This formula can be simplified substantially if the two key equilibrium relationships—purchasing power parity (PPP) and the Fisher effect (IFE)—are assumed to hold.[13] PPP implies that exchange rate changes and relative rates of inflation offset each other. As a result, the expected spot exchange rate for foreign currency (stated in terms of units of the base currency per unit of foreign currency) at time t is

$$\overline{S}_t = S_0\,(1+\overline{I})^t/(1+\overline{I}^*)^t, \tag{7}$$

where S_0 is the current spot rate, $\overline{I}$ the expected base currency inflation rate, and $\overline{I}^*$ the expected foreign currency inflation rate.[14,15] IFE implies that the nominal riskless interest rate, r, for a given currency, incorporates a premium for anticipated inflation. Thus $(1+\rho)$ can be restated as

$$(1 + r_{\text{real}})\,(1 + I)\,(1 + \text{RP}) \tag{8}$$

when r_{real} is the real interest rate and RP is the risk premium.

Substituting into (6)[16]

$$V = \sum_{t=1}^{T} \frac{\overline{CF}\,(\text{constant})_t\,(1+\overline{I}^*)^t\,S_0\,(1+\overline{I})^t/(1+\overline{I}^*)^t}{[(1+\rho_{\text{real}})\,(1+\overline{I})]^t} \tag{9a}$$

$$= S_0 \sum_{t=1}^{T} \frac{\overline{CF}\,(\text{constant})_t}{(1+\rho_{\text{real}})}. \tag{9b}$$

The problem of cash flows in different currencies and discount rates appropriate for each one collapses into a single currency calculation where the current exchange rate simply scales the flows to a common base.

Departures from PPP and IFE.   Of course, PPP does not hold exactly, and interest rates do not provide exact guides to future exchange rate changes. However, there is little evidence for major currencies subject to market forces that deviations from these key relationships are persistent or that they can be forecast.[17] As a result, the simplified approach to cash-flow estimation and valuation based on these equilibrium tendencies is quite robust for single-point expected cash-flow estimates. If various distributions of cash flows are considered, the problem becomes more complex. *Ex post* deviations from IFE will have no effect on valuation if PPP continues to hold. However, departures from PPP are likely to alter cash flows stated in constant local terms, as well as the real exchange rate at which they can be converted into the base currency. This is because they result in changes in the relative prices of inputs or outputs sold or sourced in different countries. Further, the deviations themselves are likely to relfect changes in relative prices within countries, with important implications for cash flows.

It is much more likely that firms can forecast trends in relative prices of certain inputs and outputs as opposed to overall deviations from PPP, since relative price changes hinge on microlevel changes in productivity, scarcity, or substitutability of the good or factor in question. Furthermore, given the evidence that PPP holds quite well over the long run, these relative price shifts are likely to result in larger impacts on project values than divergences from PPP. These relative price shifts can be incorporated readily by changing project cash flows in either (9a) or (9b), but (9b) is more transparent since it abstracts from offsetting inflation and exchange rate changes.

Where exchange rates are forecast to diverge from PPP because of exchange controls or trade barriers, explicit joint estimates of the local currency cash flows and exchange rates are required. These can be stated in either real or nominal terms since the key element is the change in the real exchange rate (deviation from PPP) and not the absolute exchange rate and level of inflation. Typically, the impact of PPP deviations in such cases will not be symmetric, since price controls or other market interventions are likely to be systematically related to the PPP departures.

Contractual Cash Flows

Contractual nominal cash flows including interest on debt and tax rebates based on historical cost depreciation can be discounted at a nominal rate appropriate to the currency in question and converted to the base currency by multiplying the resulting present value by the current spot rate,

$$V = S_0 \sum_{t=1}^{T} \frac{\overline{\text{CF}}\ (\text{current})_t}{[(1 + r)\,(1 + \text{RP})]^t}\ , \tag{10}$$

where $(1 + r) = (1 + r_{\text{real}})\,(1 + I)$ and I is for the currency in which the flows are denominated.[18]

For major currencies, where interest rate parity and the Fisher effect tend to hold, market interest rates are appropriate. Where market interest rates do not reflect generally held inflation and exchange rate expectations as a result of credit controls or exchange restrictions, an offshore rate (if available) or an estimated rate must be used.

Deviations from IFE. Any unanticipated change in exchange rates, whether it represents a departure from PPP or not, changes the present value of contractual flows. Anticipated changes reflected in the interest rate will have no effect on the value of interest-bearing contractual claims, but will change the value of non-interest-bearing claims, such as depreciation and other tax shields based on historical cost allocations.

APPLYING APV TO FOREIGN PROJECTS

The APV approach, outlined earlier, provides a "divide and conquer" approach to capital budgeting. Financial contributions to a project's value are recognized separately and explicitly, the total present value is the sum of the present values of the basic project cash flows, and the treatment of the various financing effects can be generalized to incorporate the special situations encountered in evaluating foreign projects. In particular, the cash flows can be separated into operating and contractual components, as well as into those components that can be estimated independently for the project and those that depend on systemwide cash-flow and tax interactions. This breakdown is illustrated in the following general equation:

$$\text{Adjusted present value} \qquad\qquad \text{APV} \tag{11}$$

$$=$$

$$
\text{Noncontractual operating flows}
\begin{cases}
\text{Capital outlay} & \displaystyle\sum_{i=1}^{N} S_0^i \sum_{t=0}^{T} \frac{I_t^i}{(1 + \rho_1)^t} \tag{11a} \\[2em]
+ \\[1em]
\begin{array}{l}\text{Remittable after-tax} \\ \text{operating cash flows}\end{array} & \displaystyle\sum_{i=1}^{N} S_0^i \sum_{t=1}^{T} \frac{\overline{\text{CF}}_t^i\,(1 - \tau)}{(1 + \rho_2)^t} \tag{11b}
\end{cases}
$$

$$
\left\{
\begin{array}{l}
\end{array}
\right.
$$

+

Contractual operating flows
$$\sum_{i=1}^{N} S_0^i \sum_{t=1}^{T} \frac{\text{CONT}_t^i (1 - \tau)}{(1 + \rho_3)^t} \quad (11c)$$

Depreciation tax shields
$$\sum_{i=1}^{N} S_0^i \sum_{t=1}^{T} \frac{\text{DEP}_t^i (\tau)}{(1 + \rho_4)^t} \quad (11d)$$

+

Contractual flows

Tax shields due to normal borrowing
$$\sum_{i=1}^{N} S_0^i \sum_{t=1}^{T} \frac{\text{INT}_t^i (\tau)}{(1 + \rho_5)^t} \quad (11e)$$

+

Financial subsidies or penalties
$$\sum_{i=1}^{N} S_0^i \sum_{t=1}^{T} \frac{\Delta\text{INT}_t^i}{(1 + \rho_6)^t} \quad (11f)$$

+

Operating flows dependent on firm's overall tax and cash-flow position

Tax reduction or deferral via interaffiliate transfers
$$\sum_{i=1}^{N} S_0^i \sum_{t=1}^{T} \frac{\text{TR}_t^i}{(1 + \rho_7)^t} \quad (11g)$$

+

Additional remittances via interaffiliate transfers
$$\sum_{i=1}^{N} S_0^i \sum_{t=1}^{T} \frac{\text{REM}_t^i}{(1 + \rho_8)^t} \quad (11h)$$

where superscript i denotes currency i and S_0^i is the current spot rate for currency i.

Each of the terms is discussed in greater detail below. We assume that operating flows are stated in constant terms and hence discounted at a real rate, while the contractual flows are stated in current terms and hence are discounted at the relevant nominal rate. Appropriate risk premiums for the various components are discussed later.

Capital Outlay (11a). The elements of this term are unambiguous for items purchased by the firm, but are more complex for capital items sourced internally. The major obstacle in the latter case is calculating the true incremental cost to the system, which may differ substantially from the registered book value of the item in question. Contractual capital costs should be distinguished from non-contractual costs and discounted at nominal rates.

Capital expenditures often are paid out of accumulated funds from existing operations whose use is restricted by exchange controls or because special tax advantages will be forfeited or additional U.S. taxes imposed if the funds are remitted rather than reinvested. The APV framework lends itself readily to incorporating the incremental value of a project resulting from its ability to employ such funds. Since the operating cash-flow term already captures project cash flows that will be available for remittance, taxed as if they are remitted, the use of restricted funds simply reduces the investment outlays (11a) by the difference between their face value and the present value of these funds if remitted via the best alternative mechanism.

Operating Cash Flow (11b). In the domestic case, there is little difficulty in defining after-tax operating cash flows. They are the total project cash flows less U.S. taxes. Whether they are reinvested in the project or not makes no difference, since all flows are deemed available to the corporate cash pool. With foreign projects, there are two major issues in defining operating cash flows: (1) whether to use project cash flows or only those flows remitted to the parent, and (2) what taxes to assume, since these will be a function of financing and remittance decisions. The first distinction arises because of foreign exchange restrictions and ceilings on profit remittances; the second because of the interactions of various national tax systems.

Clearly, the only cash flows of value to the parent are those available for remittance in one form or another, not necessarily those actually remitted. Furthermore, after-tax flows must take into account the incremental taxes to the entire corporation. However, the specific choice of ways to deal with the two issues is a question of managerial art—the solution should be straightforward, easy to apply, and likely to bring to management's attention the most critical issues.

There are two basic approaches. One is to begin with the most favorable set of assumptions regarding taxation and remittability and, in later terms of the APV equation, to subtract the present values of reductions due to specific restrictions or international tax interactions. The other is to start with conservative assumptions regarding remittability and taxation, later adding the present value of gains resulting from various mechanisms for circumventing restrictions or deferring taxes. I prefer the second alternative for the pragmatic reason that if a project is attractive under conservative assumptions, there is no need to proceed with the far more complex set of calculations regarding tax and remittance adjustments that require consideration of the total corporate cash flow and tax situation.[19]

The conservative approach includes in the first term only those cash flows available for remittance through normal channels—for example, amortization of investment and repatriation of earnings—but not those that can be obtained only through transfer pricing or other mechanisms for circumventing restrictions. The tax rate applied to these flows is either the parent rate or the foreign rate, whichever tax system imposes the largest tax liability. This implicitly assumes that all operating cash flows are remitted immediately to the United States and that the parent has no excess foreign tax credits. Any additional value derived by circumventing restrictions on cash remittances, deferring U.S. taxes, or offsetting excess foreign tax credits can be incorporated in additional terms. Since depreciation tax shields are captured in a separate term, after-tax cash flows are simply pretax flows multiplied by one minus the relevant tax rate.

A further and perhaps more serious issue in the computation of operating cash flows is the difficulty of measuring the true incremental cash flows of a project in an interdependent multinational system. For example, the establishment of a manufacturing plant in a country previously served by exports will result in an erosion of profits elsewhere in the system, but it may also create new profit opportunities for other parts of the system that provide intermediate or complementary products. This difficulty is exacerbated by departures from arm's length transfer pricing among units, some of which may result from conscious manipulation of tax and exchange control systems, but most of which result from the near impossibility of allocating the joint costs and benefits associated with "soft" factors of production, such as technology and managerial expertise used by more than one unit of the corporation. Clearly, an attempt should be made to measure incremental cash flows to the total system. Further, in keeping with conservative tax and remittance assumptions, interaffiliate flows should be valued as closely to an arm's length value as possible.[20]

Contractual Operating Flows (11c). Some elements of operating costs or revenues, as well as capital costs, may be set contractually. Typically, this will be true only for a relatively short period, and the distinction is thus immaterial for capital budgeting. However, where long-term sourcing or sales contracts are involved, explicit recognition of the contractual cash flows is called for.[21]

Depreciation Tax Shields (11d). This contractual cash flow is deterministic, subject to the corporation's ability to use or to sell the tax shield, given investment outlays. The relevant tax rate and set of tax rules that should be used are those binding at the margin, as noted above.

Interest Tax Shields (11e). For a variety of reasons, including the availability of concessionary credit, the existence of tax or exchange considerations that favor remittances in the form of interest payments, and the desire to hedge currency or political risks, foreign projects are often financed with a different and typically higher proportion of debt than the corporation as a whole. Further, the debt issued to finance the project often exceeds the increment to overall debt capacity provided by the project. Thus approaches that directly utilize the project capital structure in computing a weighted-average cost of capital are likely to overstate the worth of the project, but a weighted average based on the total firm's capitalization also is likely to be misleading. In the APV equation, in contrast, the second term captures the tax shields associated with a project's incremental contribution to corporate debt capacity. The costs or benefits of "overborrowing" at the project level for reasons of currency risk, concessionary credit, or remittance restrictions are treated explicitly in later terms.

Financial Subsidies or Penalties (11f). The value of subsidies in the form of concessionary credit or penalties resulting from local financing requirements can be computed by comparing the present value of the total pretax payments on the debt, including interest and principal, discounted at the rate that would apply if the same debt were issued to competitive capital markets with the face value of the debt. For example, if a project is eligible for a concessionary loan at 6 percent instead of a market rate of, say, 9 percent, (11f) would be the difference between the present value of the total pretax payments on the 6 percent debt discounted at 9 percent and the face value of the debt.[22]

Ability to Reduce or to Defer Taxes (11g). The base case operating cash flows, term (11b), incorporate conservative assumptions regarding the taxation of project cash flows—that they will be taxed at the U.S. rate or the local rate in the foreign country, whichever results in the greater tax liability. In many cases, an MNC can reduce taxes from this level by combining profits from countries with relatively low and high taxes, by shifting expenses and revenues among its affiliates, or simply by reinvesting profits in low-tax countries and deferring the additional U.S. taxes. In principle, the present value of these tax changes can be readily incorporated in an APV term, although computing them may require a complex corporate tax model. However, reversing the analysis to calculate a "break-even" value for term (11g) may show that a readily attainable degree of tax reduction is all that is required. Thus the full analysis can be avoided.

Ability to Circumvent Restrictions on Remittances (11h). The base case operating flows, term (11b), include only those operating flows available for remittance. Thus they will be less than project flows whenever there are binding remittance restrictions. In many cases, however, the restricted flows can be transferred out through interaffiliate pricing, management fees, special export programs, or other mechanisms. The value of these remittances, typically less than the face value of the funds in question, can be incorporated in another APV term. Again, a major advantage of the "divide and conquer" approach is that it makes explicit the impact on project value of remittance restrictions and alternative ways around them. Even where the exact possibilities for transferring restricted funds are not known, a "break-even" value for term (11h) can be computed, thus showing what proportion, in present value terms, of the restricted profits would have to be transferred to make the project marginally attractive.

RISK PREMIUMS FOR FOREIGN PROJECTS

Although the APV approach does not require that the effects of financial structure be reflected in the discount rate, the discount rate for each term must reflect both the rate of interest (real in the case of operating flows, nominal in the case of nominal flows) and a risk premium. According to current capital market theory, this risk premium should reflect only the systematic risk of the project. Depending on the openness of the base country capital market, this systematic risk should be measured relative to the firm's home country market portfolio or relative to the world market portfolio. As shown by Lessard [13], the systematic risk of projects in various countries differs substantially from U.S. and world perspectives, but much more so for other single-country versus world perspectives. From a single-country perspective, foreign projects will tend to have less systematic risk than domestic projects, although this may not be true if the more appropriate world base is used. In countries where local conditions are extremely uncertain, but not highly dependent on the world economy, the total risk of the project will be substantially greater than its systematic risk from any perspective other than the local one. Thus even apparently risky projects may not require greater than normal risk premiums.

The suggestion that cash flows from projects in politically unstable countries should not require large risk premiums is at odds with general practice. Many firms attach large risk premiums to such projects. However, the difference is often more semantic than real. A common approach to evaluating foreign projects is to discount most likely (modal) rather than expected (mean) cash flows at a risk-adjusted rate. For projects with a significant risk of expropriation or large losses due to changes in the economic structure of a country, the mean will be substantially lower than the mode. Thus the discount rate is being used to shift cash flows toward their expected values to discount them by a risk premium. Such "risk adjustments," however, introduce biases, and the more explicit approach that captures the effect of risks on expected cash flows, as well as on their valuation, is preferable.[23]

Appropriate discount rates for each major category of the APV terms are discussed below.

Noncontractual Flows (ρ_1 and ρ_2): Capital Outlays. Since these flows are not contractually fixed in any currency, but vary depending on the interactions of inflation and exchange rates, as well as on a host of other factors, I have argued that they should be stated in terms of units of constant purchasing power and discounted at the real rate of interest plus a risk premium reflecting their systematic risk. However, determining this systematic risk represents a major challenge. In many cases, there are no host country firms in the same industry with shares traded in an active market to provide beta estimates. Furthermore, formal or informal approaches for estimating fundamental betas are likely to be hampered by a lack of experience with similar projects. In addition, beta estimates estimated empirically will relate the volatility of equity values, reflecting both operating and contractual cash flows. Hence it is necessary to "back out" the relevant betas for the various components. This is not an insurmountable task, though, since the contractual flows are relatively safe and can be assumed to be discounted at a rate close to the riskless rate. Thus the adjustment involves "unlevering" beta, not only for financial leverage, but also for depreciation tax shields.

Contractual Flows $(\rho_3-\rho_6)$. The critical element in discounting these flows is determining the appropriate nominal interest rate for (near) riskless debt. Undoubtedly there is some risk of default associated with the various contractual flows, and hence a risk premium may be required. Nevertheless, as a first approximation, the corporation's borrowing rates in unregulated markets can be used. Technically, the depreciation tax shields are subject only to the risk that the firm cannot make use of them. This may be serious in certain cases, but in general if the firm cannot take the deductions directly, it can carry them forward or backward in time or, in the ultimate case, transfer them to another firm through mergers. Roughly speaking, then, ρ_4 will involve only a small risk premium and can be approximated by the interest rate on the firm's debt in the currency in question. Similar arguments apply to interest tax shields and financial subsidies.

System-Dependent Operating Flows $(\rho_7$ and $\rho_8)$. Although part of these flows are tax savings due to transfer pricing or earnings retention decisions, they are not contractually denominated except to the extent that the profit shifting also changes depreciation tax shields. Thus in practice it might be necessary to separate the term into an operating and contractual component, with the appropriate inflation and risk adjustments for each element. The amount available for remittance through these channels will depend directly on project operating cash flows and thus, although the risks of being able to remit these additional funds are unlikely to be highly systematic, the discount rate applicable to operating flows, ρ_2, appears to be a reasonable choice.

CONCLUSIONS

The APV approach provides a generalized framework capable of incorporating most of the special financial considerations that arise in evaluating foreign projects. Its attractiveness vis-à-vis traditional approaches, which attempt to force all these factors into a single term, rests only in part on its conceptual superiority. Much of its attraction lies in its transparency and simplicity of use in certain situations.

In practice, capital budgeting involves a great deal of trial and error with various "what if" questions. Furthermore, many uncertain outcomes are never reduced to specific cash flows, but instead are dealt with by testing the sensitivity of cash flows to changes in a particular assumption and by judging whether a particular variable is likely to exceed a "break-even" value. The ability to separate the various terms greatly facilitates such analyses. In most cases, only the operating cash-flow streams will need to be run under a variety of scenarios. Similarly, if there is uncertainty with respect to the appropriate discount rates, most of it will center on the risk premium for the operating cash flows, and thus sensitivity analysis can concentrate on these flows. The distinction between real and nominal flows allows a substantially simplified treatment of inflation and exchange rates, but it also serves to highlight the differential impact of these factors on the two types of flows.

While the assumptions of purchasing power parity and interest rate parity undoubtedly break down for certain countries or currencies, they provide the best set of base case single-point estimates. If deviations from these relationships are explicitly considered, a careful attempt to model the effect of these deviations on the cash flows themselves is called for. Treating them as independent in either a scenario or simulation approach is fallacious and is likely to result in more serious errors than assuming that the naive parity conditions hold.

The explicit separation of contractual and noncontractual cash flows in various currencies lends itself to sensitivity or simulation approaches for determining the impact of exchange rate changes or a project's present value, valuable both for capital budgeting and foreign exchange exposure analysis.

While these considerations clearly favor the APV approach, they do not call for its use in all situations. Little will be lost in using a single discount rate that is roughly consistent with APV solutions for small, recurring projects with few or no financing interactions. However, even in this case, the APV framework provides the ideal basis for computing these hurdle rates for decentralized use. Any strategic decision that involves financial complexities, though, should be evaluated in the more complete fashion outlined.

NOTES

1. See Eiteman and Stonehill [6], Rodriguez and Carter [22], Shapiro [25], and Folks [7] for summaries of the factors distinguishing domestic and foreign projects. An early paper that raised most of these questions was Stonehill and Nathanson's [29].

2. Rodriguez and Carter [22] demonstrate how weighted-average measures using project or subsidiary capital structures are misleading when there is financial "layering" within the corporation.

3. Shapiro [26] provides a detailed derivation of a weighted-average rule for international projects that takes many of these factors into account. However, it is exceedingly complex, and the resulting hurdle rate is likely to differ across projects and over time.

4. Naumann-Etiene [17] provides a good review of the early literature on this topic.

5. Eiteman and Stonehill [6] suggested a dual hurdle rate approach. Although they have dropped it in their subsequent edition, it continues to be advocated by others.

6. See, for example, Pomper [20].

7. Alder [1] provides the most complete treatment of this issue.

8. See Adler [1] and Adler and Dumas [2] for a discussion of valuation in such cases. Although the APV from the viewpoint of a single investor will not in general be the appropriate investment criterion for the joint venture, it will be appropriate for valuing that project from the single investor's viewpoint. In practice, there may be no rule that satisfies both participants in the joint venture. In such cases, project acceptance depends on bargaining among the participants, where each may use an APV measure to evaluate their share.

9. See, for example, Adler and Dumas [2, 3], Agmon and Lessard [4], and Stapleton and Subrahmanyan [28].

10. The VAP, an extension of the first Miller-Modigliani proposition, was introduced by Schall [24] and, although not given the same name, by Myers [16]. For an excellent statement, see Haley and Schall [11, pp. 202–208].

11. In practice, virtually all international ventures can be considered joint ventures in the sense that the local government's income taxes are risky equity claims and locally issued debt typically carries some project-related risks. In these cases, the local government's valuation of a venture may differ from that of the international firm, but these effects will usually be swamped by other adjustments, such as shadow prices for foreign exchange and labor and the recognition of positive and negative externalities.

12. For a succinct definition of these relationships, see Giddy [9], Frenkel [8], and Solnik [27]. See Dornbusch [5] for a more complete discussion of the underlying economic theory.

13. For an excellent review of the theory and evidence regarding purchasing power parity, see Officer [18]. Levich [15] reviews the evidence regarding the degree to which the forward rate is an unbiased predictor of future spot exchange rates and of interest rate parity, conditions that jointly imply IFE.

14. The classical PPP relationship is defined in terms of certain, contemporaneous variables. Giddy [10] and Solnik [27] discuss the expectational form.

15. This formula can be altered readily to accommodate varying rates of inflation over time.

16. If PPP does not hold exactly, equation (9a) includes the covariances among cash flows, inflation, and exchange rates and does not reduce to (9b). However, if the cash flows in constant terms are (relatively) independent of inflation and the exchange rate, the approximation is satisfactory.

17. Roll [23], for example, finds no evidence that deviations from PPP persist or can be forecast.

18. The value of riskless contractual flows is unaffected by uncertainty regarding the exchange rate since it can be locked in by borrowing or lending an equivalent flow at the nominal market interest rate.

19. This assumption is analogous to the "default value" approach suggested by Folks [7].

20. Vernon and Wells [31] and Robbins and Stobaugh [21] provide further illustration of the difficulty of measuring incremental cash flows at a system level.

21. See Lessard [12, pp. 354–356] for a discussion of contractual and noncontractual cash flows and their implications for corporate exposure to exchange rate changes.

22. Pretax cash flows are used since it is assumed that the use of concessionary debt will require a matching reduction in other corporate borrowings. Thus the additional interest tax shields of the concessionary debt will be offset by reduced interest tax shields on corporate borrowing at market rates. The tax shields gained and lost will not match exactly if debt capacity is defined in terms of book values. Even if defined in terms of (net present value of) cash flows, the offset will be inexact since the proportion of the debt service flows that is interest will differ for the concessionary debt and borrowings at the market rate with the same present value. In most cases, however, the error is small.

23. Eiteman and Stonehill [6] follow a third approach, "adjusting" cash flows until they are of equivalent risk to those of domestic projects and then discounting them by the domestic "cost of capital." This is similar to taking certainty equivalents of cash flows and discounting them by the riskless rate. While in many ways it is theoretically more appealing than to discount expected cash flows by a risk-adjusted rate, there are no operational, yet reasonably precise ways to do this.

REFERENCES

[1] Adler, M. "The Cost of Capital and Valuation of a Two-Country Firm," *Journal of Finance* (March 1974).

[2] Adler, M., and Dumas, B. "Optimal International Acquisitions," *Journal of Finance* (March 1975).

[3] Adler, M., and Dumas, B. "The Microeconomics of the Firm in an Open Economy," *American Economic Review* (February 1977).

[4] Agmon, T., and Lessard, D.R. "Financial Factors and the International Expansion of Small-Country Firms," in Agmon and Kindleberger, eds., *Multinationals from Small Countries*. Cambridge, Mass.: M.I.T. Press, 1977.

[5] Dornbusch, R. "Monetary Policy under Exchange Rate Flexibility," in *Managed Exchange Rate Flexibility*. Boston: Federal Reserve Bank of Boston, Conference Vol., No. 20, 1979.

[6] Eiteman, D.K., and Stonehill, A.I. *Multinational Business Finance*, 2nd ed. Reading, Mass.: Addison-Wesley Publishing Company, 1979.

[7] Folks, W.R., Jr. "Critical Assumptions in Evaluating Foreign Investment Projects," paper submitted at Nijenrode conference, August 1979.

[8] Frenkel, J.A. "A Monetary Approach to the Exchange Rate: Doctrinal Aspects and Empirical Evidence," *Scandinavian Journal of Economics* (May 1976).

[9] Giddy, I. "The Cost of Capital in the International Firm," unpublished working paper, Columbia University, 1976.

[10] Giddy, I. "An Integrated Theory of Exchange Rate Equilibrium," *Journal of Financial and Quantitative Analysis* (December 1976).

[11] Haley, C.W., and Schall, L.D. *The Theory of Financial Decisions.* New York: McGraw-Hill Book Company, 1979.

[12] Lessard, D.R., ed. *International Financial Management.* New York: Warren, Gorham, & Lamont, 1979.

[13] Lessard, D.R., ed. "World, Country and Industry Relationships in Equity Returns: Implications for Risk Reduction through International Diversification," *Financial Analysts Journal* (January/February 1976).

[14] Lessard, D.R., ed. "Transfer Prices, Taxes, and Financial Markets: Implications of Internal Financial Transfers within the Multinational Firm," in R.B. Hawkins, ed., *Economic Issues of Multinational Firms.* JAI Press, 1979.

[15] Levich, R.M. "The Efficiency of Markets for Foreign Exchange," in Lessard, ed., *International Financial Management.*

[16] Myers, S.C. "Procedures for Capital Budgeting under Uncertainty," *Industrial Management Review* (Spring 1968).

[17] Naumann-Etiene, R. "A Framework for Financial Decisions in Multinational Corporations—A Summary of Recent Research," *Journal of Financial and Quantitative Analysis* (November 1974).

[18] Officer, L.H. "The Purchasing Power Theory of Exchange Rates: A Review Article," *IMF Staff Papers* (March 1976).

[19] Ornstein, J., and Vora, K.T. "Foreign Investment Projects in Multinational Firms," Master's thesis, Sloan School of Management, M.I.T., December 1978.

[20] Pomper, C.B. *International Investment Planning: An Integrated Approach.* Amsterdam: North-Holland Publishing Company, 1976.

[21] Robbins, S.M., and Stobaugh, R.B. *Money in the Multinational Corporation.* New York: Basic Books, 1973.

[22] Rodriguez, R.M., and Carter, E.E. *International Financial Management.* Englewood Cliffs, N.J.: Prentice-Hall, 1979.

[23] Roll, R. "Violations of Purchasing Power Parity and Their Implications for Efficient International Commodity Markets," in M. Sarnat and G.P. Szëgo, eds., *International Finance and Trade,* Vol. 1. Cambridge, Mass.: Ballinger Publishing Company, 1979.

[24] Schall, L.D. "Asset Valuation, Firm Investment, and Firm Diversification," *Journal of Business* (January 1972).

[25] Shapiro, A.C. "Capital Budgeting for the Multinational Corporation," *Financial Management* (May 1978).

[26] Shapiro, A.C. "Financial Structure and the Cost of Capital in the Multinational Corporation," *Journal of Financial and Quantitative Analysis* (November 1978).

[27] Solnik, B. "International Parity Conditions and Exchange Risk," *Journal of Banking and Finance* (August 1978).

[28] Stapleton, R.C., and Subrahmanyan, M.G. "Market Imperfections, Capital Market Equilibrium, and Corporation Finance," *Journal of Finance* (May 1977).

[29] Stonehill, A.I., and Nathanson, L. "Capital Budgeting and the Multinational Corporation," *California Management Review* (Summer 1968).

[30] Taggart, R.A., Jr. "Capital Budgeting and the Financing Decision: An Exposition," *Financial Management* (Summer 1977).

[31] Vernon, R.A., and Wells, L.T. *Manager in the International Economy*, 3rd ed. Englewood Cliffs, N.J.: Prentice-Hall, 1976.

7 CRITICAL ASSUMPTIONS IN EVALUATING FOREIGN INVESTMENT PROJECTS

William R. Folks, Jr.
University of South Carolina

This paper addresses certain critical aspects in the technology of the financial analysis of foreign investment projects by the investing concern. Recent pedagogy in the field [2] indicates the desirability of a two-stage or double-hurdle approach to the analysis of such projects. The first hurdle that a project must surmount is an indication of its viability in the local investment environment. The overall project cash flows in local currency are developed from market data and engineering and production studies, and a determination is made using payback, present-value, internal rate-of-return considerations, or whatever, as to whether or not the project is viable in a local economic sense. Failure to meet the local viability test results (or ought to result) in project rejection, regardless of the apparent profitability of the project at the parent.

The second hurdle requires the project to prove its viability in terms of cash flow to the parent. For a number of reasons, outlined in the next section, the stream of cash flows realized by the parent differs in timing and amount from that realized by the subsidiary. To this possibly materially different set of cash flows, a second payback, present-value, or rate-of-return test is applied, resulting in a decision as to the viability of a project from the parent's point of view. Failure to pass this viability test would result in project rejection, regardless of the local viability test result.

Thus foreign investment projects are placed in double jeopardy under this financial evaluation system. From a local economic viewpoint, the project should earn a return sufficient to meet the cost of capital in local terms committed to it; the local cost of capital (including the cost of imported foreign capital) should approximate the economic return that the local society expects from investment projects. A project that fails this test, and whose viability from a parent standpoint depends on financial legerdemain to trick up a reasonable return, is, *de minimis,* politically unwise and socially indefensible to the extent that it consumes local capital more profitably deployed elsewhere. Further, a project must eventually earn a return to the parent sufficient to justify its funding costs. It cannot in the long run be a shareholder-wealth maximizing investment strategy to accept overseas projects whose return to the parent does not cover the costs of funds committed to it. It is assumed, of course, that the parent flow analysis includes a financial evaluation of any hidden benefits that may be attributed to the project in the future.

The two-stage approach is not universally accepted. Pomper [3] uses "maximization of the present value of consolidated cash flow as the objective function for this model." An adjustment, similar to that suggested in the next section, is made for nonparent cash flows by utilizing an objective function weight (normally $\leqslant 1$) to represent the value to the parent of a cash flow generated outside the parent. Thus Pomper in reality uses a modified parent flow analysis.[1] Shapiro emphasizes primarily parent company flows:

> *The capital budgeting model presented here only recognizes cash flows back to the parent, and it is the opportunity yield on these repatriated funds that is relevant.*[2]

In a most recent survey, Bavishi [1] reports on the practices in foreign investment project analysis of a number of firms based in the United States. Only 37 percent of the 156 firms in his survey analyze both project and parent cash-flow streams. Some 42 percent consider only subsidiary flows, while 21 percent look at parent flows only. In the light of these findings revealing a wide diversity of corporate practice, this paper will review the task of identifying parent company cash flows for investment project analysis, since failure to develop parent company flow figures is more extensive and possibly more expensive, and since the development of parent company cash flows is more complicated and technical in nature. In particular, aside from some general principles enunciated by Shapiro [6] and the prototype project analysis developed by Eiteman and Stonehill [2], there is little guidance on how to develop a detailed analysis of parent flows. In such an analysis, parent flows are not only determined by project flows and environmental factors (such as exchange rate changes and exchange control regulations), but also by managerial decisions relating to certain aspects of the project, such as transfer prices, royalties and fees, and how the project is financed, among others. This paper concentrates on developing some general principles on which to set managerial parameters for any project and then makes suggestions for a set of default parameters to be used in the analysis of projects that allows for comparability of the analyses generated. As Pomper [3] has elegantly attacked the transfer pricing and fee issues, this paper concentrates on the areas of financial structure, dividend policy, and terminal value assessment, hitherto unexplored in the context presented here.

METHODOLOGICAL CONSIDERATIONS IN IDENTIFYING PARENT COMPANY CASH FLOWS

Analysis of parent cash flows begins with a complete analysis of project cash flows, operating under the configuration chosen by management. *Pro forma* balance sheets, income statements, and cash budgets need to be developed for any local units involved (at least on an incremental basis), based on the financing pattern and technology charges indicated by the managerial parameters. Thus, while a project flow analysis may ignore financing charges, the parent analysis would charge the local cash flow with debt repayments and interest expense, among others. Local flows obviously cannot be converted directly at the projected exchange rates, nor can simple adjustments be made. Rather, as Shapiro indicates:

> In general, incremental cash flows to the parent can be found by subtracting world-wide parent company cash flows (without the investment) from post-investment parent company cash flows. [6, p. 7]

As noted, the development of actual parent cash-flow figures requires the creation of a set of assumptions regarding certain managerial decisions that impinge on these flows. There are two general approaches toward making such assumptions. The first would be to use the incremental cash flows that are actually generated from the configuration of the project as it is expected to be operated. Actual cash flows to the parent materialize as, among others,

1. Dividends and capital repatriation
2. Interest on parent loans and repayment of principal
3. Contribution generated by incremental sales to the subsidiary or lost on sales replaced by the subsidiary
4. Cost savings on incremental purchases from the subsidiary

5. Royalties, licensing fees, and other payments for use of technology or trademarks
6. Management fees

Complicating the analysis is the fact that, in a globally integrated operation, certain cash flows generated by the project may flow into other subsidiaries rather than the parent, and adjustments are needed to reflect the value realized by the parent.

The actual amount of the period-to-period cash flows realized by the investment project are subject both to external uncertainty and to management control. Assumptions regarding future economic conditions, exchange rate changes, and political developments need to be specified. Exchange rate assumptions, in particular, are critical, both in the context of their direct impact on the dollar value of local currency cash flows as projected and their (possibly more important) impact on local currency flows through altered product market conditions.

A variety of techniques are available for the analysis of such uncertainties in cash-flow streams. If the uncertainty is not viewed as major, a firm may well be content to approximate such uncertainties by use of expected values. Given the complexity and interplay of the problem, however, the analyst may use a simulation based on subjective or analytically developed probabilities. The mechanics and interpretation of the results of such analyses are well known [7].

The primary thrust of this paper involves the development of the internal plumbing of the analysis that results from the managerial assumptions made regarding project capital structure dividend and reinvestment policies, and other decisions that are under managerial control and that specifically determine parent cash flows in a given external environment. The thrust of this methodology is to develop a set of consistent assumptions that can be applied (as far as practicable) to all project analyses. In contrast to analyzing the project using the set of assumptions that would be managerially reasonable, this approach attempts to come up with a reasonable and conservative set of general assumptions that will allow any and all project analyses to be compared directly. Thus the set of cash flows to the parent that are used for further analysis are not those that will flow to the parent, but rather a set of hypothetical cash flows that would flow to the parent were the project financed and managed according to the basic assumption set. Hereafter, these fundamental analytic assumptions will be referred to as the default assumptions; these assumptions are those to be invoked automatically for any capital project analysis, just as the default parameters for a computer program are used automatically whenever alternative program parameters are not specified. The set of cash flows to the parent that are developed under the default assumptions or norms are referred to as normalized cash flows.

The controlling assumption in determining the timing of these normalized cash flows is that they represent the cash flow to the parent that is fully realized or realizable.[3] The controlling assumption regarding amount is that the value must be free of all taxes, either local or parent. In other words, the parent-normalized cash flow is credited with an amount when it is returned to the parent directly or may be utilized by the parent in any other unit without further reduction in value (except for the costs of transfer into the locus of use).

Given the range of assumptions available to specific investment projects, failure to standardize analysis through the use of a set of default assumptions may lead to incorrect project selection. Projects should be rated on their capability to throw off parent company–controlled cash and should not be penalized by assumptions of reinvestment or suboptimal financing plans.

AN ILLUSTRATION OF THE DEFAULT ASSUMPTION APPROACH: THE CASE OF DIVIDEND ASSUMPTIONS

Let us apply the two principles for determining parent cash flows to the consideration of a company that receives a portion of its cash flow in the form of dividends. Clearly, the amount of the dividend that the parent receives must be adjusted downward for any withholding taxes paid locally and any incremental tax liability incurred by the parent. If the dividend payment generates usable foreign tax credit, the tax saving would increase the net cash flow associated with the dividend. The appropriate cash inflow to the parent is clearly not generally equal to the cash outflow of the subsidiary paying the dividend, which in turn may or may not be equal to the earnings of the subsidiary, which in turn is not normally equal to the cash flow generated by the project.

We further apply these general principles to determining the default assumption for the level of dividends to be considered as declared by the subsidiary from its earnings. Three general subsidiary dividend policies for analysis may be identified as candidates for the default assumption:

1. *Corporate target dividend rate.* As has been indicated in the literature,[4] many companies set a specific dividend target (equal to a percentage of earnings, or some other measure) for application to all subsidiaries. Provided such a dividend policy is viable for each subsidiary where investments are under consideration, this approach has the virtue of applying a uniform standard to all projects.
2. *Anticipated actual dividend flows.* A projection is made as to what the dividend to the parent actually will be, and the parent is credited only with these flows.

3. *Maximum feasible dividend flows.* Under the exchange control laws and investment codes of the host country, limits may be placed on the amount of dividends that can be declared. The parent is credited with the maximum dividend declarable under these regulations each year, whether or not it is anticipated that the dividends will be paid.

For purposes of analysis, the use of maximum feasible dividend flows is indicated as a default assumption, invoking the principle of crediting the parent with fully realizable cash inflows. Whether or not the dividend is actually paid, the dollar cash flow that would be generated by dividend payment is disposable to the parent for global deployment. This maximum feasible dividend should be adjusted only for certain specific reasons:

1. In periods when the project under investigation requires additional cash inflows from the parent and payment of the dividend would create a tax liability, the dividend should be adjusted. The same result could be achieved by assuming the dividend is paid, charging the parent the total amount of the new outflow, and crediting the parent with the tax liability savings as an inflow. Where the local currency outflows are less than the anticipated dividend, the parent receives the net local currency residual as a dividend, which is fully adjusted for a tax liability. Where the local currency outflows are greater than the anticipated dividend, the outflows are assumed first to be funded through blocked funds, then through local financing within parameters specified by the financing plan, and, finally, through parent-fund injections in dollars, which are cash outflows to the parents.
2. In the periods when payment of the maximum feasible dividend would require violation of the norms of the financing plan, the dividend is adjusted. If, for example, local currency cash flow is not sufficient both to meet contractual debt obligations and to pay dividends, the amount of the dividend credited under the analysis is reduced to the level feasible for the given cash flow. Local currency debt can be incurred to meet dividends subject to limitations on its usage.

The approach developed above also has ramifications for determining the cash outflow required for initiating new investments in countries where there is a stream of repatriatable funds generated from existing operations. The approach recommended involves the reduction of the initial dollar outflow of the investment by the amount of tax savings that nondeclaration of dividends generates. Such an approach represents one solution to the difficult problem of incorporating deferral of U.S. taxes in the analysis of foreign investment projects.

Basically, the benefit of the deferral is allocated to the investment project that makes use of deferred funds. If a given project requires infusion of funds in subsequent periods, any tax savings on the use of local funds generated by the project are credited to the project. On the other hand, if the tax savings from deferral cannot be used in the project under analysis but in subsequent projects, the benefit is placed with the subsequent project. The existence of other profitable investment opportunities in the country of an investment is not relevant for analysis of the parent company cash flows from a specific investment. If one project is dependent on another (Project B can be undertaken only if Project A is chosen), the analyst should look at an analysis of Project A alone (under a maximum feasible repatriation scheme) and an analysis of Projects A and B together as one project, with deferral benefits of using *Project A's* cash flow to fund Project B incorporated into the analysis of the joint project.

In joint ventures, where relationship with a partner constrains dividend declaration, or other projects where the capability to declare dividends is restricted by loan covenant, the actual allowable or planned dividend schedule determines the maximum feasible dividend for analytic purposes, just as exchange restrictions or investment codes may determine dividend level.

Return of capital is also a possible method for remitting funds to the parent. If dividends are at all linked to earnings, the amount of cash flow is likely to exceed unit earnings for a particular period, because of depreciation flows. Liquidation of a portion of the capital of an overseas subsidiary is complicated in its taxation effects, but the same general principles should apply. Where return of capital is feasible, it should be assumed that it takes place at the maximum permissible rate and should be fully tax-effected, including any taxation on previously reinvested earnings. Final return of capital is discussed in the section on terminal value.

An added complication is that incremental cash inflows occur in related third-country subsidiaries, resulting from purchase of inputs from the new venture for further processing and sale or supplying of output to the new venture. Such operations may also require incremental investment from the parent to the third-country subsidiary or alteration in local funding patterns, which leads to alteration in subsequent dividend patterns. These cash flows should not be directly converted to dollars, but rather analyzed for their impact on the availability of funds for dividend remission; thus for each subsidiary where such flows take place, it would be necessary to determine the net change in realizable parent company cash flow. If cash flow should be captured in a country that did not restrict remission of profits, the incremental cash flow would be treated as a fully repatriatable dividend, and the after-tax dollar amount would be credited to the project as a cash inflow. Although it is highly unlikely that an investment would be structured to capture cash flow where funds were already blocked, in such a case, flows would be valueless immediately to the parent (although some increment in the terminal value would be made through increments to the terminal value of the subsidiary capturing the flow). The approach of Pomper [3] discussed at the beginning of this article might be appropriate, although the analyst ought not to attribute to the project any subjective benefits based on reinvestment opportunities.

Thus, to reiterate, the parent is credited with a cash flow at the time it is realized in the parent or is realizable to the parent. The amount to be credited to parent cash flow is the amount realized or realizable by the parent after payment of all taxes and other transfer costs needed to bring funds to the parent, but not those costs for employment elsewhere.

THE CRITICAL DEFAULT ASSUMPTIONS: FINANCIAL STRUCTURE

It is well recognized that cash flow to the parent for a foreign investment project is a function of how the project is financed. Specific project financing, possibly at subsidized rates, may both reduce required parent company commitment of funds and free up additional cash for investment. Local funding may be used for working capital financing or, where capital markets are more developed, for some permanent funding. Funding from international bank credits may be tailored to the project cash flow for repayment of principal and interest payment. Funds provided by joint venture partners also reduce the level of parent company investment.

The funding of a foreign direct investment project cannot readily be divorced from the capital budgeting analysis. There are two sets of assumptions that need to be made. First, how is the project as a whole to be financed? Second, in what form is the contribution by the parent to be made (loan or equity)?

With regard to the first of these issues, there are two reasonable candidates for the default assumption. One approach would be to use the actual capital structure of the project analysis. Thus, if the actual financing plan called for a contribution by the parent of 30 percent of required project funding, this contribution would represent parent cash outflow (adjusted for taxes that might arise from contributions in kind, etc.). The second approach would be to adopt a standardized capital structure for all projects; thus, even if the parent provides only 30 percent of project funds, under this approach the parent might be charged with 40 percent as an outflow, if the standardized capital structure called for such a contribution.

Because of an inherently inseparable connection between the project and its financing, and in the belief that a project should be credited for positive benefits if its financing allows for expedited or enlarged cash flows to the parent and penalized if the financial structure delays or reduces such flows, I suggest utilization of a modified version of the first assumption and analysis of the investment project using the specific capital structure that is developed for it. The two major modifications to be made to this approach involve using a special default assumption for the parent contribution to the project and adjusting the capital structure artificially to reflect the repayment of external debt according to a set of subassumptions that utilize funds generated by the project according to a predetermined hierarchy of repayment rules.

The principles underlying the repayment rules are twofold: First, all contractual payments for debt or lease financing are assumed paid according to schedule, and, second, no other funding is repaid unless payment is made with funds that are otherwise blocked. In no instance is cash flow to the parent reduced to make advanced debt repayments.

Suppose, for example, we are analyzing an investment project requiring $100 million in financing, with the actual financial structure developed in Table 1. In determining the cash flow to the project after financing charges (a determination necessary before the availability of cash flow for servicing parent debt and paying parent dividends is known), it is assumed that both the supplier credits and the Eurocredit are paid down according to the precise schedule developed in the credit agreements. Were there any local currency financing with contractually determined repayment schedules, such as a local bond issue by the subsidiary, net project cash flows would further be reduced as indicated. Even if the Eurocredit could be rolled over if necessary, such an additional financial capability would not be reflected in the analysis.

Table 1. Financial Structure for Sample Project

1. Local currency line of credit from loan institutions	$ 10,000,000
2. Credit from suppliers (two years' grace; principal and interest amortized over five annual installments thereafter)	20,000,000
3. Eurocredit (interest payable at spread over LIBOR semiannually; three years' grace on principal; thereafter seven equal repayments of principal)	35,000,000
4. Parent contribution	
a. Dollar loan to subsidiary	20,000,000
b. Parent equity investment	15,000,000
Total financing	$100,000,000

The end result of this sort of financing policy assumption is that the capital structure of the project, for analytic purposes, changes over time, with a concentration in the funding sources of parent company contribution and local currency borrowings. Local currency borrowings may be expanded in two situations. First, service of other contractual debt obligations may exceed cash flows in a particular period. In that case, rather than injecting additional funds from the parent, it would be considered proper to increment local currency funds usage, up to limits prescribed by local lending norms. Second, if there exists a capability of making a payment to the parent, but insufficient funds are available at the subsidiary, it is appropriate to substitute locally borrowed funds in the capital structure, once again up to the limits prescribed by local norms. Local borrowings may be reduced as one use of blocked funds.

We turn now to the development of the structure (loan versus equity) of the parent's contribution to the project. The question here is whether to use a standardized loan-equity ratio or to vary this ratio from project to project. In most cases, it appears that it is advantageous to finance initially with parent loans to subsidiaries as much as possible, as, in effect, the repayment of the loan is viewed as a more feasible form of capital repatriation than is a reduction of initial equity contribution. Further, in some cases, interest payments and dividends are subject to different withholding rates at the source. In any case, it can be determined by a subanalysis whether debt or equity funding by the parent is favored. In cases where the debt injection appears superior, I would recommend analyzing the project as if it were funded using a corporatewide maximum debt-equity ratio (some have suggested that companies may be comfortable with ratios as high as four to one). [4, p. 57] Where equity injections seem indicated, the project should be analyzed using a minimum debt-equity ratio. Thus the process is a two-stage one: First, we determine whether the project environment favors use of debt or equity, and, second, we set our default capital structure at either the corporate maximum or minimum debt-equity ratio.

Since one purpose of debt injection is to provide the ability to withdraw funds rapidly through repayment, we would consider parent debt to be repaid, for analytic purposes, as rapidly as legally allowable, even to the extent of increasing use of local currency debt for its repayment. In any project of consequence, other lenders will probably restrict repayment of parent debt to a preset schedule. If such is the case, the project analysis would incorporate this schedule.

To illustrate our default assumptions, suppose the parent of the project whose financial structure is shown in Table 1 is free to vary its debt-equity ratio up to a maximum of four to one. If it is determined that debt represents the most attractive channel for repatriating funds, the project would be analyzed as if the parent had contributed $28 million in debt and $7 million in equity.

One aspect of project analysis that has received significant prior attention [6, pp. 12-13, 2, pp. 289-295] is the problem of analyzing the impact of dividend and other funds flow restrictions on the parent cash flow. Limitations on dividend levels, blocking of dividends declared, and restrictions on technology payments may all be used by local exchange authorities to reduce outflows needed to service foreign direct investment. Such limitations invariably result in the accumulation of a pool of local currency funds, which are at least temporarily of no value to the parent and, therefore, because they are not realized or realizable to the parent, cannot be credited immediately.

The existence of this pool of funds does, however, influence the value of future flows to the parent, since the funds may be deployed locally, earn a return, and raise the future earnings and/or investment base that can be used to increase future dividend flows. If dividends limitations are related to registered investment and earnings retained in the subsidiary are allowed to increment registered investment, higher dividends may be paid in later periods. If dividend restrictions are related to earnings level, the earnings from reinvestment of blocked funds would raise the future earnings base and thus future dividends. Finally, accumulation of funds may raise the terminal dollar value of the investment.

Thus a default assumption is needed with regard to the utilization of blocked funds. I recommend that blocked funds first be deemed as used to reduce any existing local currency debt and then be considered as invested at the local risk-free rate. Crediting the investment project with a higher return, based on the availability of unspecified local reinvestment opportunities, violates the essential principle of crediting an investment project only with the impact on parent flow attributable directly to the project. In special cases, such as Brazil, where special accounts are available (under Resolution 432) for deposit of funds generated against future repayment of hard currency debt, such opportunities should be built into the analysis as a channel for blocked funds.

Use of the local risk-free rate for analysis of the return on blocked funds offers an interesting situation when applied to the analysis of a capital investment project to be funded completely with blocked funds. The initial parent company outflow is zero because the project requires no incremental parent funding. The benefit of such a project is represented by the increase in local currency cash flow (and earnings) generated by the project over and above the cash flow generated if used for investment at the risk-free rate or repayment of local debt. Such increments would, if the dividend remittance allowables are tied to earnings or registered capital, provide some future parent return. Thus, the project is most likely to have a positive parent net present value.

To summarize the critical financing assumptions in their default mode:

1. *Capital structure.* Utilize the specific capital structure of the project, with repayment of all nonparent external debt and local term debt assumed to occur as scheduled.

2. *Local flexible financing.* Consider this financing as a source of future funds, up to specified limits, to meet shortfalls in funds flow needed to service contractual debt obligations and to pay dividends.

3. *Parent contribution.* Determine the environmental desirability of debt versus equity and assume that the parent contribution maximizes use of debt or equity according to the result.

4. *Parent loan repayment.* Assume that parent loan is repaid as rapidly as project funds throwoff allows and possible restrictive covenants permit.

5. *Dividends.* Assume that dividends are paid at the earliest possible moment that funds throwoff and exchange control restrictions permit.

6. *Reinvestment of blocked funds.* Assume that blocked funds are first used to reduce local currency funds requirements and are then invested at the local risk-free rate.

THE CRITICAL DEFAULT ASSUMPTIONS: TERMINAL VALUE AND EXPROPRIATION

Determination of the horizon date for a foreign investment project is to some extent a matter of managerial preference. Clearly, the horizon date must be sufficiently far into the future to cover the time horizon of any particular funding programs tied to the project, but also sufficiently close to the present to allow the projection of a realistic economic and political scenario. After elimination of project-tied financing, the capital structure becomes relatively simplified and amenable to analysis. With project financing through Euromarkets generally no more than fifteen years in maturity, I would recommend that the basic corporate time horizon be somewhere between ten and twenty years. Even if cash flows are considerable beyond the project horizon date, these cash flows may be incorporated in the assessment of a terminal value.

It is the terminal value default assumption that is critical. One possible approach would assume that the project is liquidated at market prices and that all funds remaining after creditor satisfaction are repatriated as feasible to the parent. Such an approach would require an assessment of the local market value of the project, the cash flow available locally after payment of any taxes upon liquidation, the amount of such local funds blocked and their final disposition, and the parent country tax implications of the return of these funds to the parent, among other factors. What would then enter parent cash flows would be the net repatriated proceeds in dollars of a complete liquidation of the project.

However, the liquidation value of a foreign direct investment project may not fully represent the value of that investment as a going concern. As an alternative, I would suggest using a certainty equivalent approach to the assessment of terminal value. Given the capital structure and cash flows generated by the project, the question would be asked of the analyst, "What is the maximum amount the company would pay at the horizon date, in after-tax parent dollars, for an investment project with the operating characteristics and financial structure of this project?" Such an approach allows the analyst to discount implicitly the future parent flows that the project will generate, as well as adjusting this value for the sometimes considerable intangible benefit of a presence in, and the operating experience of, the host country and the global market and strategic advantages of having the particular investment. Such intangibles do have a significant value to the parent. Evaluation of such nonmonetary consequences in terms of dollar equivalents is a well-known decision-analytic technique.[5] Although the number generated may be somewhat imprecise logically as opposed to liquidation value, it is certainly superior conceptually.

Expropriation also requires the assessment of a terminal value for the project. Techniques for incorporation of expropriation probabilities in project analysis have been developed [6, pp. 9–12]. The thrust in the terminal value assumption issue is the determination of the cash flow to the parent in the event of an expropriation. The analyst should attempt to measure the financial terms of the expropriation, to apply it to the default capital structure, and to develop a residual value in cash to the parent (present and future flows), incorporating any tax savings or additional taxes resulting from the expropriation. In a similar way, the value of the flows should be adjusted for nonmonetary consequences in a particularly tricky way. The alternative to accepting the investment is not taking the investment. Thus loss of the investment through expropriation reduces the company to the same position as if it never took the investment. The only nonmonetary consequences are those that arrive from having the investment and then losing it.

THE DISCOUNT RATE ASSUMPTION

Approaches to the determination of the appropriate discount rate to use for project cash flows may involve using either a risk-adjusted discount rate based on the capital asset pricing model or on the more traditionally developed marginal weighted-average cost of capital. The use of a risk-adjusted measure is conceptually difficult when applied to parent company flows only, since investors may focus on returns developed from consolidated financial information rather than from parent company structure only. However, the cash outflows associated with parent flows are generated with funds raised according to the capital structure of the parent only. Any risk adjustment made to these flows should be based on the covariance of the parent flows with returns available to investors in the parent company markets, *de minimis*, or, if one assumes some international mobility of capital, with returns on a market portfolio of domestic and international stocks available to investors in the parent's country. The covariance of project returns with such a market return is *a priori* not normally equal to the covariance of parent returns with market.

A relatively simpler discount rate to utilize is the after-tax marginal weighted-average cost of capital to the parent, using as weights the proportion of various financing alternatives in the parent capital structure only (with transparent separation of funds sources, such as the use of a finance subsidiary, ignored). Funds supplied by third-country subsidiaries should not be costed at the local exchange risk-adjusted cost. Rather, the parent company realizable equivalent (i.e., the amount of dollars that the parent company would receive from these funds if remitted) should be taken as the amount invested by the parent, and the parent company realizable value of interest payments and principal repayments should be taken as the parent company inflow. Inclusion of parent-guaranteed debt in the weighting process is a more difficult problem. If, for example, the parent routinely raises debt in international capital markets for global dispersion, such funds are a portion of the company's permanent financing and should be included in the averaging process. On the other hand, guarantees for specific debt associated with the project should not cause that debt to be incorporated into the pool of total parent investable funds. Rather, the debt should be considered part of the project financial structure as analyzed earlier. If, in any project scenario, the parent is called on to repay the debt with parent company funds, such parent payments are incorporated as parent outflows.

Although Bavishi [1] reports that only 40 percent of his responding firms use net parent value for analysis, such an approach is recommended for capital budgeting if firms are not capital-rationed, and it is necessary for the calculation of a profitability index if the firm's access to funds is restricted. For this reason, we suggest its use for project decision making.

CONCLUSIONS

The suggestions developed above for the analysis of parent company cash flows represent an attempt to develop a methodology that will put different, possibly competing, projects on the same analytic footing. Parent return is a function of both external environmental factors and of managerial decisions. Failure to standardize assumptions regarding managerial parameters will lead to inconsistent project analysis. In particular, assumptions regarding managerial parameters may lead to failure to credit the investment project with realizable parent funds. For example, if a 60 percent dividend payout rate for the project is adopted, projects in which a higher payout is feasible are penalized for the most part, for local currency reinvestment at the risk-free rate will normally lead to a lower return in dollars than the parent company discount rate. Such a resultant reduction in net present value may cause rejection of an acceptable project or the preference of a competing project in another country.

While the suggestions above do attempt to fill a void in the analysis of foreign investment projects, they are offered primarily as a focus for future debate and alteration. Further advances in the theory of multinational capital structure, which may incorporate empirical results in international diversification with segmented and quasi-segmented capital markets, may suggest alternative default assumptions or may even prove some of them irrelevant and unnecessary.

However, at present, financial analysts will be required to prepare specific project analyses, despite the present theoretical incompleteness. Certainly, the suggestions developed above offer a reasonable starting point for the development of standardized corporate procedures.

NOTES

1. See the next section for further comments regarding Pomper's method.

2. Shapiro [6, p. 16] ; italics are his.

3. This assumption is explicitly made by Shapiro [6] as well.

4. See Robbins and Stobaugh [4, pp. 75–96] for a discussion of remittance practices.

5. The approach as mentioned is used by Pomper [3] for adjusting flow values. Schlaifer [5, pp. 52–53] reviews the principle.

REFERENCES

[1]   Bavishi, Vinod B. "Capital Budgeting Study among US MNCs Indicates Current Practices/Trends," *Business International Money Report* (June 8, 1979), pp. 194–195.

[2]   Eiteman, David K., and Stonehill, Arthur I. *Multinational Business Finance,* 2nd ed. Reading, Mass.: Addison-Wesley Publishing Company, 1979.

[3]   Pomper, Claude B. *International Investment Planning: An Integrated Approach.* Amsterdam: North-Holland Publishing Company, 1976.

[4]   Robbins, Sidney M., and Stobaugh, Robert B. *Money in the Multinational Enterprise.* New York: Basic Books, 1973.

[5]   Schlaifer, Robert. *Analysis of Decisions under Uncertainty.* New York: McGraw-Hill Book Company, 1969.

[6]   Shapiro, Alan B. "Capital Budgeting for the Multinational Corporation," *Financial Management* 7 (Spring 1978), pp. 7–16.

[7]   Stobaugh, Robert B. "How to Analyze Foreign Investment Climates," *Harvard Business Review* (September-October 1969), pp. 100–108.

III CAPITAL ALLOCATION MODELING

8 MULTICRITERIA APPROACHES TO DECISION MODELING

Roy L. Crum
University of Florida

Frans G. J. Derkinderen
The Netherlands School of Business

As described in most finance and economics textbooks, the process of asset selection by business organizations and models intended for identifying appropriate allocations of scarce resources are based upon a number of usually implicit assumptions. These involve such things as the availability and quality of information, the capabilities of decision makers to process this information properly, the motivations under which management operates, and the dynamic or intertemporal characteristics of corporate operations. Conforming to the maxim of the positivist philosophy, criticisms of and objections to these models of asset selection, when based on deviations of their underlying assumptions from observable conduct by operating managers, are traditionally considered to be largely irrelevant; the positivists believe that the ability to derive economically "correct" resource allocations is the sole criterion upon which the validity and usefulness of a model can and should be judged. Nevertheless, in the past few years the frequency and intensity of such objections have increased. Greater attention is now being directed by researchers to the question of what constitutes a "correct" allocation of scarce corporate resources in the business environment of the 1980s [18, 11].

From the perspective of the behavioral scientists, before this question can be answered it is necessary first to focus attention on the significant attributes of the business entity: The pressures and power structures, the various value systems and internal motivations, and the dynamics of the decision process are of critical importance for defining the feasibility of any proposed methodology or the "correctness" of any resource allocation scheme. Only with this information, the behavioralist believes, can the usefulness of a model or other approach to the problem of asset selection be adequately judged, since the context in which it will be employed delimits its potential contribution.

We believe that the variety inherent in managing a modern corporation in today's business environment, variety that tends to be either ignored or at least downplayed in most finance books, lends credence to the necessity to include at least some elements of the behavioralists' point of view. Thus in this paper we propose to investigate the asset selection process from the perspective of the decision maker who is subject to the day-to-day realities and pressures of the business world.

In the next section of the paper, the assumptions underlying the exploration are developed. These assumptions act together to define the context of the decision-making process. An appreciation of the forces acting upon a manager and the state of partial ignorance under which he is called upon to operate gives a different perspective of the resource allocation problem from the one usually encountered in a finance textbook. For the present purpose, the most relevant implications of the assumptions are that the decision maker must react to competing and often conflicting forces that threaten to pull apart the organization and that, consequently, multiple decision criteria are indicated. In fact, it is shown in the third section that the normal single-criterion models appearing in the finance literature cannot adequately capture the relevant dimensions of the problems facing management. Thus it is not surprising that they have not been well received by the intended beneficiaries: the decision makers themselves.

The fourth section of the paper focuses attention on identifying the types of criteria that may be important for allocating resources under uncertainty when the multidimensional nature of the process is embodied in the analysis. Because of the conflicts and tradeoffs inherent in a multicriteria approach, some suggestions are offered in the fifth section about how the analysis should be structured and what criteria should be selected both to extract the most information from available data and to assure adherence to at least the spirit of generally accepted financial theories.

Using this discussion of analytical procedures as a basis, the sixth section is devoted to a survey of modeling philosophies and methodologies that have been suggested in the literature for handling the multiple-criteria problem. Strengths and weaknesses of each approach are presented from both the theoretical and the operational perspective. It is seen that one approach dominates the others, but that several offer significant advantages that may be important for particular applications.

The paper indicates in the seventh section the orientation that we believe is desirable to assume in modeling the resource allocation process. Concluding comments are then given concerning appropriate directions for future research in this area. It is apparent that the problems that will be encountered are great and that the tradeoffs that must be made are difficult, but it is equally clear that the potential rewards of success are very high.

ASSUMPTIONS REQUIRED TO ENHANCE REALISM

To capture the essence of the decision context, several assumptions are required about the characteristics and capabilities of individual participants, the manner in which the various individuals interact within the confines of the firm, and the linkages between the company and the external environment. While not an exhaustive list of reasonable postulates, the assumptions discussed below are sufficient to describe the main lines of both the environment and the internal organization of the corporation and thus to serve the purpose at hand.

Usually the structural form taken by decision models in finance assumes the maximization of a single fixed objective (shareholder wealth, NPV, EPS, etc.) given a set of known alternatives, the outcomes of which are described by knowable density functions. Also, managers are presumed to have the ability to interpret available information correctly and to perform any computations necessary to permit attainment of the optimum or highest level with respect to the objective. This process can be called rational optimization and serves as the basis for most of the current finance theories of market operations.[1]

Unfortunately, decision makers are incapable of achieving this idealized state of objective rationality: The human mind cannot formulate and solve the complex problems required for its accomplishment considering the multitude of possibilities. Also, knowledge of the available alternatives, as well as other information, is incomplete, so that the boundaries of the "true" feasible set are unknown. Under these circumstances, in which only a subset of the feasible region is recognized, decision makers operate on the principle of limited or bounded rationality [28]. This leads to the situation of bounded or constrained optimization, the solutions of which are wrongly interpreted to be the "best" possible—they are "best" only in the sense that given the cognitive and informational limitations, no better alternatives can be identified. It is important to note that the "best" obtainable alternative under conditions of bounded rationality is inferior to the solution *assumed* possible by the objective rationality of current finance models.

The above discussion has identified the first three important assumptions about decision making in the firm:

1. Decision makers can only operate under the principle of bounded rationality.
2. Decisions must be made on the basis of incomplete information.
3. Decision makers are not always successful in interpreting correctly and reacting appropriately to available information.

Another characteristic of decision making in a firm is that although a decision may be made at a point in time, the process leading up to that decision is an inherently intertemporal phenomenon with distinct behavioral implications. It is probable that the person who makes the ultimate decision is neither the one who collected the supporting information nor the one who provided the input data. In fact, it is likely that these data were generated by people in various departments, representing different levels within the company and having differing motivations, including selfish interests in the outcome of the selection process. With this type of situation, the danger that personal prejudices will be introduced and information will be filtered before being passed along is manifest. This point is particularly critical when it is realized that it is extraordinarily difficult for higher-level managers to prevent this "gaming" as information flows through the firm.

Since there are often time constraints associated with the need to finalize "the budget," the search for other alternatives with which to compare a project tends to be truncated. Put another way, when a manager finds an alternative that appears to be acceptable for a particular purpose, there is a tendency to end the search process for other (perhaps superior) candidates.[2] Thus two additional assumptions of corporate behavior have been identified:

4. Multiple levels within the hierarchy of the firm are involved in the decision process so that internal politics and power struggles, as well as multiple-value frameworks, tend to bias or contaminate the information flows.
5. The decision process is best described as a sequential search so that when a solution is found that appears to be acceptable to the decision maker, there is a tendency to end the search process.

Two particularly important issues of relevance for the present discussion are related to what can be called the stakeholder concept [1, 14]. The traditional point of view of finance is that the goal of the firm is the maximization of shareholder wealth [5]. The desires and interests of other groups with a stake in the continued prosperity of the corporation—employees, management, suppliers, customers, local communities, etc.—are treated as constraints affecting the primary objective. Such things as the increasing militancy of trade unions, consumer protection legislation, and other similar forces are generating expanding interest in treating the concerns of other stakeholders more as objectives in and of themselves rather than as constraints. Even if this trend is not supportable by traditional economic theory, the fact remains that companies are showing more interest in it. This is evidenced by the fact that, for instance, General Telephone and Electronics has now set up stakeholder committees charged with monitoring the continuing welfare of the various groups and ensuring that their interests are considered explicitly in the decision process.[3]

Another related development is the realization that management and the owners of the firm are often different groups with what may be noncoincident motives and value systems. Agency theory, for instance, looks at this issue from the perspective of contractual relationships between the parties [26, 5]. This view of a corporation as the nexus of a complex series of contractual arrangements appears to be an attempt to come to grips with the power tradeoff implications of the stakeholder concept. Thus we can identify two additional assumptions that are important for describing the operations of businesses:

6. Stakeholders exert often conflicting pressures on management that cannot be ignored if effective action and, at least in the long run, internal harmony within the firm are to be achieved.
7. There is a separation of ownership and management of the corporation.

When the dynamic characteristics of the decision process are considered, particularly given the seven assumptions discussed above, several other fundamental realities come into play. In a world of uncertainty with incomplete information available, strategic management dictates that good current decisions be defined not only in terms of effective utilization of available information (the classical conception), but also in terms of their built-in flexibility to enable the firm to react appropriately when new information is obtained in the future [2] — that is, the future consequences of current decisions must be considered explicitly as part of the initial decision process. This is complicated by the fact that recent research has shown that decision makers are not uniformly risk averse (as is almost universally assumed) [7]. In fact, risk attitudes appear to be very situation-dependent and can change over time. The primary driving factors leading to shifting risk attitudes have been identified as targets or aspiration levels and the risk of ruin [7]. As decisions are aggregated over time, various outcomes combine to present a different profile with respect to achievement of the desired target and the implications for ruinous loss. Thus two more reality-enriching assumptions are:

8. The decision process is dynamic so that future consequences of current actions, including their implications for corporate flexibility, have to be taken into consideration.
9. Decision makers are not uniformly risk averse, and their preferences change from context to context, as well as over time.

Focusing directly on the characteristics of the decision alternatives themselves, the normal view is that they are independent (or mutually exclusive), exhibit transitivity, and have a criterion value expressible in terms of monetary return [5]. For some alternatives, these assumptions may be questionable from a practical perspective. How does one measure the monetary return from building a new parking lot or from investing capital in pure research? Obviously these alternatives have some benefit to the firm (or perhaps to a particular stakeholder group associated with the company), but expressing the benefits in terms of a measure of monetary return would be arbitrary, artificial, and at best a strain on the credibility of the analysis. Without this measure, though, it is impractical to evaluate alternatives in the traditional single-criterion framework. A multidimensional analysis with more than a single criterion is one feasible way in which these alternatives can be evaluated more rationally. A problem then arises, since transitivity is basically a unidimensional concept and thus cannot be guaranteed to hold if there are multiple criteria. This point, incidently, appears to have been overlooked in most of the literature on multiobjective decision making [21].

The assumption that alternatives can be stated in such a way that they are either independent or mutually exclusive presents few problems if complete information is available—then it is always feasible to define independent or mutually exclusive alternatives by proper definition of "the project." In the absence of complete information, one may not always be able to achieve this state of affairs. Realizing this, the possible consequences of dependencies should be considered explicitly in the decision-making process. Thus the last assumptions made to achieve more realism in the resource allocation or asset selection process are:

10. Some decisions cannot credibly be assigned a monetary return.
11. Transitivity of alternatives does not necessarily hold in all situations.
12. It may not always be possible to define alternatives so that they are either independent or mutually exclusive.

With these twelve primary assumptions, the variety of the environment and the organization have been enhanced in such a way that it is now realistically possible to derive further insight into the decision process.

IMPLICATIONS OF THE ASSUMPTIONS FOR DECISION MODELS

The most striking implication of the set of assumptions given above that is ignored or assumed away by most finance theories is that the firm is not a monolithic entity, always presenting a single face to the world. It does not possess all needed information, nor does it have the ability to process what information it can obtain in a timely manner so as to extract all relevant intelligence. Rather, it is composed of a set of individuals, many of whom have conflicting motives and different value systems, who must make decisions on the basis of partial ignorance. Since the person or persons responsible for making a decision are not necessarily the owner [5], the criteria or criterion used to make the decision likely differs from those proposed by economic theory. In fact, with various power groups contending for a larger share of the benefits, it is evident that multiple criteria are used in the corporate decision process.

Nonmonetary benefits, such as prestige, power, and perquisites, tend to become relatively more important to decision makers as they rise to more senior positions within the firm and become concerned with the fulfillment of Maslow's higher-level needs [24]. In this light, managers are probably far more concerned with an adequate resolution of conflicts between the multiple decision criteria and with sufficient harmonization with respect to the various power groups (including stockholders) than they are with the pursuit of single-minded maximization of shareholder wealth. In fact, when there are multiple criteria, it is not even possible to optimize in the traditional sense. Optimization implies the ability to rank order the alternatives according to the sole criterion and to identify the one(s) with the highest ranking. With multiple criteria, ranking according to the criteria may not (and usually will not) result in an unambiguous identification of a clearly superior alternative. The best that can be hoped for in this case is the identification of nondominated alternatives in the Pareto-optimality sense. Thus, for situations in which multiple decision criteria are used to evaluate alternatives, it is not possible for managers to conform to conventional economic theory and to maximize the wealth of the shareholders.

Carrying this argument to its logical conclusion, it is often stated that decision makers are better represented as satisficers than as optimizers [28]. By this, it is meant that aspiration levels, representing "satisfactory" performance for each criterion, are established *a priori*, and alternatives are investigated until a solution is obtained by which all targets are met or exceeded. At that point, the search process terminates. Unfortunately, significant conceptual difficulties are encountered when attempting to reconcile this satisficing approach to decision making with the precepts of traditional economic theory.

Although it apparently follows from the assumptions about the firm discussed above, we do not believe that satisficing defined in this, the traditional, way, represents the process by which decision makers should select assets and allocate resources. Nor do we believe that this type of behavior is required by the assumptions. No sensible person would satisfice when adequate data and the ability to process them properly are available: Under those conditions, the person could optimize. With incomplete information and operating under bounded rationality, it should still be possible to achieve a constrained optimum or to identify nondominated alternatives. But this brings to the fore the problems of identifying appropriate decision criteria to use in the selection process and of setting appropriate targets for each.

Managers normally perceive a range of factors by which their personal success will be judged. Signals about these factors may come from incentive compensation system measures, from bond indenture requirements, or from other similar sources. The manager will then tend to define "good" performance in terms of the variables and to set targets for each.[4] To the extent that the goals of the firm are made congruent with the personal objectives of the decision makers, these various targets can serve as adequate proxies or indications of good corporate performance. With incomplete information and assuming that managers themselves possess knowledge that is unavailable to the shareholders of the firm or to the capital market in general, it would be extremely difficult at best for anyone to question the efficacy of the resource allocations actually made: No one else knows what is achievable (optimum) either. The danger that exists is that the targets or aspiration levels will be set too low and that even if the allocation meets or even exceeds all targets, incorrect signals about the company's future prospects may be transmitted to the market place.[5] Thus setting appropriate targets to convey the correct signals is of primary importance.

IDENTIFYING CRITERIA AND SETTING APPROPRIATE ASPIRATION LEVELS

It is dangerous to try to generalize too far in defining appropriate criteria for use in the decision-making process. However, five distinct classes can be identified into which most criteria suggested in the literature can be grouped. By selecting factors from each class and by structuring the analysis according to the specific requirements of the situation, the most important dimensions of the dynamic resource allocation process can be captured. If careful attention is paid to a balance of criteria from each of the five classes, the information content of the analytical procedure and the signals generated by it should be concentrated and channeled in the right direction.

The first class of criteria encompasses prescreening or filter variables that serve to eliminate alternatives without the need for further analysis. Recent empirical studies have shown that managers tend to utilize filter rules to eliminate projects that have serious implications of bankruptcy for the firm, regardless of the countervailing potential they may have for high returns [20]. Other preemptive factors might include management decisions to refrain from investments in specific countries, from utilization of certain scarce or controversial resources, or any other similar strategic proscription. It may be arguable that the use of such filter rules is not always in the best interest of the firm. The preemptive negative weights implied by this rule should perhaps be replaced with less restrictive penalties; in this way, the nature of the tradeoffs required for acceptance or rejection of the project can better be ascertained. Nevertheless, to the extent that decision makers are risk averse and desire preliminary screening rules, the first class of criteria can accommodate them.

Measures of aggregate performance over time, such as net present value, internal rate of return, and profitability index, are included in the second class of criteria. Most of the measures suggested in the finance literature as appropriate decision criteria probably fall within this class. It is important to note that by aggregation these measures eliminate intertemporal information and assume that the purpose of the decision model is to establish an allocation plan for the entire planning horizon. That is, the focus of the model is not on making an initial decision that may be updated in the future, but rather on the specification of all decisions to be taken during the period without updating at a later point in time. In the absence of complete information about the future, this implicit assumption may be of questionable merit.

Other measures suggested as appropriate decision criteria fall in the third class, criteria that ensure corporate stability and harmony. Included in this class are such things as maintenance of earnings per share, achieving adequate return on book equity each period, balancing various growth rates, preserving liquidity and financial ratio relationships. Criteria from within this class are important for steering indenture provisions and perhaps incentive compensation. However, it is probably more usual in the finance literature to consider these criteria as constraints on the allocation rather than as separate goals or objectives. Whichever way they are viewed, it seems clear that managers consider them to be quite important, and thus they should be evaluated explicitly by decision models.

With few (if any) exceptions, the first three classes encompass all decision criteria that are normally found in the literature of finance. It is our belief, however, that the list is inadequate for making effective decisions in a world characterized by as much uncertainty as appeared in the late 1970s and is fore-

casted for the 1980s. In this respect, the evolving concepts of strategic management can lend insight to the modeling process through what can be called
strategic positioning of the firm.[6] What is called for is a shifting of major emphasis of the resource allocation process from long-range planning to making the
best possible current decisions, considering the available information, that
should also lead to adequate flexibility as events unfold and the firm is called
upon to react appropriately. Strategic positioning recognizes explicitly that it is
not realistic to assume that ample knowledge about future threats and opportunities is available when initial decisions must be made. Taking this into account
from the first, the emphasis is concentrated on stimulating upside potential as
the future unfolds and at the same time mitigating downside adversities [11].

A rather subtle point needs further elaboration at this point. The purpose of
analytical models for decision making under uncertainty is usually stated in
terms of increasing the efficiency of the process by structuring consistently the
perceptions of the decision maker. That is, probabilistic information (predomi-
nately derived subjectively) about the expected path of development over time
of the projects can be structured by a properly designed model so that all intelligence from these data is extracted and applied consistently to the problem of
resource allocation. The resulting model solution is then efficient in the sense
that it is the logical outcome of the input information and will result in the
maximum benefit to the firm *if the underlying probabilistic information is correct.* The fact that there is an *ex ante* probability of 1.0 that the information is
incorrect[7] (and thus an alternative allocation would perhaps be superior) is considered to be irrelevant—what is called for is a model that makes decisions
consistent with *a priori* expectations alone. Strategic management takes the position that this is *not* the most efficient (and probably not the most effective) use
of resources, since it ignores a vital piece of reliable information that has potentially serious ramifications for the corporation: Almost invariably the input
information *will be wrong ex post* and other variables identified as important
after the fact probably have not even been taken into consideration. Strategic
positioning is an explicit attempt to include the ramifications of this further
information in the current decision process.

The fourth class of criteria, then, is concerned with strategically positioning
the firm so as to maximize the number of feasible options that lead to favorable
outcomes available to the company in the future as a result of current decisions.
By focusing attention on the impact of current decisions from the perspective of
both profitable exploitation of present options and future room to maneuver,
the firm can position itself most advantageously.

The other part of strategic positioning that is also required to achieve these
favorable conditions, however, is segregated into the fifth class of criteria: factors
that tend to minimize the number of feasible paths that lead to unfavorable out-

comes down which the corporation could have to go in the future as a result of current decisions. Thus factors from these last two classes work together to position the firm from two complementary strategic perspectives: enhanced upside potential and reduced downside adversities.

SELECTING APPROPRIATE CRITERIA

Clearly, the contribution to making good decisions by utilizing criteria from these last two classes is potentially very significant. Unfortunately, it is difficult to enumerate specific criteria that can generally be assigned unambiguously to these two classes. The reason is that the strategic positioning concepts are very situation-dependent. Without explicit consideration of the decision context— the strengths and weaknesses of the firm, the opportunities and threats it faces, the resources at its disposal, etc.—generalizations about appropriate descriptive criteria are unwarranted. Nevertheless, as demonstrated below, guidance can be given to aid a decision maker in selecting appropriate strategic positioning factors.

It is important to realize that emphasizing the necessity to consider the specific attributes of the decision context does not imply that each problem is so different from all others that it is unique. In fact, it should be possible to identify broad categories of problem situations that have sufficient points in common to justify giving similar guidance to the manager. The scheme by which these categories of relatively homogeneous problem situations are identified should be based on discriminating factors that have the ability to distinguish between situations that require quite different actions to remedy effectively. Breaking down the problem situations into more than just a single category, each one of which is differentiated from all others but which at the same time possesses sufficient internal consistency to permit generalized guidance to be given, is the essence of a typological approach to problem-solving.[8] Using this approach, guidance can be given and situationally appropriate decision criteria can be identified based on important similarities with other members of the same category. In this way, the unjustified generalizations that quite often are prone to come from other nontypological analytical procedures can be avoided.

The use of a typological approach, although not necessarily lessening substantially the problem of ascertaining reasonably reliable input data for each of the selected criteria, will at least be helpful in interpreting the information in question. While objective verification of information entering the decision process would be desirable, this is usually not attainable. Thus the manager is forced to rely on subjective estimates of perhaps crucial factors upon which the resource allocation process depends. In these circumstances, a good rule to follow is to introduce as much intersubjectivity, or corroborating external evidence for the perceptions of the individual, into the process as possible as a substitute for arbitrary hypersubjectivity [10, 13]. For structuring perceptions with intersubjective content, the manager should look for supporting signals received from outside himself. Through this perception-corroboration process, the chances of being on the right track are enhanced, and the ability to live with the uncertainties inherent in the decision process is increased.

Often these intersubjective perceptions will involve taking into account qualitative factors, as well as quantitative data. Indeed, at times it may turn out that the most important aspects of the problem situation are qualitative. It is thus an unavoidable consequence of the nature of the input information that one needs to fall back on the comparative approach. In this regard, a well-defined benchmark or reference point is required to make adequate comparisons consistently [9, 11]. Anchoring the analysis to such a benchmark also serves to increase the degree of intersubjective credibility of the process and therefore to strengthen the reliability of the outputs.

In the business environment of the 1980s, characterized by more complexity and increased dynamics, it often will be difficult for a decision maker to ascertain reliably the *magnitude* of changes that the firm needs to make to improve its position. But it is vital that the manager be able to sense for key strategic issues the *right direction* in which the company should move [11]. This is generally possible for the talented entrepreneur; otherwise, management would be a pure art without substantial scientific elements.

We believe that careful selection of decision criteria from all five classes, a conception of the warranted direction in which to move for each criterion, and the use of intersubjective information anchored to a suitable reference point should usually lead to adequate guidance, at least in crucial strategic matters. Thus it should also result in good current decisions from the perspective of exploiting present options in accordance with the perceived direction, while at the same time safeguarding future flexibility.

MODELING METHODOLOGIES TO SOLVE THE MULTICRITERIA PROBLEM

The essential nature of the resource allocation problem described above is far richer than is normally conveyed by traditional financial models. As demonstrated above, a central feature of the decision-making process is the need to consider explicitly the tradeoffs between multiple criteria, only some of which reflect conventional economic factors. When modeling these complex relationships, there are numerous methods available by which a manager can structure the analysis so as to make the asset selection decision on the basis of multiple criteria. As a survey of the major approaches taken by these methods, in the discussion that follows, five broad categories of decision models are examined in turn with due consideration given to their strengths, weaknesses, and potential for implementation.

Perhaps the simplest category can be called heuristic classification. With this approach, several figures of merit (or demerit), representing the characteristics of the projects under consideration according to various criteria, are calculated. Strike-out rules are then employed to eliminate projects that do not meet minimum threshold requirements for each criterion. From among the remaining feasible projects, a capital budget is tailored based on heuristics deemed appropriate for the problem at hand. Although this is the easiest method to employ (and we suspect the most prevalent), it tends to be more subject to problems of hypersubjectivity and an inconsistent application than other methods. There is always the danger that the heuristics chosen might reflect more the prejudices of the individual manager, and thus be almost void of intersubjectivity, than they reflect the strategic requirements of the company. If derived in an appropriate manner so that they are compatible with the essence of vital theories, heuristics can be useful tools in the decision process, assuming that proper care is taken to utilize reliable input data adequately.

Philosophically related to the first category, but less arbitrary in some ways, the second approach involves more formalized satisficing behavior. The decision maker establishes *a priori* a set of thresholds or bounds, one for each criterion, that an acceptable allocation must satisfy. An extended search is then conducted to identify various combinations of projects that meet all of the planning requirements. A capital budget can then be chosen based on management's preferred combination rather than on the basis of hypersubjective *a priori* heuristics. Quite often the search process will terminate when the first or only a few feasible combinations are identified, and there is no way to tell if a substantially better combination exists. This methodology is the one usually employed in conjunction with simulation studies and is designed simply to ascertain a "satisfactory" resource allocation scheme [17].

While it is fairly easy to employ and is less hypersubjective than the first category, this satisficing approach is not entirely satisfactory from the perspective of economic theory when operating under conditions of bounded rationality. *A priori*, it is unlikely that a decision maker will know what the feasible set looks like or what is attainable in terms of the objectives to be met. If sufficient information is available to enable the manager to discern a "satisfactory" solution, there should also be enough data to conduct an exploration of the extreme points of the feasible region. Why, then, should a decision maker satisfice when a more favorable outcome can be attained?

The third category of models moves into the realm of optimization. Defining each criterion to be a decision variable and assigning *a priori* weights to each, the resource allocation problem is treated as a mathematical program with a single objective function. In this way, the limits of the attainable set can be probed and shadow prices can be used to investigate the tradeoffs. However, since some objectives are inherently contradictory and it may even prove impossible to attain an intersubjectively grounded threshold level for some criteria, the likelihood of encountering an infeasible problem is high. Thus, operationally, this method may be fraught with difficulties [19].

A more refined variant of single-criterion optimization for the purposes at hand is goal programming [23]. In this, the fourth category, the decision maker arrays a hierarchy of goals, assigns *a priori* targets and priorities, and proceeds to maximize in turn the goal with the highest priority. Several criticisms of goal programming have appeared in the literature, but the fact remains that targets, or aspiration levels, have been shown to be important determinants of managerial behavior and that priority schemes are commonly encountered in business. Still, however, the sometimes subtle distinction between "goals" and "constraints" is worrisome because the economic consequences of deviations from the target are not the same for each one. That is, a penalty is applied to deviations on either side of a goal, but a nonbinding constraint incurs no penalty [3].

In the fifth category, the decision problem is treated as a vector maximization problem for which nondominated solutions are sought [16, 27]. These Pareto-optimum solutions are then examined by the decision maker, and the one most closely corresponding to his preferences is selected. This methodology *preserves the essential multicriteria nature of the selection problem until the moment of selection,* and no priorities or weighting schemes are required *a priori.* Unless it is possible to employ discrete variables, however, this methodology can generate a large number of solutions from which to choose. Also, since, after determining nondominated combinations, some priority or weighting scheme must be employed to make the selection, this method is not free from a managerial preference function.

CHOOSING AN APPROPRIATE MODELING METHODOLOGY

It is our belief that establishing weights and priorities should be an important part of the decision process *ex ante.* Using a typological approach to criteria selection for *all* classes of criteria (not just for the last two classes) and employing intersubjectively grounded input data should give the decision maker an indication of the relative importance (and therefore the weight) of each criterion for achieving the strategic position desired by the firm. Thus these preliminary preceptions of weights and priorities, taken together from a strategic perspective, form a departure point to which the analysis can be anchored.[9]

Sensitivity analysis of the various solutions can give further insight into the dynamics and nature of the tradeoffs required. By revealing the impact of incorrect input information on the outcome of the decision, sensitivity analysis can lead to a better perception of the extent of flexibility and the consequences of changing circumstances that would be associated with a current alternative. This is helpful for incorporating strategic positioning philosophy into the decision process.

Since one of the most crucial parts of the decision-making process can be characterized as trading off multiple criteria against each other, preserving the essential multidimensional nature of the problem to the point of actual selection of an alternative by the manager is called for. Of the five categories of modeling methodologies, only the first two and the last inherently possess this characteristic. Several fundamental objections were made against satisficing approaches (the first two categories) that we believe render them less useful than other methods. Even preservation of the multicriteria nature of the problem does not offset these disadvantages. With the fifth category, multiple-criterion programming (vector maximization), the major drawback is not so fundamental. It is true that conventional vector maximization algorithms might generate a large number of nondominated solutions from which to choose. In this case, a natural inclination of managers would be to employ some type of heuristic to narrow further the range of options. There are fewer objections to this than there are to applying the heuristic approach to the complete set of alternatives since only nondominated options are considered, but a less arbitrary approach would be desirable.

Recent theoretical breakthroughs have resulted in an algorithm for finding nondominated integer solutions to multiple-criterion problems [30, 22]. The number of nondominated integer solutions is far less than for continuous problems, so this major criticism can be eliminated. Also of significance, for purposes of resource allocation decisions, the algorithm under discussion possesses a further desirable characteristic in that it is possible to input a weighting scheme and to ascertain a unique nondominated solution that is the best obtainable with that set of weights. Thus a decision maker can converge on a small number of nondominated solutions that should move the firm in the intended direction. Selecting the most desired option from among these alternatives should prove far easier than with conventional vector maximization approaches. Also, it is likely that the ramifications of making an "inferior" choice from the reduced set of alternatives will be far less serious than they might otherwise be.

To the best of our knowledge, only two studies have been written that utilize this new approach for resource allocations [6, 8]. They are based on an interactive algorithm that permits extensive interaction between the decision maker and the computer [22]. It is our conviction that neither this approach nor any other modeling method would prove operationally successful without the capability to interact on a real-time basis with the model [31]. The ability to explore quickly and thoroughly "what if" questions and to perform extensive sensitivity analyses of the various options available to the company generates insights, feed forward, and feedback into the dynamics and the ramifications of the process. This ability, along with preserving the essential multidimensional nature of the problem, makes interactive Multiple Objective Discrete programming—MOD programming—superior to other methodologies suggested in the literature as an aid for making resource allocation decisions.

In all fairness, however, this discussion would not be complete without also mentioning interactive decision-making systems linked to a goal programming solution algorithm [25]. These enhanced interactive goal programming-based approaches are substantially superior to methodologies other than the MOD programming described above. Since there are many more things than the way the model is constructed that will impact on its usefulness in practice, we believe that careful selection of criteria or goals and the setting of targets using the so-called theory of the displaced ideal [4] will at least enable the quality of decisions based on the enhanced goal methods to be of a similar order of magnitude as those made by MOD programming.

Conceptually, however, the edge must be given to the latter. There are so many variables that can disturb the whole trial in practice; so why not conduct it in the most defensible way possible with respect to programming methodology? Already, too many sources of errors exist with the possible danger of noneffi-cient, if not noneffective, solutions: Why enhance this risk?

CONCLUSIONS

Our reasons for writing this paper were based on a desire to explore the modeling philosophies inherent in various methods for allocating scarce resources suggested in practice or in the literature. We wanted to be able to outline the required characteristics of an approach that would conform most closely to the spirit of what is called for by the nature of the problem. Interactive MOD programming appears to us to meet these requirements. This is not to say, however, that other approaches have little merit or that they are of necessity substantially inferior. It is likely that other methodologies, such as enhanced interactive goal programming, are capable of achieving satisfactory resource allocations when employed properly. Further research is required to assess the benefits and difficulties in an operational setting with the various approaches before a methodology can be demonstrated as definitely superior. New and better approaches may be developed in the future, but for the time being we believe that interactive MOD programming is the best choice for the applications under discussion.

NOTES

1. Keen [21] provides an excellent discussion of the evolution of this concept.

2. For more information on this sequential search process in firms, see Simon [28, 29] and Fleming [15].

3. Details about the existence of these stakeholder committees were given to one of the authors during a meeting with financial executives.

4. Management by objectives is a classical example of this process.

5. For more information about signalling theory, see Ross [26].

6. An excellent discussion of the evolution of strategic management can be found in Ansoff *et al.* [2]. Strategic positioning in the sense called for here is developed in Derkinderen [9] and Derkinderen and Crum [11].

7. Since there are an infinite number of possible outcomes, the probability of any specific one occurring – including the one forecasted – is zero. This does not mean that talented entrepreneurs are not usually roughly right, only that they are never *exactly* right along all relevant dimensions. Attention is being directed to the implications of not being exactly right, which clearly would be more serious for large deviations from the *ex post* results than for small ones.

8. Derkinderen and Crum [11] present an expanded discussion of a strategically grounded typological approach with several example applications.

9. The need for a strategic perspective and the manner in which this process works is described in detail in [11].

REFERENCES

[1]   Ansoff, H. Igor. *Corporate Strategy*. New York: McGraw-Hill Book Company, 1965.

[2]   Ansoff, H. Igor; Declerck, Roger P.; and Hays, Robert L., eds. *From Strategic Planning to Strategic Management*. London: John Wiley & Sons, 1976.

[3]   Carleton, Willard T.; Dick, Charles L., Jr.; and Downes, David H. "Financial Policy Models: Theory and Practice," *Journal of Financial and Quantitative Analysis* (December 1973), pp. 691–709.

[4]   Colson, Gerard, and Zeleny, Milan. *Uncertain Prospects Ranking and Portfolio Analysis under the Conditions of Partial Information*, Mathematical Systems in Economics, Vol. 44. Cambridge, Mass.: Oelgeschlager, Gun & Hain Publishers, 1980.

[5]   Copeland, Thomas E., and Weston, J. Fred. *Financial Theory and Corporate Policy*. Reading, Mass.: Addison-Wesley Publishing Company, 1979.

[6]   Crum, Roy L.; Derkinderen, Frans G.J.; and Klingman, Darwin D. "Multicriteria Optimization for Locating Direct Foreign Investments," paper presented at the 1979 meeting of the Southern Finance Association, November 1979.

[7]   Crum, Roy L.; Laughhunn, Dan J.; and Payne, John. "Risk Preferences: Empirical Evidence and Its Implications for Capital Budgeting," in

Derkinderen and Crum, eds., *Risk, Capital Costs, and Project Financing Decisions.*

[8] Crum, Roy L., and Derkinderen, Frans G.J. *Strategic Modeling for Corporate Investment.* Boston: Pitman Publishing, 1981.

[9] Derkinderen, Frans G.J. "Pre-Investment Planning," *Long Range Planning* (February 1977).

[10] Derkinderen, Frans G.J. "Intersubjectiviteit in het beslissingsproces," Nijenrode Research Memo 8–78, 1978.

[11] Derkinderen, Frans G.J., and Crum, Roy L. *Project Set Strategies.* Boston: Martinus Nijhoff Publishing, 1979.

[12] Derkinderen, Frans G.J., and Crum, Roy L., eds. *Risk, Capital Costs, and Project Financing Decisions,* Nijenrode Studies in Business, Vol. 6. Boston: Martinus Nijhoff Publishing, 1981.

[13] Derkinderen, Frans G.J., and Crum, Roy L. "The Use of Intersubjective Corroboration in Decision Making: Overview and Perspective," CSFM Research Report 2–80, Center for Strategic Financial Management, Gainesville, Fla., 1980.

[14] Derkinderen, Frans G.J., and Crum, Roy L. "Capital Budgeting as an Open System Process," in Frans G.J. Derkinderen and Roy L. Crum, eds., *Readings in Strategies for Corporate Investment.* Boston: Pitman Publishing, 1980.

[15] Fleming, John E. "Study of a Business Decision," *California Management Review* (Winter 1966), pp. 51–56.

[16] Geoffrion, A.M. "Proper Efficiency and the Theory of Vector Maximization," *Journal of Mathematical Analysis and Applications* 22, pp. 618–630.

[17] Gershefski, G. "Building a Corporate Financial Model," *Harvard Business Review* (July–August 1969), pp. 61–72.

[18] Hastie, K. Larry. "One Businessman's View of Capital Budgeting," *Financial Management* 3 (Winter 1974), pp. 36–44.

[19] Johnsen, E. *Studies in Multiobjective Decision Models.* Lund, Sweden: Studenlitteratur, 1968.

[20] Joy, O. Maurice, and Barron, F. Hutton. "Behavioral Risk Constraints in Investment Analysis," in Derkinderen and Crum, eds., *Risk, Capital Costs, and Project Financing Decisions.*

[21] Keen, P.G.W. "The Evolving Concept of Optimality," in M.K. Starr and M. Zeleny, eds., *TIMS Studies in the Management Sciences: Multiple Criteria Decision Making,* Vol. 6. Amsterdam: North Holland Publishing Company, 1977.

[22] Klingman, Darwin; Ross, G. Terry; and Soland, Richard M. "A General Model for Multicriteria Facility Location Problems and an Interactive Heuristic Algorithm for Solving the Model," technical report, Analysis, Research and Computation, Inc., Austin, Texas, October 1978.

[23] Lee, Sang M. *Goal Programming for Decision Analysis.* Philadelphia: Auerbach Publishers, 1972.

[24] Maslow, A.H. *Motivation and Personality,* 2nd ed. New York: Harper & Row, 1970.

[25] Nijkamp, Peter, and Spronk, Jaap. "Goal Programming for Decision-Making: An Overview and a Discussion," Erasmus Universiteit Rotterdam, September 1977.

[26] Ross, Stephen A. "The Determination of Financial Structure: The Incentive Signalling Approach," *Bell Journal of Economics* (Spring 1977), pp. 23–40.

[27] Roy, B. "Problems and Methods with Multiple Objective Functions," *Mathematical Programming* 1, pp. 239–266.

[28] Simon, Herbert A. *Models of Man.* New York: John Wiley & Sons, 1957.

[29] Simon, Herbert A. *Science of the Artificial.* Cambridge, Mass.: MIT Press, 1969.

[30] Soland, R.M. "Multicriteria Optimization: A General Characterization of Efficient Solutions," Rapport Techniques EP 77-R-8, Ecole Polytechnique de Montreal, Montreal, Quebec, 1977 (to appear in *Decision Sciences*).

[31] Wagner, G.R. "A Survey of Uses and Users of a Contemporary Planning System," Execucom Systems Corporation, Austin, Texas.

9 FLEXIBILITY OF CORPORATE PLANNING MODELS IN THE CASE OF CHANGING OBJECTIVES

Reinhart Schmidt
Kiel University, West Germany

Strategies considering future business environments must attach great importance to economic and social change. Occurring within the firm and the environment, such changes may not only give reasons for the revision of plans, but also for the adaptation of the company's planning system.

A firm's objective system is of special importance in economic and social change because the firm as an *organization* can be defined as an objective-oriented formation. Objectives are established by individuals and groups within the firm or by the influence of outside individuals and groups on the process of objective formulation within the firm. The resulting objective system thus is a complex system, characterized by a formal subsystem:

1. The firm as a whole with one or several objectives
2. Departments with one or several objectives

and by an informal subsystem:

3. Groups with one or several objectives
4. Individuals with one or several objectives

Though this paper does not look at the informal subsystem, the interdependence between the two subsystems must be remembered. People entering and leaving the firm, changes in personalities over the lifetimes of individuals, and reallocation of individuals within the organizational hierarchy are one reason why the objective system changes.

Another reason for changes in the objective system is economic and social change within the environment of the firm. The firm's strategy aims at survival [15, p. 45], which mainly means adapting the firm to its environment. To ensure this adaptation, the firm must not only change its strategic objects and instruments, but also change its objective system. The attempt to be in accordance with the environment leads to the definition of a firm as a goal-seeking system [23, p. 495]. The organizational structure and the multiplicity of goals specify this system as a multilevel-multigoal system [23, p. 494].

The objective-setting process within the firm is dynamic and evolving. The changing nature of this process has been stated in detail by Johnsen [13, p. 150]. A formalized, especially a computerized, planning system must be able to match changing objectives. One approach to fulfilling this requirement is the concept of planned change [1] in connection with organizational change. Another approach, which also reflects the uncertainty of the future, is the flexibility approach, where a planning system is built so that changing requirements may be fulfilled without changing the system.

In this paper we follow the second approach, focusing on the influence of changing objectives on the flexibility of the planning system. First, we investigate the nature of the change process with respect to objectives. Next, we look at possibilities of ensuring flexibility of a computerized planning system. Finally, corporate planning models are discussed with regard to changing objectives. An example is given by applying the planning-system for mathematical applications on a dialogue basis (PLASMA) [32].

THE PROCESS OF CHANGING OBJECTIVES

The importance of changing objectives may be demonstrated by a new evaluation of data that Heinen [10] collected (the number of interviewed managers was 25). In Table 1 we have computed the percentages of different preference structures of objectives.

The changing structure of objectives can be demonstrated empirically: Suppose we are planning to substitute nonowner-managers for owner-managers in a given firm. Then the figures in Table 1 show that 55.6 percent of the owner-managers would vote for profit as a goal of highest priority. On the other hand, after having been substituted for the owner-managers, only 37.5 percent of the nonowner-managers would vote this way.

Objectives are expressed by goals [8]:

- Being related to an object
- Having one or several attributes
- Being measured on a certain scale
- Being overcome by an objective function

Changing objectives then means a variation of the object structure, the attributes, the scale, the objective function, or perhaps the goal values.

The process of changing objectives can be investigated on two levels:

1. At the level of a given decision process, objectives can be changed by the search process *within* the decision process. There is empirical evidence that objectives change after the beginning of the problem-solving process and before its end [7, 8, p. 245]. This statement is true even without considering preference articulation, which is the main problem in multiple-criteria decision making by interactive methods. If *a priori* articulation of preferences, interactive articulation of preferences, or *a posteriori* articulation of preferences [11, p. 30ff.] are adequate, this question is *embedded* in the question of changing objectives within the given decision

Table 1. Managers' Preference Structures of Objectives

Preference Structure of Objectives	Nonowner-Managers	Owner-Managers	All 25 Managers
$P > G > S$	12.5	22.2	16.0
$P > S > G$	25.0	33.4	28.0
$G > P > S$	12.5	22.2	16.0
$G > S > P$	0.0	11.1	4.0
$S > G > P$	50.0	11.1	36.0
$S > P > G$	0.0	0.0	0.0
Total percent	100.0	100.0	100.0

Explanation: P = profit; G = growth; S = safety.

process. It seems to us that the change of objects, attributes, scale, and objective function has at least the same importance as the problem of multicriteria decision making by interactive methods. It may be useful to look back at Cyert and March [2], who stressed the search—also for goals—within a given decision process. The conclusion of this discussion is that *in the case of modeling one must permit variation of objectives within a given decision process.*

2. At the level *between* two decision processes, objectives can be changed by the search-learning process [13, p. 295]. Regarding the latter, it is an unsolved problem if the approach of Simon—aspiration levels—or the approach of Lindblom—muddling through—describes the changing objectives correctly [15, p. 41]. Perhaps the combination of Simon's concept with the theory of adapting aspiration levels [29] contributes to a better construction of the decision process. From the modeling point of view, the changing objectives at the level between decision processes are much more important than the changes within a given decision process. One reason for this is the generally longer time span between different decisions, which requires processing more information from the environment than in the case of a singular decision process. Czeranowsky and Strutz [3] give empirical evidence that firms change goals over time.

THE FLEXIBILITY OF CORPORATE PLANNING SYSTEMS

It is not only changing objectives that compel corporate planning systems to be flexible. This is apparent if one looks at the elements of a formalized planning system [32]:

1. The *models* are logical structures of the object areas to be portrayed. Such a structure can exist without specifying an objective; for instance, there may be a number of equations, and the objective function may not yet have been specified.
2. The *data* are the numerical values that can be inserted into the model structure. Values and priorities of goals can be viewed as data as well.
3. The *methods* can be defined as solution mechanisms to solve the combination of model and data. Algorithms are special types of methods.

The distinction between models, data, and methods leads to seven flexibility types for a computerized planning system [31, p. 97]:

1. Flexibility of *data:* Several data constellations should be applied to a given model structure and solution method.

2. Flexibility of *methods:* The efficiency of different methods should be investigated in the case of given model structure and data constellation.

3. Flexibility of *models:* Different model formulations should be compared with respect to a given method and data constellation.

4. Flexibility of *methods and data:* A given model structure should be confronted with different combinations of solution methods and data constellations. Here one needs decision rules for assigning a specific solution method to a specific data constellation.

5. Flexibility of *models and data:* A given solution method should be applied to different combinations of model structures and data constellations.

6. Flexibility of *models and methods:* A given data constellation is the numerical basis for combinations of different model structures and solution methods.

7. Flexibility of *models, methods, and data:* The planning system must be able to combine model structure, data constellation, and solution method in an adequate manner.

The values of goals and constraints are understood as parts of the data constellation. Therefore, in the case of changing objectives, flexibilities of types 1, 4, 5, and 7 are required: Flexibility of data (type 1) means the ability of the planning system to adapt a given model structure to changing objectives, whereby the solution method must not be altered. Flexibility of methods and data (type 4) is necessary *if changing objectives require a change in the solution method* — e.g., the transition from linear programming to goal programming. Flexibility of models and data (type 5) matches changing of objectives if the solution method can handle a change in model structure too. Type 7 flexibility ensures adequate adaption if the changing objectives require both a new model structure and a new solution method.

The flexibility approach to planning systems can be demonstrated by Figure 1, in which the process of planning, realization, and control is divided into eight steps in the case of model-based decision making. There are two types of feedback (comparable to the two levels of changing objectives):

1. Feedback *before* making a decision: This type of feedback allows changing alternatives and restrictions, reformulating the model, changing the data constellation, and changing the model solution.

2. Feedback *after* decision and realization: This type of feedback is the expression of the learning process, which theoretically continues ad infinitum.

Steps 1 (problem recognition), 2 (alternatives and restrictions), and 6 (decision) are executed by people, while in steps 3 (model structure), 4 (data constel-

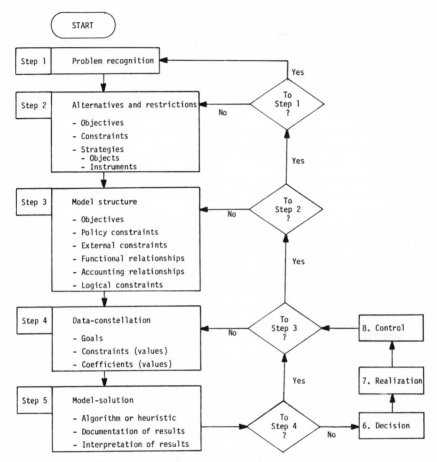

Figure 1. Model-Based Decision Making

lation), 5 (model solution), and 8 (control), there can be an interaction between people and computers.

Flexibility of a computerized system thus requires:

- Flexibility at step 3, allowing change of the model structure on a dialogue basis [31]
- Flexibility at step 4, allowing use of alternative data constellations, especially defining goals in an interactive manner [18]
- Flexibility at step 5, characterized by choosing different algorithms [32, 31].

With respect to flexibility at step 5, several algorithms have been implemented in the PLASMA system—i.e., LP (without parametric programming), goal programming (interactive version of [17]), and multiobjective linear programming [35]. It is intended to expand the bank of methods to interactive methods of multiobjective linear programming.

Figure 2 demonstrates connections between solution methods that in part require a special formation of objectives (for the inclusion of uncertainty methods see [30, p. 491]). These connections are important for the system to be able to handle special types of changing objectives.

To investigate the possibilities of changing objectives in detail, Table 2 contains a documentation of model characteristics with respect to the type of equations and the type of objective function (for structuring objective functions, see [4]).

From Table 2 we see that the functional possibilities shrink if we start at modeling objectives and end at accounting relationships (identities). In a broader sense, policy constraints can be viewed as similar to objectives. This is of importance in the case of changing objectives within corporate planning models. Such models generally consist of many policy constraints, and changes of these con-

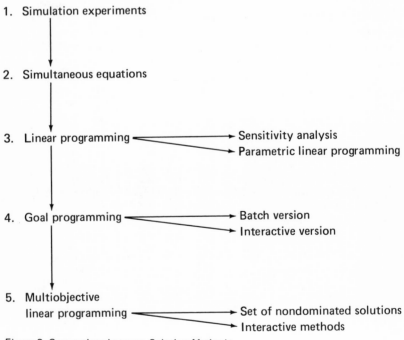

Figure 2. Connections between Solution Methods

Table 2. Connections between Types of Model Equations and Modes of Action

Model Characteristics	Mode of Action			
	Maximizing	Approximizing	Satisficing	Fixing
Objectives	OBJ.MAX	OBJ.APP	OBJ.SAT	OBJ.FIX
Policy constraints	–	POL.APP	POL.SAT	POL.FIX
External constraints	–	–	EXT.SAT	EXT.FIX
Logical constraints	–	–	LOG.SAT	LOG.FIX
Functional relationships	–	–	–	FUN.FIX
Accounting relationships	–	–	–	ACC.FIX

straints may occur more frequently than changes of the real objectives. This statement leads to the conclusion drawn by Eilon [5] that a clear distinction between goals and constraints is not possible in many cases.

A computerized planning system should allow changes between the different functional characteristics of Table 2 in an interactive manner. This requires an automated assignment of the solution method to a given change of model and data. For instance, in PLASMA a change from OBJ.MAX to OBJ.APP automatically leads to the substitution of linear programming by goal programming. The development of more user-oriented computerized planning systems requires:

1. The approximation of model formulation to natural problem solving—i.e. the understanding of natural language
2. The connection of models with large data banks and with the decision maker or the decision group, respectively
3. The automatic switch from one solution method to another due to the existing model and data

CORPORATE PLANNING UNDER CHANGING OBJECTIVES

There is much empirical evidence that individual managers have different objectives [10, p. 37ff., 3] and that the objectives of top management differ from those of divisional management [20]. Recalling the debate on interactive multiple-criteria problem-solving, it is interesting to note that the cited investigations state *a priori* rankings of goals. Thus it seems to be in accordance with business (at the moment) to go first from simulation models [34, 27, 30, 6, 24] to linear programming [30, 28 (mixed integer), 21, 24, 33] and then to expand the model to goal programming [12, 17, p. 207ff., 26, 19, 9]. Models using multiple-objective linear programming begin to appear [16].

The changing of objectives and the influences on the strategies of the firm have been demonstrated by Lee and Lerro [19]. In the following, we use the *same* data to demonstrate the flexibility of the planning system to adapt to changing objectives. In Figure 3 we present a copy of the model input at the terminal (all computations have been carried out by a PDP 10 at Kiel University). The PLASMA syntax allows summing up ("SUMME") and multiple indexing. In the case of goal programming, the decision variables $X(I)$ are completed by deviational variables after the model structure of Figure 3 has been produced.

SATZ BUDGET ALLOCATION
[SUMME OUTLAY(I,J)*X(I) FUER I=1,15] = BUDGETGOAL(J) FUER J=1,4

SATZ INTERPERIOD TRANSFER OF FUNDS
[SUMME (OUTLAY(I,1)+OUTLAY(I,2))*X(I) FUER I=1,15]
                                                           = CUMBUDGETGOAL(2)
[SUMME (OUTLAY(I,1)+OUTLAY(I,2)+OUTLAY(I,3))*X(I) FUER I=1,15]
                                                           = CUMBUDGETGOAL(3)
[SUMME (OUTLAY(I,1)+OUTLAY(I,2)+OUTLAY(I,3)+OUTLAY(I,4))*X(I)
                             FUER I=1,15] = CUMBUDGETGOAL(4)

SATZ NET PRESENT VALUE
[SUMME PRESENTVALUE(I)*X(I) FUER I=1,15] = PRESENTVALUEGOAL

SATZ INCOME
[SUMME INCOME(I,J)*X(I) FUER I=1,15] = INCOMEGOAL(J) FUER J=1,4

SATZ CASH FLOW
[SUMME CASHFLOW(I,J)*X(I) FUER I=1,15] = CASHFLOWGOAL(J)
                                                              FUER J=1,4

SATZ PROJECT LIMITATION
X(I) <= 1FUER I=1,15

Figure 3. A Financial Planning Model Expressed by PLASMA Syntax

The manipulation of all data—inclusive goal data—can be executed in an interactive manner. This is done by manipulating a data bank, which contains:

- Coefficients (OUTLAY, PRESENTVALUE, INCOME, CASHFLOW)
- Constants (none in the example given)
- Goal values (BUDGETGOAL, CUMBUDGETGOAL, PRESENTVALUE-GOAL, INCOMEGOAL, CASHFLOWGOAL)

The established goals are grouped as follows:

1. Budget allocation (B)
2. Transfer of funds between periods (T)
3. Net present value (P)
4. Income (I)
5. Cash flow (C)

For BUDGETGOAL and CUMBUDGETGOAL an overachievement should be prevented, while for PRESENTVALUEGOAL, INCOMEGOAL, and CASH-FLOWGOAL underachievement is not wanted. That means that the first two goal groups require high priorities of the variables d^+, while the following three goal groups call for high priorities of the variables d^- (see the meaning of d^- and d^+ in [17]).

Thus, five priority classes can be created—one priority class for each group of goals. Within a given priority class, weights can be assigned; e.g., the deviational variables d^+ of the group BUDGET can be weighted:

$$8 \cdot d^+{}_{\text{BUDGET(1)}} + 4 \cdot d^+{}_{\text{BUDGET(2)}} + 2 \cdot d^+{}_{\text{BUDGET(3)}} + 1 \cdot d^+{}_{\text{BUDGET(4)}}.$$

In Tables 3 and 4 we present results of eight model runs with different objective structures. Results are reported:

- For different priority structures (see runs 1, 2, and 3 in Table 3)
- For different budget values (full budget in runs 1, 2, 3, and 7, half budget in runs 4, 5, 6, and 8)
- For different weights *within* each of the five priority classes [equal weights in runs 1 to 6, descending weights (= 8, 4, 2, 1) in runs 7 and 8]

Inspection of Tables 3 and 4 demonstrates the special effect of cutting the budget of each year by 50 percent (compare runs 1 with 4, 2 with 5, and 3 with 6). It can also be seen that several decision alternatives are more robust to changing objectives than others. Thus interactive goal programming—using a flexible modeling syntax and a flexible data manipulator—can help to meet the requirements of changing objectives.

Table 3. Optimal Project Structure with Respect to the Structure of Objectives

Run	Objective \ Project No.	1	2	3	4	5	6	7	8	9	10	11	12	13	14	15
1	BTCIP.FULL.ONE	1	1	0	0	0.3	0.5	1	0.3	0.9	0	0.5	1	1	1	0
2	CBTIP.FULL.ONE	1	1	0	0	0.4	0.8	1	0	0.7	0	0.5	1	1	1	0
3	PICTB.FULL.ONE	1	1	1	0	0	0.6	0.1	0.3	1	1	1	1	1	1	0
4	BTCIP.HALF.ONE	0	1	0	0	0	0	1	0	0.7	0	0.4	0	1	0.3	0
5	CBTIP.HALF.ONE	1	1	0	0.5	0.4	0	1	0	0.5	0	0.4	1	1	1	0
6	PICTB.HALF.ONE	1	1	1	0	0	0	1	1	1	0	1	1	0.9	1	0
7	BTCIP.FULL.UNEQ	1	1	0	0	0.3	0.2	1	0.5	1	0	0.5	1	1	1	0
8	BTCIP.HALF.UNEQ	1	0.5	0	0	0	0	0.6	0	1	0	0.4	0	1	0.3	0

Explanation of objectives: BTCIP = B >> T >> C >> I >> P; FULL = full budget; HALF = half budget; ONE = weights are equal to one; UNEQ = weights within each goal group descending from period 1 to 4.

Table 4. Underachievement of Priorities at Different Priority Levels

Run	Objectives / Priority Level	1	2	3	4	5
1	BTCIP.FULL.ONE	0	0	22.0	6.9	93.3
2	CBTIP.FULL.ONE	0	22.0	53.9	36.0	111.6
3	PICTB.FULL.ONE	0	5.4	80.8	411.2	220.8
4	BTCIP.HALF.ONE	0	0	576.7	659.6	5.0
5	CBTIP.HALF.ONE	0	333.2	779.6	96.2	110.8
6	PICTB.HALF.ONE	0	9.4	115.9	1093.8	466.5
7	BTCIP.FULL.UNEQ	0	0	200.0	60.0	82.7
8	BTCIP.HALF.UNEQ	0	0	2821.5	80.0	687.9

Note: For an explanation of objectives, see Table 3.

CONCLUSIONS

Considering strategies of adapting a firm to its environment, one must take changing objectives into account. It has been shown that the incorporation of changing objectives into the modeling process is necessary and possible. From the practical point of view, changing objectives require a flexible computerized planning system. Elements and structure of such a system have been discussed, and an example of interactive goal programming has been presented. Future research must concentrate on integrating multiple-criteria decision making beyond the goal programming concept.

REFERENCES

[1] Bennis, W.G. "Theory and Method in Applying Behavioral Science to Planned Organizational Change," *Journal of Applied Behavioral Science* 1 (1965), pp. 337–359.

[2] Cyert, R.M., and March, J.G. "The Behavioral Theory of the Firm: A Behavioral Science-Economics Amalgam," in W.W. Cooper *et al.*, eds., *New Perspectives in Organization Research.* New York: John Wiley & Sons, 1964.

[3] Czeranowsky, G., and Strutz, H. "Ergebnisse einer empirischen Untersuchung über Unternehmensziele," in H. Jacob, ed., *Zielprogramm und Entscheidungsprozess in der Unternehmung.* Wiesbaden: Gabler, 1970.

[4] Dinkelbach, W. "Ziele, Zielvariablen und Zielfunktionen," *Die Betriebswirtschaft* 38 (1978), pp. 51–58.

[5] Eilon, S. "Goals and Constraints in Decision-Making," *Operational Research Quarterly* 23 (1972), pp. 3–15.

[6] Francis, J.C., and Rowell, D.R. "A Simultaneous Equation Model of the Firm for Financial Analysis and Planning," *Financial Management* 7 (Spring 1978), pp. 29–44.

[7] Hamel, W. *Zieländerungen in Entscheidungsprozessen.* Tübingen: Mohr, 1974.

[8] Hauschildt, J. *Entscheidungsziele.* Tübingen: Mohr, 1977.

[9] Hawkins, C.H., and Adams, R.A. "A Goal Programming Model for Capital Budgeting," *Financial Management* 3 (Spring 1974), pp. 52–57.

[10] Heinen, E. *Das Zielsystem der Unternehmung.* Wiesbaden: Gabler, 1966.

[11] Hwang, C.L., and Massud, A.S.M. *Multiple Objective Decision Making – Methods and Applications.* Berlin: Springer-Verlag, 1979.

[12] Ijiri, Y. *Management Goals and Accounting for Control.* Amsterdam: North-Holland Publishing Company, 1965.

[13] Johnsen, E. "Experiences in Multiobjective Management Processes," in M. Zeleny, ed., *Multiple Criteria Decision Making.* Berlin: Springer-Verlag, 1976.

[14] Johnsen, E. "Multiobjective Management in the Small Firm," in S. Zionts, ed., *Multiple Criteria Problem Solving.* Berlin: Springer-Verlag, 1978.

[15] Keen, P.G. "The Evolving Concept of Optimality," in M.K. Starr and M. Zeleny, eds., *Multiple Criteria Decision Making.* Amsterdam: North-Holland Publishing Company, 1977.

[16] Lawrence, K.D., and Lawrence, S.M. "A Multiple Objective Linear Programming Model for Corporate Financial Management," paper presented at TIMS/ORSA meeting, Atlanta, Georgia, 1977.

[17] Lee, S.M. *Goal Programming for Decision Analysis.* Philadelphia: Auerbach, 1972.

[18] Lee, S.M. "Interactive Goal Programming: Methods and Application," in S. Zionts, ed., *Multiple Criteria Problem Solving.* Berlin: Springer-Verlag, 1978.

[19] Lee, S.M., and Lerro, A.J. "Capital Budgeting for Multiple Objectives," *Financial Management* 3 (Spring 1974), pp. 58–66.

[20] Lorsch, J.W., and Allen, S.A. *Managing Diversity and Interdependence.* Cambridge, Mass.: Harvard University, Graduate School of Business Administration, 1973.

[21] Machado, E.L., and Carleton, W.T. "Financial Planning in a Regulated Environment," *Journal of Financial and Quantitative Analysis* 13 (1978), pp. 759–777.

[22] March, J.G., and Simon, H.A. *Organizations.* New York: John Wiley & Sons, 1958.

[23] Mesarovic, M.D.; Sanders, J.L.; and Sprague, C.F. "An Axiomatic Approach to Organizations from a General Systems Viewpoint," in W.W. Cooper *et al.*, eds., *New Perspectives in Organization Research.* New York: John Wiley & Sons, 1964.

[24] Metz, M. *Bilanz- und Ergebnisplanung für internationale Unternehmen.* Frankfurt am Main: Lang, 1978.

[25] Nijkamp, P., and Spronk, J. "Interactive Multiple Goal Programming: Method and Application," Centre for Research in Business Economics, Erasmus Universiteit Rotterdam, Report 7812/F, June 1978.

[26] Osteryoung, J.S. "Multiple Goals in the Capital Budgeting Decision," in J.L. Cochrane and M. Zeleny, eds., *Multiple Criteria Decision Making.* Columbia: University of South Carolina Press, 1973.

[27] Powell, J.R.P., and Vergin, R.C. "A Heuristic Model for Planning Corporate Financing," *Financial Management* 4 (Summer 1975), pp. 13–20.

[28] Rychel, D.F. "Capital Budgeting with Mixed Integer Linear Programming: An Application," *Financial Management* 6 (Winter 1977), pp. 11–19.

[29] Sauermann, H., and Selten, R. "Anspruchsanpassungstheorie der Unternehmung," *Zeitschrift für die gesamte Staatswissenschaft* 118 (1962), pp. 577–597.

[30] Schmidt, R. "Zur Planungsflexibilität bei der Planung von Bankbilanzen", in H.N. Dathe *et al.,* eds., *Proceedings in Operations Research* 6. Würzburg: Physica, 1976.

[31] Schmidt, R. "Zur Verbindung von Modellen, Methoden und Daten bei Unternehmensplanung mit EDV," in H. Müller-Merbach, ed., *Quantitative Ansätze in der Betriebswirtschaftslehre.* Munich: Vahlen, 1978.

[32] Schmidt, R., and Janowski, W. "Zur Gestaltung computergestützter Planungssysteme," *Zeitschrift für Betriebswirtschaft* 47 (1977), pp. 417–436.

[33] Valero, F.J., and Vilá, D.V. "An Integrated Corporate Planning Model Using Mixed Integer Programming," paper presented at EURO III, Amsterdam, 1979.

[34] Warren, J.M., and Shelton, J.P. "A Simultaneous Equation Approach to Financial Planning," *Journal of Finance* 26 (1971), pp. 1123–1142.

[35] Zeleny, M. *Linear Multiobjective Programming.* Berlin: Springer-Verlag, 1974.

10 INTERACTIVE MULTIPLE GOAL PROGRAMMING AS AN AID FOR CAPITAL BUDGETING AND FINANCIAL PLANNING WITH MULTIPLE GOALS

Jaap Spronk
Erasmus University Rotterdam, The Netherlands

In this paper, we consider capital budgeting and financial planning as decision problems involving a multiplicity of goals. Furthermore, we will investigate the usefulness of a number of multiple-objective programming methods for the solution of these problems.

Capital budgeting and financial planning both deal with the selection of capital investment projects. Capital budgeting can be described as follows [19, 34]: Given the net present value of a set of independent investment alternatives, and given the required outlays for the projects in each of the time periods of the planning horizon, find the subset of projects that maximizes the total net present value of the accepted ones while simultaneously satisfying a constraint on the outlays in each of the periods.

The first mathematical programming formulation of the capital budgeting problem has been provided by Weingartner [33]. The model can be written as

$$\left.\begin{array}{ll} \max & \displaystyle\sum_{j=1}^{n} b_j \cdot x_j, \\[2em] \text{subject to} & \displaystyle\sum_{j=1}^{n} c_{tj} \cdot x_j \leqslant C_t \quad \text{for } t = 1, \ldots, T; \\[2em] & 0 \leqslant x_j \leqslant 1 \quad \text{for } j = 1, \ldots, n; \end{array}\right\} \tag{1}$$

where b_j denotes the net present value of project j, and where c_{tj} is the outlay required for project j in period t. The maximum permissible expenditure in period t is given by C_t. The fraction of project j accepted is given by x_j. This fraction can be required to be either zero or one, by which the linear programming problem turns into an integer programming problem. Both problems have been dealt with in detail by Weingartner [33, 34]. This formulation has been adapted and extended in various ways. Other constraints, for instance, capacity, liquidity, and manpower, have been added, different objective functions have been proposed, uncertainty has been explicitly dealt with, and so on. Financial planning can also be seen as an extended capital budgeting problem. In financial planning, capital investments, financing, and dividend options are considered simultaneously [21].

As will be shown in the second section, there are several motives to treat capital budgeting and financial planning as decision *problems* involving a multiplicity of goals. *First,* by undertaking (capital) investments, one is offering income in one period in order to receive (hopefully more) income in a future period. Income in each of the periods can thus be seen as a separate and mutually conflicting flow of goal variables. *Second,* in an uncertain world, investing involves taking risks. Clearly, apart from its (expected) income characteristics, an investment project should be described by some measure of its riskiness. The decision maker, having the possibility to choose different subsets from the set of all his investment opportunities, can influence both expected income and total risk involved. Thus "risk" can be viewed as another goal variable. Obviously, this holds true both for investments in the public sector and in the private sector. However, in the latter case, modern capital market theory provides tools to aggregate all future and uncertain income flows in one measure, the market value of the firm. This subject will be dealt with in more detail in the second section. *Third,* in general, objectives different from those mentioned above influence decisions concerning the selection of investment projects. This is especially true for the public sector, where the existence of multiple goals in project selection has long been recognized, as is witnessed by the widespread use of cost-benefit and cost-effectiveness analysis.[1] But also the private enterprise is, and should be, dealing with a complex of multiple goals, which changes over time [9]. In consequence, private project selection should be seen as a decision problem involving multiple goals. Several authors recognized this fact and presented a variety of capital budgeting and financial planning models, which explicitly deal with multiple goals. A sample of these models is discussed in the third section, in which we also discuss a number of characteristics of capital budgeting and financial planning, which constitute sources of difficulties for the application of multiple-objective programming methods.

In the fourth section, we describe a new, interactive procedure, called Interactive Multiple Programming [25]. We will show that this procedure has a number of attractive properties, especially for capital budgeting and financial planning. Notably, most of the problems arising from this field of application can be solved in a straightforward manner.

The fifth section will be devoted to a well-known, originally single-objective financial planning model, which has a firm basis in the theory of finance.[2] We sketch how such a model can be translated into an Interactive Multiple Goal Programming model. The final section gives a summary statement of the main conclusions.

WHY MULTIPLE GOALS?

It is not necessary, at least not here, to repeat the three capital investment selection problems formulated by Lorie and Savage [19]. In most proposals for the solution of these problems, some form of the discounted present (or future) value criterion plays an important role. Discounting can be regarded as perhaps the oldest and certainly the most widely used multiple-objective decision method. In this view, K_t, the sum of the cash flows in period t ($t = 1, \ldots, T$) associated with the investment plan to be chosen, is considered to be a separate goal variable, which should be maximized. By assigning *a priori* weights (i.e., discounting factors) to each of these goal variables, the desirability of the investment plan can be expressed in a single-valued measure, the discounted (present or future) value of the investment plan. Unlike the case of many other multiple-objective decision problems, the use of *a priori* weights (i.e., discounting factors) in this case can be theoretically justified through the existence of a price mechanism. The latter, which in fact is the capital market, determines "prices" (i.e., discounting factors) for lending and borrowing money.

Most theories that deal with the correctness of the use of the present value criterion start with the *a priori* assumption that the firm is (and should be) maximizing its owners' (stockholders') wealth. Then the firm, which is supposed to be confronted with a set of economically independent investment opportunities, cannot make its investment decisions independently of its owners' consumption decisions. In this view, investment is "not an end in itself but rather a process for distributing consumption over time" (see Hirshleifer [12] for a more detailed discussion). To reach an optimal solution, both the firm and its owners can (and should) also consider the exchange opportunities offered by the capital market.

For the certainty case, Hirshleifer [12] has shown "that the present-value rule for investment decisions is correct in a wide variety of cases." One of these cases occurs when investment opportunities are independent and the capital market is perfect. In some cases, the present-value rule is only correct in a formal sense, because "the discounting rate used is not an external opportunity but an internal shadow price which comes out of the analysis" [12, p. 352]. Unfortunately, there are also cases for which the present-value rule fails to give correct answers. According to Hirshleifer [12, p. 352], this is only true "for certain cases which combine the difficulties of non-independent investments and absence of a perfect capital market."

In an uncertain world the analysis becomes much more complicated. The main problem[3] is the description of the capital market, valuating uncertain future income streams. One of the best-known descriptions is given by the capital asset pricing model (CAPM), as developed by Sharpe, Lintner, and Mossin. The CAPM, which essentially is a one-period model,[4] has produced results that have been shown empirically to be reasonably close approximations of the valuation of uncertain income streams by capital markets. The same model can be applied to the valuation of the firm's capital investment projects. Given an economically independent project, and given the firm's objective to maximize its stockholders' wealth, the firm does not have to worry about the unsystematic risk of the projects, because "it is of no value to its owners." Accordingly, the discount factor to be used can be expressed in terms of the risk-free interest rate, the market price of risk, and the project's covariance with the market [3]. In consequence, different projects will require different discount factors.

Clearly, there are very good theoretical reasons to use some variant of the present-value rule in evaluating investment plans. Nevertheless, the theoretical justification of its use is certainly not complete. As mentioned above, this even holds for the relatively simple certainty case.[5] For the world of uncertainty, very promising results have been provided by the development of the capital asset pricing model. As noted already, this is a one-period model. To our best knowledge, a generally accepted multiple-period version of this model does not exist yet. Besides these apparent theoretical shortcomings, there are also some practical problems in applying the present-value rule.[6] The most notorious of them is the requirement of economic independence, both between the projects to be evaluated and the existing operations of the firm and between the projects themselves. Within the same firm, such independence is a not very frequent occurrence. Another important problem is the determination of the "correct" discounting factor. Obviously, in an uncertain world, where interest rates may change over time, this is not a very easy task.

Nevertheless, since the cash-flow streams generated by the firm are being valued by the capital market, the firm's project-selection rules should take this valuation into account. An alternative to the above-mentioned present-value rules might be to treat the expected level, as well as both the systematic and the unsystematic risk of each period's sum of cash flows,[7] as separate goal variables. The prices (discounting factors) are thus not fixed on an *a priori* basis, but rather become the results of one of the interactive procedures, described in the third and fourth sections. A problem with this method is the large number of goal variables—that is, three per period (or two if the unsystematic risk is not considered to be a goal variable) times the number of periods (T). We will return to the latter problem and discuss some possible solutions later.

As mentioned in the introduction, private enterprise has to deal with a complex of multiple goals, which changes over time. So objectives, different from the owners' wealth maximization, may influence the decisions concerning the selection of investment projects. Because the present-value rules are built on the assumption that the firm should be maximizing its owners' wealth, the question becomes whether these rules can still be used if the firm has to deal with a complex of multiple goals.

A first possibility is to adopt the present-value criterion and to ignore all other goal variables. It is clear that such a relentless approach by no means guarantees optimal values for these other goal variables. On the contrary, it is possible that one or more of them are so badly served that the risk-return characteristics of the income streams, induced by the investment, change, and with them the present value of the investment. So one may even wonder whether the contribution to the owners' wealth resulting from this procedure is optimal. For example, the present-value rule does not discriminate among projects with the same present value but with different time patterns in their cash-flow streams. Not all participants (and possibly not all owners either) will be indifferent. The same holds for the firm's unsystematic risk. The capital market is insensible for this risk because of the ability to diversify it. Owners and other participants of the firm do not always have the possibility of compensating for the unsystematic risk factor. This alone is an important reason to treat this factor as another criterion in the evaluation of projects.

Another, often-proposed procedure is to formulate criteria for the goal variables not accounted for in the present-value rule and to apply them to the set of alternative investment opportunities *before* the present-value rule. This implies that the former criteria have preemptive priority above the present-value criterion, which obviously is not always what is wanted by the decision maker.

A better approach is to deal with all goal variables simultaneously. When this is done by means of interactive procedures, the decision maker has the possibility of investigating the tradeoffs between the goal variables in a systematic way. We return to this later.

MULTIPLE-OBJECTIVE MODELS FOR CAPITAL BUDGETING AND FINANCIAL PLANNING

Sample

In this section, we discuss a sample of capital budgeting and financial planning models, which explicitly deal with multiple goals. These models will be characterized both by their technical and their (financial) economic properties.

One of the easiest ways to deal with multiple goals is to single out one of them to maximize, while requiring minimum values for the other goal variables. Such an approach was followed, e.g., by Robichek, Ogilvie, and Roach [27], who extended the capital budgeting problem by imposing constraints on each period's level of earnings induced by the accepted projects. The objections against such a procedure are clear. It assumes that all goals formulated as constraints are equally important and, moreover, that they have absolute priority over the goal variable that is being maximized.

During the very early stages of the development of goal programming, it was suggested several times that this technique could be an important means of dealing with capital budgeting and financial planning involving multiple objectives. For instance, Ijiri, Levy, and Lyon [14] argued that their linear programming model for budgeting and financial planning could be combined with goal programming approaches to break-even budgeting. Indeed, a considerable number of authors have used goal programming in financial planning and goal programming models. (An extensive list of references can be found in Nijkamp and Spronk [24]). Its use in these fields corresponds with the decision maker's reality. In this respect, Ashton and Atkins [2] state that "it is natural in financial planning to speak in terms of targets and goals; many of the indicators of company performance such as dividend cover, liquidity, or return on capital employed have target ratios adopted by customs and practice." Nevertheless, the employment of goal programming is not without difficulties. Notably, its need of a considerable amount of *a priori* information to be given by the decision maker should be mentioned. This shortcoming of goal programming clearly paved the road for other procedures.

An important concept, which has been shown to be very useful in multiple-objective programming, is formed by the so-called efficient (or Pareto-optimal) solutions. A solution is defined here as the $(m \times 1)$ vector of values attained respectively by each of the m goal variables g_i, $i = 1, \ldots, m$ for a given combination of the instrumental variables. An efficient solution then is characterized by the fact that none of the goal values can be improved upon without deteriorating one or more of the other goal values. Typically, there is no unique efficient solution. In fact, there is, in general, a whole set of efficient solutions from which the ultimate solution still has to be chosen. The identification of (all) efficient solution for a given problem is sometimes referred to as the vector-maximum problem. Sealey [29] describes a bank financial planning model that has been formulated as a vector-maximum problem. The relevant goal variables are assumed to be profit and solvency, where the latter is defined by two distinct (although related) goal variables: (1) the capital adequacy ratio (defined as the ratio of required to actual bank capital) and (2) the risk asset to capital ratio. The instruments are the amounts to be invested in each of the six available types of assets. Furthermore, the model is subject to a number of constraints, relating to capital adequacy, diversification, required reserves, and to the balance sheet. For this example, Sealey has found a set of seventeen efficient solutions from which the decision maker has to choose a final solution.

This approach seems attractive. Nevertheless, a few important disadvantages should be mentioned. For instance, one may wonder whether for a given goal variable, more is always preferred to less (or vice versa). In many financial planning problems, goal variables like growth size, level of liquidity, amount of leverage, and several other ratios are considered to be important. For none of these goal variables is it obvious that they should be either maximized or minimized. Of course, one may maximize (or minimize) these kinds of goal variables subject to additional constraints, delimiting their values. As will be shown in the next section, there are more flexible solutions to this problem. A more serious problem consists of the fact that, in general, the number of efficient solutions is very large. The identification of them thus requires a considerable (and sometimes even prohibitive) amount of computer storage space and time.

Furthermore, the number of efficient solutions easily exceeds the information-processing capacity of the decision maker. The solution to this problem is offered by some of the so-called interactive procedures, which are based on a mutual and successive interplay between a decision maker and an expert (or analyst).

Candler and Boehlje [4] describe a two-period capital budgeting model in which the alternative activities consist of (1) two investment projects, to be undertaken either in period 1 or in period 2, (2) the "opportunity to put cash in the bank," (3) net tax-free cash at the end of the planning horizon, (4) the value of the assets at the end of the planning horizon, (5) dividends paid to share-holders, and (6) pollution. At the same time, the latter four activities have been defined as goal variables, each of which has to be maximized or minimized. Moreover, dividends have been restricted to maintain at least the current level. Furthermore, the dividends have been restricted to increase at a given (linear) rate. The outcomes of the existing operations have been assumed to be given and fixed and, consequently, to be independent of the investment projects. This problem has been formulated as a deterministic vector-maximum problem. The feasible region of the activity vectors x is described by linear (in)equalities in x. Some of the elements of x are integer. Because the goal variables g_j (x), $j = 1$, . . . , 4, are at the same time activity variables, they can be expressed on a linear scale only. Candler and Boehlje aim at efficient (Pareto-optimal) solutions. The ultimate solution is to be found by an (unstructured) iterative and interactive approach.

Chateau [7] gives a numerical example of a capital budgeting problem with multiple goals.[8] The problem is to choose from a set of investment projects, some of which are indivisible. Internal capital rationing is assumed to have the highest priority. Furthermore, three other goals are assumed (an acceptable level of cash, a desired level of dividend disbursement, and a minimum target asset value). These goals are expressed entirely in present values.

This problem has been formulated as a deterministic, mixed-integer, goal pro-gramming model employing preemptive priority factors. Chateau shows the results for a variety of objective functions, including the one originally used by Weingartner. Although Chateau finds merit in the goal programming model's flexibility, he also mentions a number of its disadvantages. In his opinion, "The ordering and weightings on *a priori* ground and in absolute or relative terms may constitute a rigidity factor of the goal programming approach."[9] Not surpris-ingly, he proposes an interactive procedure. However, for this he has chosen an approach that also requires very detailed information from the decision maker — i.e., marginal rates of substitution for multiple criteria.

With regard to multiple-objective decision models, many interactive proce-dures have been shown to be very powerful tools in the process of searching for a final (compromise) solution. However, as mentioned above, financial planners usually express their preferences in terms of goals and targets. Therefore it seems useful to search for interactive procedures that correspond to this use. An attempt in this direction was made by Ashton and Atkins [2]. They describe an interactive procedure based on goal programming, in which both weights and targets are changed parametrically. Two important technical problems they have met are the choice of the metric distance in the goal program and the consider-able number of goals that is being used in their financial planning model. They developed a three-stage methodology that could deal with these problems in an ad hoc way. In their opinion (with which we wholeheartedly agree), a specific methodology is necessary for financial planning problems involving multiple objectives. Moreover, in view of the possible applications in this field, the efforts to find such a methodology seem to be justified.

Ashton and Atkins described an eight-period financial planning model incorporating a set of investment opportunities and financing alternatives available to the firm. Furthermore, the model contains a number of accounting variables that correspond with the U.K. tax law and accounting standards. For each of the planning periods, eight goal variables are defined (six of which are ratios). Thus the problem contains a total of sixty-four goal variables. Such a large number of goal variables constitute a source of difficulties in using multiple-objective programming methods. This, and other problems arising from this field of applications, will be dealt with in the next subsection.

Some Common Problems

A number of characteristics of capital budgeting and financial planning with multiple objectives will be discussed next. We will focus on those characteristics that may interfere with the application of multiple-objective decision methods.

In the complex organization that the firm has become today, capital budgeting and financial planning involve decisions at multiple hierarchical levels, to be made by a multiplicity of decision makers. Partly because of these reasons, the problem becomes one with multiple objectives. Thus, formally, one should speak about multiple-level, multiple-person, multiple-objective decision problems. Here we concern ourselves mainly with the multiple-objective nature of the problem, abstracting from multiple-decision levels and assuming a single decision maker. In some cases, however, we will indicate in which way the latter two aspects (i.e., the multiplicity of decision levels and of decision makers) may determine and influence the features of the multiple-objective decision problem at hand.

Large Numbers of Goal Variables. In capital budgeting and financial planning, the number of goal variables can easily grow unmanageable. Even if the firm considers a small number of goal variables (say two or three) to be important, these goal variables need to be formulated for each of the time periods within the planning horizon. Also, it may be necessary to define the same kind of goal variables separately for different divisions of the firm. It is clear that in this way, the number of goal variables becomes considerably more than "the magical number seven plus or minus two," which is often mentioned in the literature on multiple-objective decision making as the maximum number of goal variables that can be handled by the decision maker.

One possibility to reduce the number of goal variables is to replace each set of analogue time-indexed goal variables by some kind of aggregate. In contrast with the discounting procedure, which has its roots in the theory of finance, there are generally no procedures that aggregate these time-indexed goal variables in a theoretically sound way. Nevertheless, some aggregators may be useful in practice. To mention just a few, one could use the goal variables' average, or only the goal variable defined for the end of the planning horizon, or the maximum growth rate of the goal variable, or the minimum, and so on. Of course, it is necessary that the chosen aggregate have some practical meaning to the decision maker. If such an aggregate cannot be found for all goal variables, one has to accept, besides each other, time-indexed goal variables, together with goal variables that themselves are aggregates of other goal variables. It may be that the decision maker considers these goal variables to be incomparable. The way out is to use time-indexed goal variables only. This, of course, brings us back to where we started: an unmanageable number of goal variables.

A possibility to deal with a large number of goal variables is to divide the set of goal variables into a number of subsets, each containing goal variables of approximately the same importance. Then the multiple-objective decision problem can be solved for one of these subsets, subject to (flexible) constraints on the goal variable in the other subsets. Next, the multiple-objective decision problem can be solved, given the outcomes of the former decision problem. If the second problem cannot be solved satisfactorily, the first problem has to be solved again, subject to less restrictive constraints, and so on, until a satisfactory final solution has been found.[10]

More Not Always Preferred to Less. As mentioned in the preceding subsection, it is not always true that a goal variable needs to be either maximized or minimized. It may well be that the decision maker strives for a given target goal level or that he wants the goal variable to be clenched between an upper and a lower limit. Most existing interactive procedures can deal with these situations in a fairly rigid way only. Interactive Multiple Goal Programming, as described in the next section, offers a more flexible approach.

Ratios as Goal Variables. In the examples given earlier, many goal variables are ratios, being nonlinear functions of the instrumental variables. This may cause problems in multiple-objective programming approaches. Consider, for example, the following goal constraint in a goal programming formulation:

$$g_i(x)/g_2(x) - g^+ + g^- = g^* \qquad (2)$$

where g^* is the target ratio of per period profit, $g_1(x)$, to per period sales, $g_2(x)$. Both $g_1(x)$ and $g_2(x)$ are assumed to be linear in x, the vector of instrument values. As usual, g^+ and g^- measure, respectively, the over- and underattainment of the target ratio value g^*. It is clear that cross multiplication by $g_2(x)$ yields a nonlinear constraint, which requires special treatment. Detailed discussions on this topic can be found in Charnes and Cooper [5] and Kornbluth [17]. The latter also indicates that the presence of ratios complicates the solution of vector-maximum problems.

Capital Rationing. The situation in which constraints (for each of the periods of the planning horizon) have been imposed on the required outlays for the projects is commonly called *capital rationing.* According to Weingartner [35], most authors have interpreted capital rationing as a market-imposed limitation on the expenditures a firm may make (*external* capital rationing). Within this interpretation, two situations can be distinguished: (1) Neither the firm nor its owner(s) have access to financial markets, and (2) only the firm is supposed to be rationed by these markets. Weingartner [35] argues that, in reality, capital rationing is unlikely to exist for the private enterprise.

This leads to another interpretation of rationing: the so-called internal (or self-imposed) capital rationing. A firm may refuse to attract additional funds because it thinks the conditions offered by the market are unfavorable. A factor causing this refusal may be that there is an important disagreement between the firm and the market with respect to the prospects of the firm. Another reason for a firm to impose limits on its expenditures may be that its current owners do not want to lose their control over the firm.

Capital budgeting models incorporating capital rationing constraints can also be used in situations quite different from those described above. Indeed, Weingartner [35, p. 1404] states that his "contributions have been directed at utilizing the information content of the programming formulation as an aid to decision making and not as a positive theory of financial markets." In the managerial process of capital budgeting within firms, limits are frequently set on *plans* for expenditure on capital account. According to Weingartner [35, p. 1428], this is done for planning and control purposes, and, consequently, it is not properly a case of capital rationing. In our opinion, it is better not to treat the expenditure limits in this case as "hard" constraints, as they are in most of the current programming formulations, but rather as "soft" constraints, as provided, for instance, by the goal programming formulation.

Indivisible Projects. A frequently adopted assumption in capital budgeting and financial planning is that some or all of the investments are indivisible, which means that they cannot be undertaken in part. Generally, in mathematical programming formulations, this requirement is translated by means of integer $(0, 1)$-variables (see, e.g., Weingartner [34]).

The existence of $(0, 1)$-variables may give rise to problems in multiple-objective programming methods. In general, integer multiple-objective programming methods are not straightforward extensions of continuous multiple-objective methods. A survey of integer multiple-objective methods is given by Zionts [37, 38].

Uncertainty. Because of the very nature of capital budgeting and financial planning, one might want to use stochastic variants of multiple-objective programming methods (see, e.g., Charnes and Cooper [5]). An interesting possibility then is to treat chance constraints as goal variables within an interactive framework. Such a framework, together with its pros and cons with respect to the problems described above, is presented in the following section.

INTERACTIVE MULTIPLE GOAL PROGRAMMING

Interactive Multiple Goal Programming (IMGP) is a further extension of the well-known goal programming approach initiated and further developed by Charnes and Cooper. These authors present an overview of the development of the field of goal programming in a recent study [6] . Our approach is mainly taken from a survey report by Nijkamp and Spronk [24] .

In general, a multiple-goal program can be formulated as

$$
\left.
\begin{aligned}
&\text{minimize } f(\mathbf{y}^+, \mathbf{y}^-) \\
&\text{subject to} \\
&g(x) - \mathbf{y}^+ + \mathbf{y}^- = \mathbf{b} \\
&x \in R, \quad R = \{x | h(x) \leqslant \mathbf{h}\} \\
&\mathbf{y}^+, \mathbf{y}^- \geqslant 0 \\
&\text{and } y_i^+ \cdot y_i^- = 0 \quad \text{for } i = 1, \ldots, m
\end{aligned}
\right\} \tag{3}
$$

where f is the (dispreference) function with the positive (y_i^+) and the negative (y_i^-) deviations from the aspired levels (b_i) of the goal variables $g_i(x)$ as arguments $(i = 1, \ldots, m)$. The feasible area R of the instrumental variables x is bounded by the set of constraints $h(x)$. In general, the minimand f is assumed to be convex. The feasible area is also assumed to be convex. In many cases, both the goal variables $g(x)$ and the constraints $h(x)$ are assumed to be linear in x. We then have

$$
\left.
\begin{aligned}
g(x) &= A \cdot x \\
h(x) &= B \cdot x
\end{aligned}
\right\} \tag{4}
$$

where A is a matrix of order $(m \times n)$, B is a matrix of order $(k \times n)$, and $\mathbf{x}$ is an n-dimensional vector. As shown in Nijkamp and Spronk [24], the following general form for the function f can be deduced from the Minkovski metric:

$$f(y^+, y^-) = \left\{ \sum_{i=1}^{m} \alpha_i^+ \cdot \left[\frac{y_i^+}{b_i} \right]^p + \sum_{i=1}^{m} \alpha_i^- \cdot \left[\frac{y_i^-}{b_i} \right]^p \right\}^{1/p} \tag{5}$$

It is easily seen that equation (5) is a weighted (by α_i^+ and α_i^-) and standardized form of the l_p metric. That is, for $p = 1$ we get an absolute value metric, for $p = 2$ an Euclidean metric, and for $p \to \infty$ an approximation of the Chebychev (minimax) metric. In multiple-goal programming, the weighting factors α_i^+ and α_i^- may be replaced by preemptive priority factors, by which lexicographic orderings can be handled [24].

In our opinion, goal programming is one of the stronger multiobjective programming models available. It has a close correspondence with decision making in practice. Furthermore, it has some attractive technical properties.

Several empirical findings from decision-making practice are, in our opinion, rather convincing to demonstrate the practical usefulness of multiple-goal programming. As mentioned by several authors, the method corresponds fairly well to the results of the behavioral theory of the firm. In practice, decision makers are aiming at various goals, formulated as aspiration levels. The intensity with which the goals are striven for may vary for each goal; in other words, different "weights" may be assigned to different goals.[11] The use of aspiration levels in decision making is also reported by scientists from other fields, for instance, psychology (for a short overview, see Monarchi et al. [22]). In the same way, preemptive priorities are also known in real-life problems. Support for this essentially lexicographic viewpoint is provided by Fishburn [10] and Monarchi et al. [22]. A more concrete example of the correspondence of multiple-goal programming and practice is provided by Ijiri [13], who regards multiple-goal programming as an extension of break-even analysis, which is widely used in business practice.

The above plea for multiple-goal programming is of a somewhat theoretical nature. However, the operational usefulness of multiple-goal programming has also been recognized in practice, as shown by the many applications that have been reported in the literature (see Nijkamp and Spronk [24] for an overview).

One of the technical advantages of multiple-goal programming is that there is always a solution for a well-defined problem, even if some goals are conflicting, provided the feasible region R is nonempty. This is due to the inclusion of the deviational variables y_i^+ and y_i^-. These variables show whether the goals are attained or not, and in the latter case they measure the distance between the realized and aspired goal levels. Another advantage of multiple-goal programming is that it does not require very sophisticated solution procedures. The linear goal programming problems especially can be solved by easily available linear programming routines.

An important drawback of multiple-goal programming is its need for fairly detailed *a priori* information on the decision maker's preferences. Goal programming requires the definition of aspiration levels, the partition into preemptive priority classes, and the assessment of weights within these classes. We agree with those scholars advocating interactive approaches. These methods are based on a mutual and successive interplay between a decision maker and an analyst. Interactive methods require neither an explicit representation or specification of the decision maker's preference function nor an explicit quantitative representation of tradeoffs among conflicting objectives. Obviously, the solution of a decision problem requires that the decision maker provide information about his priorities regarding alternative feasible states, but in normal interactive procedures only limited information is asked for, which moreover can be provided in a stepwise manner. The task of the analyst is to display all relevant information especially about admissible values of the criteria and reasonable compromise solutions. Unfortunately, most of the usual interactive approaches lack some of the advantages of "traditional" multiple-goal programming, such as the possibility of including preemptive priorities. Furthermore, multiple-goal programming can handle situations of satisficing behavior, which is in contrast with most existing interactive methods. This situation, combined with the often-shown power of the traditional approach to include piecewise linear functions (cf. Charnes and Cooper [6]), justifies the effort of seeking an interactive variant of the traditional approach.

A Brief Description of Interactive Multiple Goal Programming

In this subsection, we present the general lines of a new, interactive variant of multiple-goal programming (IMGP). In the next subsection, we list some of the main features of IMGP. A more detailed description is given in an earlier report [25]. IMGP is capable of including all advantages of multiple-goal programming. For instance, preemptive priorities and piecewise linear functions can be handled in a straightforward way. Furthermore, the interactive process imitates practice in formulating aspiration levels, assessing priorities, and seeking a solution and readjustment of the aspiration levels. The method needs no more *a priori* information on the decision maker's preference structure than do other interactive multiobjective programming models. However, all available *a priori* information can be incorporated within the procedure.

Step 0.   First identify the goal variables $g_i(x)$, $i = 1, \ldots, m$ as a linear or piece-wise linear function of x, the vector of instrumental variables $x_1, x_2, \ldots, x_n$. We assume the $g_i(x)$ to be concave in x. Then specify the feasible set R, which is assumed to be convex and within which an optimal solution must be found. When the decision maker's preferences can be described by a preference function f (note, however, that we do not make any attempt to do this), this function should be a concave of both $g_i(x)$, $i = 1, \ldots, m$ and x_1, $i = 1, \ldots, n$. An optimal solution is then defined by

$$\left.\begin{array}{l} \max f = f\{g_i(x), i = 1, \ldots, m\}, \text{ subject to} \\[2mm] x \in R. \end{array}\right\} \qquad (6)$$

To simplify this brief exposition, we assume further that

$$\frac{\partial f}{\partial g_i} > 0 \text{ for } i = 1, \ldots, m. \qquad (7)$$

Thus we presuppose that a higher value of each of the goal variables is preferred to a lower value of (the same) goal variables.[12]

Step 1.   Next maximize successively each of the m goal variables $g_i(x)$ separately and denote the maxima by g_i^* and the m corresponding combinations of the instrumental variables by x_i^*, $i = 1, \ldots, m$.

   It is not possible to find a feasible value of $g_1(x)$ that exceeds g_i^*. On the other hand, it is not necessary to accept a value of $g_i(x)$ that is lower than $g_i^{\min}$, defined as

$$g_i^{\min} = \min_{j=1}^{m} \{g_i(x_j^*)\}, \qquad (8)$$

the lowest value of $g_i(x)$ resulting from the successive maximizations of the goal variables. In IMGP we define a "solution" S as a vector of minimum values imposed on each of the goal variables. Therefore it is clear that a final solution S^* must be found between the "ideal" (but mostly infeasible) solution I and the "pessimistic" solution Q, which are defined respectively as

$$I = [g_1^*, g_2^*, \ldots, g_m^*]$$

and

$$Q = [g_1^{\min}, g_2^{\min}, \ldots, g_m^{\min}]. \qquad (9)$$

To facilitate the notation, we have included the optimistic solution I and the pessimistic solution Q in the $(2 \times m)$ potency matrix P.

Step 2.   For each goal variable $g_i(x)$, the decision maker may have defined aspiration levels g_{ij}, $j = 2, \ldots, k_i - 1$, with the following property:

$$g_i^{\min} < g_{i2} < g_{i3} < \cdots < g_{ik_i-1} < g_i^*. \qquad (10)$$

Furthermore, we define

$$g_{i1} = g_i^{min} \text{ and}$$
$$g_{ik_i} = g_i^*. \qquad\qquad \Big\} \qquad (11)$$

In the following steps, these goal values are used in constructing trial solutions $\hat{S}_i$, which have to be evaluated by the decision maker. Because proposed goal levels are sometimes considered as being too high, we need the auxiliary vector δ, whose elements $\delta_j, j = 1, \ldots, m$ correspond to the m goal variables. We define δ_j as the difference of the lowest level of $g_j(x)$ being *rejected* by the decision maker and the highest level of $g_j(x)$ being *accepted* thus far. At the first stage of the procedure, no proposals have been made and, consequently, no goal level has been rejected. Therefore we put $\delta_j = 0$ for $j = 1, \ldots, m$ during the first step.

Step 3. Define the starting solution as

$$S_1 = [g_{11}, g_{21}, \ldots, g_{m1}], \qquad (12)$$

which is thus equal to the pessimistic solution defined in equation (9). Present this solution together with the potency matrix P_1 to the decision maker.

Step 4. If the proposed solution is satisfactory to the decision maker, one may accept it; if not, continue with step 5. Define R_i as the subset of R defined by the goal levels in S_i.

Step 5. The decision maker then has to answer the following question: "Given the provisional solution S_i, which goal variable should be improved first?"[13]

Step 6. Let us assume that the decision maker wants to augment the jth goal variable. Then construct a new trial solution S_{i+1}, which differs with respect to S_i only as far as the value of the jth goal variable is concerned (denoted by $g_j(x)_{\hat{S}_{i+1}}$ and $g_j(x)_{S_i}$, respectively).

If $\delta_j = 0$, no proposed value of $w_j(x)$ has been rejected thus far, by which we can propose the next higher aspiration level listed in step 2. *If* $\delta_j > 0$, a value of $g_j(x)$ that exceeds the current solution by an amount δ_j has been rejected by the decision maker. In this case, define[14]

$$g_j(x)_{\hat{S}_{i+1}} = g_j(x)_{S_i} + \frac{1}{2} \cdot \delta_j. \qquad (13)$$

When a provisional value for $g_j(x)$ has been calculated in one of both above-mentioned ways, we introduce the restriction

$$g_j(x) \geqslant g_j(x)_{\hat{S}_{i+1}} \qquad (14)$$

and proceed to step 7.

Step 7. Join the restriction formulated in step 6 or step 9 to the set of restrictions describing the feasible region R_j. Next calculate a new potency matrix, as in step 2, but subject to the new set of restrictions. Label this potency matrix $\hat{P}_{i+1}$.

Step 8. Confront the decision maker with S_i and $\hat{S}_{i+1}$, on one hand, and with P_i and $\hat{P}_{i+1}$, on the other hand. The shifts in the potency matrix can be viewed as a sacrifice for reaching the proposed solution. *If* the decision maker judges this sacrifice to be justified, accept the proposed solution by putting $S_{i+1} = \hat{S}_{i+1}$ and $P_{i+1} = \hat{P}_{i+1}$.

Furthermore, in the computer algorithm (see Figure 1), put $\delta_j = \frac{1}{2} \cdot \delta_j$ (which is only relevant for $\delta_j > 0$). *If* the decision maker considers the sacrifice unjustified, the proposed value of $g_j(x)$ is obviously too high. Therefore drop the constraint added in step 7 and proceed to step 9.

Step 9. We know that $g_j(x)_{S_i}$ is too low and that $g_j(x)_{\hat{S}_{i+1}}$ is too high in the decision maker's view. By definition, we thus may set δ_j equal to the difference between these two values. A new proposal value $\hat{S}_{i+1}$ is then calculated[15] by defining

$$g_j(x)_{\hat{S}_{i+1}} = g_j(x)_{S_i} + \frac{1}{2} \cdot \delta_j. \tag{15}$$

As in step 6, we add the restriction that $g_j(x)$ must equal or exceed the new proposal value, and we go to step 7 in order to calculate a new potency matrix $\hat{P}_{i+1}$.

When the decision maker is not able to indicate which single goal variable should be augmented, we assume he is at least capable of defining a set of goal variables whose values need to be augmented. In this case, the procedure must be modified slightly. This is shown in Figure 1, where we give a flowchart of the procedure.

Main Features and Possibilities of the Procedure

In this subsection, some key properties and possibilities of IMGP will be mentioned. For a more detailed discussion, see Nijkamp and Spronk [25].

In IMGP, the *goal variables* are assumed to be known and concave in the instrumental variables. The *preference function* of the decision maker is *not* assumed to be known. However, it is assumed to be concave, both in the goal variables and in the instrumental variables. Note that this preference function is not restricted to be monotone nondecreasing (or nonincreasing) in the goal variables. Clearly, those assumptions are not very restrictive. For instance, both optimizing and satisficing behavior can be incorporated.

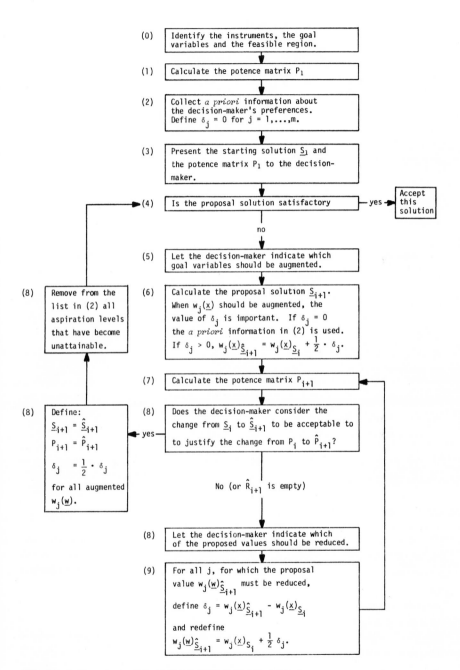

Figure 1. A Flowchart of the Extended Interactive Procedure

205

The decision maker only has to give information on his local preferences. This is done on the basis of a *solution* and a *potency matrix* presented to him. Remember that a solution is a vector of minimum values for the respective goal variables. The potency matrix shows separately for each of these goal variables the maximum value given the solution concerned. The decision maker only has to indicate whether a solution is satisfactory or not, and if not, which of the minimum goal values should be raised. He does *not* have to specify how much these goal values should be raised. *Nor* is there any need to specify weighing factors. (See also the next point.) A new solution is presented to him together with a new potency matrix. He then has to indicate whether the shifts in the solution outweigh the shifts in the potency matrix. If not, a new solution is calculated, and so on.

IMGP needs no more *a priori* information than other interactive programming models. However, all available *a priori* information can be incorporated within the procedure. In particular, *aspiration levels* and *preemptive priorities* that have been defined by the decision maker can be incorporated in the interactive process quite easily (note that IMGP offers the decision maker the opportunity to reconsider this *a priori* information during the interactive process). This ability to include *a priori* information makes IMGP also suitable for multicriteria problems that are repetitive and not important enough to warrant a permanent intervention of the decision maker.

As shown in Nijkamp and Spronk [25], IMGP converges within a finite number of iterations to a final solution, which exists and is feasible. Apart from an ϵ neighborhood, this solution is optimal. Whether this solution is unique or not depends on the decision maker's preferences. (For instance, when the decision maker is a satisficer having formulated targets attainable within the feasible region, a unique final solution does not in general exist.)

The decision maker is assumed to be able to answer the questions posed by IMGP. His answers must be consistent, although he is allowed to make some errors during the interactive process. Finally, because of the possible learning effects, the procedure must be repeated several times to be sure that a final solution is found that is as close as possible to the optimum.

Given a new (trial) solution, the maxima of the goal variables must be (re) calculated during each iteration of IMGP. This can be done with the help of any optimization method that meets the fairly unrestrictive requirements imposed by IMGP (i.e., convexity[16] of the feasible region R and concavity of the preference function and the goal variables). If the problem can be formulated in linear terms, some technical advantages can be enjoyed. Then IMGP can make a straightforward use of goal programming routines. In that case, for each proposal solution, a set of goal programs can be formulated, which differs mutually only with respect to one element in the objective function [25]. When a new solution is proposed, these goal programs are only modified with respect to some of the right-hand constants, being the respecified goal levels altered. The linear format of IMGP has all the advantages of standard multiple-goal programming discussed earlier. The easily available dual information should especially be noticed [15, 23].

AN ILLUSTRATION

The purpose of this section is to sketch how an existing financial planning model might be brought into the multiple-goal programming framework described in the preceding section. For the former, we have chosen the well-known (abbreviated version) of the LONGER model as described by Myers and Pogue [21]. The LONGER model, which has a sound basis in finance, is a static, mixed integer linear programming model, simultaneously dealing with investments (a.o. in liquid assets), financing, and dividend decisions. The model departs from two propositions: (1) The risk characteristics of a capital investment opportunity can be evaluated independently of the risk characteristics of the firm's existing assets or other opportunities. (2) The total market value of the firm is equal to its unlevered value plus the present value of taxes saved because of debt financing. The valuation of each investment opportunity has been assumed to be exogenous to the model. The simple objective assumed in the model is to maximize the current market value of the net worth of the firm (and thereby to maximize the wealth of current stockholders). However, this objective is to be maximized subject to a number of constraints, several of which reflect managerial choices and therefore, in our opinion, can better be treated as goal variables that can be traded off against each other.[17] One is a debt capacity constraint, which, according to Myers and Pogue [21, p. 589], may arise because of practical reasons that depart from the MM propositions. These reasons are (1) credit rationing, (2) managerial risk aversion, and (3) the impact of bankruptcy costs on the firm's value. This limit on debt capacity has been translated as a chance constraint, where the debt outstanding is limited to a fraction of the expected market value of total assets in each period. This fraction is determined by the "maximum acceptable probability of trouble," where "trouble" denotes the situation in which the real value of the firm's assets is less than the book value of its liabilities. Within interactive multiple-goal programming, one can deal with such a debt capacity constraint in a more flexible way. For instance, one could treat the "probability of trouble" as a goal variable to be minimized. This can be achieved by formulating a constraint corresponding with a very low "probability of trouble" (say .5). Next, reformulate this chance constraint as a goal chance constraint, after which the deviation from this constraint can be treated as a goal variable to be maximized. (Clearly, the larger this deviation is, the smaller the probability of trouble is.) In this way, the interactive procedure of the previous section can be employed, with the only modification being that the deviation calculated at each iteration should be retranslated to its corresponding probability of trouble. Of course, bankruptcy cost (for which the firm's market value has to be corrected) could be expressed as a function of the described deviation variable.

Another constraint, dealt with by Myers and Pogue, ensures a sufficiently large liquidity buffer in the financial plan "to provide a degree of flexibility in the face of uncertainties associated with future cash flows" [21, p. 593]. This constraint relates to the level of the liquidity reserve, being the sum of liquid assets and unused borrowing potential. (Note that the latter equals the deviation in the goal chance constraint on debt capacity.) Because the liquidity reserve is a random variable, it can be dealt with as above with the debt capacity constraint. Other constraints have been included by Myers and Pogue to keep track of planned dividends and accounting earnings, undoubtedly to recognize their informational content. To do so, these authors propose target compound growth rates, both for dividends and earnings. Obviously, the deviations from these growth rates can be treated by means of an interactive procedure, such as the one described in the previous section. Besides, other possibilities exist. For instance, one may treat the maximum rate of growth of dividends during the planning period as a separate goal variable to be maximized. Conversely, one may want to maximize the minimum growth rate, or both at the same time, and so on (for further details, see [30]).

CONCLUSIONS

If the firm is assumed to be directed exclusively toward the maximization of its stockholders' wealth, it can be viewed as facing a multiple-objective decision problem, because it involves trading off income in different time periods and trading off expected income versus risk. Apart from using a model describing the capital market's valuation process, one might consider using a multiple-objective decision model including expected income and systematic risk as separate goal variables for each of the periods of the planning horizon.

In contrast to the above-mentioned assumption, the private enterprise in reality is dealing with a dynamic goal complex, including the stockholders' wealth as one of the goal variables. As pointed out in the second section, such a complex can be dealt with best if the goal variables within this complex are being considered simultaneously. This conclusion again leads to the need for multiple-objective decision methods.

One of the most often proposed multiple-objective decision methods for financial planning and capital budgeting is goal programming in which a weighted combination of the deviations from a set of goal levels is to be minimized. This has proved to be a powerful and flexible method. A major drawback is its need for a considerable amount of *a priori* information on the decision maker's preferences. This handicap can be sidestepped by using interactive procedures based on a mutual and successive interplay between a decision maker and an analyst (model). We are advocating an interactive variant of goal programming (Interactive Multiple Goal Programming) because it combines the attractive properties of goal programming with those of interactive procedures. As shown in the fifth section, such a combination can be useful in the field of financial planning and capital budgeting.

NOTES

1. In spite of the merits of these techniques, it is our opinion that other techniques are better suited for the selection of public projects [see 23].

2. For this, we have chosen the abbreviated version of the LONGER model, as described by Myers and Pogue [21].

3. Because of limited space, the following discussion can only be very brief. For a more thorough discussion, we refer to Hamada [11], Rubinstein [28], and Stapleton [31].

4. To make the CAPM analysis suitable for multiperiod capital budgeting, additional assumptions should be made. See, e.g., Hamada [11]

5. Surely, this was recognized by Hirshleifer [12]. For further discussion on possible theoretical shortcomings, we refer to Adelson [1].

6. See also Derkinderen [8].

7. In practice, it may be necessary to replace these goal variables by other (proxy) variables.

8. According to Chateau, this example is an adopted version of the two-period Lorie and Savage problem as presented by Weingartner [33].

9. Furthermore, Chateau seems to suggest that goal variables should be expressible in monetary terms. In our opinion, this is not generally true for the goal programming formulation.

10. A paper (jointly with Zionts) dealing with this very subject is in preparation.

11. As shown by Lane [18, pp. 57–60], the correspondence of the behavioral theory and multiple-goal programming is not complete because the latter gives a specific interpretation of "satisfying goals as close as possible."

12. In the full description of IMGP, it is shown that cases in which $\partial f/\partial g_i$ is negative and cases in which f is not a monotone function of the $g_i(x)$ can also be included.

13. After step 9, we discuss the case in which the decision maker wants to raise more than one goal variable at the same time.

14. At this moment, the decision maker may wish to define a new aspiration level. In our opinion, it is wise to give him explicitly the opportunity to do so.

15. Also in this case, the decision maker himself may wish to define a new aspiration level.

16. However, with some minor modifications, IMGP can also be applied to discrete decision models [24].

17. In their paper, Myers and Pogue [21] state that management may wish to assign a cost to deviations from a target dividend payment and from target earnings.

REFERENCES

[1]   Adelson, R.M. "Discounted Cash Flow: Can We Discount It?," *Journal of Business Finance* 2 (1970), pp. 50–66.

[2]   Ashton, D.J., and Atkins, D.R. "Multicriteria Programming for Financial Planning," paper presented at the 23rd international meeting of TIMS, Athens, 1977.

[3]   Ballendux, F.J., and Vliet, J.K. van. "Firm Effects and Project Values," Report 7815/F, Centre for Research in Business Economics, Erasmus University Rotterdam, 1978.

[4]   Candler, W., and Boehlje, M. "Use of Linear Programming in Capital Budgeting with Multiple Goals," *American Journal of Agricultural Economics* 53 (1971), pp. 325–330.

[5]   Charnes, A., and Cooper, W.W. "Deterministic Equivalents for Optimizing and Satisfying under Chance Constraints," *Operations Research*, 1963.

[6]   Charnes, A., and Cooper, W.W. "Goal Programming and Multiple Objective Optimizations, Part I," *European Journal of Operational Research* (1977), p. 39.

[7]   Chateau, J.P.D. "The Capital Budgeting Problem under Conflicting Financial Policies," *Journal of Business Finance and Accounting* 2 (Spring 1975), pp. 83–103.

[8]   Derkinderen, F.J.G. "Investeringsproblematiek Financieel Strategisch Bezien; Enige Consequenties van Imperfecties," in Jonkhart, Schuit, and Spronk, eds., *Financiering en Belegging*.

[9]   Easton, A. *Complex Managerial Decisions Involving Multiple Objectives.* New York: John Wiley & Sons, 1973.

[10] Fishburn, P.C. "Lexicographic Orders; Utilities and Decision Rules: A Survey," *Management Science* (1974), p. 1442.

[11] Hamada, R.S. "Portfolio Analysis, Market Equilibrium and Corporation Finance," *Journal of Finance* (1969), pp. 13–31.

[12] Hirshleifer, J. "On the Theory of Optimal Investment Decision," *Journal of Political Economy* (1958), pp. 329–352.

[13] Ijiri, Y. *Management Goals and Accounting for Control.* Amsterdam: North-Holland Publishing Company, 1965.

[14] Ijiri, Y.; Levy, F.K.; and Lyon, R.C. "A Linear Programming Model for Budgeting and Financial Planning," *Journal of Accounting Research* (1963), pp. 198–212.

[15] Isermann, H. "The Relevance of Duality in Multiple Objective Linear Pro-
      gramming," in Starr and Zeleny, eds., *Multiple Criteria Decision Making*.
[16] Jonkhart, M.J.L.; Schuit, J.W.R.; and Spronk, J., eds. *Financiering en
      Belegging: Stand van zaken anno 1978*. Leiden: Stenfert Kroese, 1978.
[17] Kornbluth, J.S.H. "A Survey of Goal Programming," *Omega* 1 (1973),
      pp. 193–205.
[18] Lane, M.N. "Goal Programming and Satisficing Models in Economic
      Analysis," Ph.D. dissertation, University of Texas, 1970.
[19] Lorie, J.H., and Savage, L.J. "Three Problems in Rationing Capital,"
      Journal of Business (October 1955), pp. 229–239.
[20] Myers, S.C. "Interactions for Corporate Financing and Investment
      Decisions-Implications for Capital Budgeting," *Journal of Finance* 29
      (March 1974), pp. 1–25.
[21] Myers, S.C., and Pogue, G.A. "A Programming Approach to Corporate
      Financial Management," *Journal of Finance* 29 (May 1974), pp. 579–599.
[22] Monarchi, D.E.; Weber, J.E.; and Duckstein, L. *An Interactive Multiple
      Objective Decision-Making Aid Using Non-Linear Goal Programming*, in
      Zeleny, ed., Multiple Criteria Decision-Making.
[23] Nijkamp, P.; Rietveld, P.; Spronk, J.; Veenendaal, W. van; and Voogd, H.
      Multidimensional Spatial Data and Decision Analysis. New York: John
      Wiley & Sons, 1979.
[24] Nijkamp, P., and Spronk, J. "Goal Programming for Decision-Making,"
      Ricerca Operativa, Special Issue on Multiple Criteria Decision Making
      (Fall 1978).
[25] Nijkamp, P., and Spronk, J. "Interactive Multiple Goal Programming,"
      Report 7803/A, Centre for Research in Business Economics, Erasmus
      University Rotterdam, 1978.
[26] Nijkamp, P., and Spronk, J. "Analysis of Production and Location Deci-
      sions by Means of Multi-Criteria Analysis," *Engineering and Process
      Economics* (Spring 1979).
[27] Robichek, A.; Ogilvie, D.; and Roach, J. "Capital Budgeting: A Pragmatic
      Approach," *Financial Executive* (1969), pp. 26–38.
[28] Rubinstein, M.E. "A Mean-Variance Synthesis of Corporate Financial
      Theory," *Journal of Finance* (1973) pp. 167–181.
[29] Sealey, C.W. "Financial Planning with Multiple Objectives," *Financial
      Management* (Winter 1978), pp. 17–23.
[30] Spronk, J. "Capital Budgeting and Financial Planning with Multiple
      Goals," Report 7907/F, Centre for Research in Business Economics,
      Erasmus University Rotterdam, 1979.
[31] Stapleton, R.C. "Portfolio Analysis, Stock Valuation and Capital Budget-
      ing Decision Rules for Risky Projects," *Journal of Finance* (1971),
      pp. 95–117.
[32] Starr, M.K., and Zeleny, M., eds. *Multiple Criteria Decision Making*, TIMS

Studies in Management Sciences, Vol. 6. Amsterdam: North-Holland Publishing Company, 1977.

[33] Weingartner, H.M. *Mathematical Programming and the Analysis of Capital Budgeting Problems.* Englewood Cliffs, N.J.: Prentice-Hall, 1963.

[34] Weingartner, H.M. "Capital Budgeting of Interrelated Projects: Survey and Synthesis," *Management Science* 12 (March 1966), pp. 213–244.

[35] Weingartner, H.M. "Capital Rationing: *n* Authors in Search of a Plot," *Journal of Finance* 32 (1977), pp. 1403–1431.

[36] Zeleny, M., ed. *Multiple Criteria Decision-Making.* Berlin: Springer-Verlag, 1976.

[37] Zionts, S. "Integer Linear Programming with Multiple Objectives," *Annals of Discrete Mathematics* 1 (1977), pp. 551–562.

[38] Zionts, S. "A Survey of Multiple Criteria Integer Programming Methods," Working Paper 322, State University of New York at Buffalo, 1978.

11 CAPITAL RATIONING METHODS

John D. Forsyth
Duke University

David C. Owen
Bell Canada

The multiperiod allocation of limited resources among competing investment proposals is one of the most significant and difficult problems a business organization must resolve. The significance of the problem stems from the fact that any set of capital investments represents both a means of implementing strategic plans and a framework for developing future strategic plans. The difficulty of the problem is a consequence of a variety of factors: the implementation of investment proposals that require the use of scarce resources, the length of time required to transform a proposal into an operational investment, the need to live with capital investments that may take a number of years to recover the financial resources required for their implementation, and the lumpiness of capital investments, to cite a few illustrations. Moreover, the sheer magnitude of the capital investment budgets of business organizations can be staggering. It is not uncommon to see such budgets exceed one billion dollars per year.

This paper will report on a study of alternative approaches to the development of a capital investment plan. Basically, two approaches will be offered, a mathematical programming approach and a heuristic approach. In terms of organization, a description of the design of the study is offered; a summary and analysis of the results of the study is given; and the implications of the study's results from the point of view of management and some comments and suggestions for further study are offered in the concluding section. However, before setting out the study design, some perspective on the problem and theoretical developments will be useful.

A brief tracing of history reveals the 1950s as an interesting decade because at the beginning of that period Dean [2] popularized, if not fathered, a technique for rationing capital among competing investment proposals based on a ranking of candidates using their respective indices of net present value relative to their capital requirements. By the end of that decade, Lorie and Savage [5] articulated some weaknesses in using such a heuristic approach as ranking by net present value as a technique for selecting capital investment proposals for implementation. Furthermore, Hirshleifer [4] suggested a theoretical form for addressing the shortcomings of ranking by indices.

The 1960s saw the resolution of the problems described by Lorie and Savage when Weingartner [6] developed a mathematical programming model for allocating resources among competing proposals. The Weingartner optimization approach fostered vigorous discussions, leading to a number of extensions to his pioneering work. And, as the 1980s emerge, Weingartner's mathematical programming model remains the unchallenged theoretical basis for optimization approaches to the capital rationing problem.

While Weingartner's model offered the theoretical resolution of the capital rationing problem, it took a number of years to develop the needed apparatus to make the model operational. However, Balas [1] succeeded in developing an algorithm for solving the peculiar (zero-one) structure of the Weingartner mathematical programming model. More recently, we have seen the development of computer codes for solving large-scale mathematical programming models of the "zero-one" type. While such codes were being developed, questions emerged about the potential usefulness of a mathematical programming model in a business organization. Fogler [3], for example, suggested that there may not be the need to use sophisticated mathematical programming models for rationing capital, because a heuristic technique, such as the net present-value index, provides reasonably close approximations to solutions attainable by mathematical programming models.

Today, we are left with a haunting question:

Why is it that business organizations are not known to use the theoretical apparatus, the algorithms, and the computer codes that the academic community has produced for resolving the capital rationing problems?

It is tempting to offer some tentative hypotheses as rationales for the departure of business organizations from the work of academics. For example, it may be that the organizational cost—broadly defined—would be prohibitive. Or it may be that the input requirements to use a mathematical programming model are simply too demanding. Also, the assumed ability of any large organization to make a set of simultaneous decisions on capital investment proposals may be totally invalid. The world does not stand still once a year so as to allow management to make its set of capital allocation decisions. Indeed, the dynamics of the capital rationing may not be capable of being captured in a mathematical programming model. In any event, such a question as the one raised above cannot be answered without substantial field studies. Thus, as a modest beginning, this paper investigates the questions suggested by Fogler.

STUDY DESIGN

A simulation study was conducted to provide a comparison of a heuristic approach versus an optimization approach to capital rationing. Basically, investment proposals were generated with randomly distributed characteristics. Thus each investment proposal had associated with it a net present value and the required capital outlay(s). The investment proposals were captured in a mathematical programming model requiring the maximization of an objective function totaling the net present value of a set of investment proposals. The relevant constraints were expressed in terms of the period by period total capital available for implementing an investment plan. While other constraints may have been designed, such as, for example, interdependencies among projects and engineering time availabilities, the model focused exclusively on capital availabilities. Thus in notional terms the mathematical programming model was designed to maximize the value of the objective function subject to the relevant budget constraints. Upon solution of the model,[1] not only were the most attractive candidates identified, but also the resulting total net present value was calculated.

   As a heuristic approach, the investment proposals were ranked on the basis of the ratio of the net present value to the required investment outlay for each and every proposal. The rank ordering of the investment proposals identified the most attractive proposal as the one with the highest index. The second-ranking proposal had the second highest index. This ranking procedure was followed until a complete rank ordering of investment proposals was obtained. Then investment candidates were selected—by this ranking index—until the ceiling provided by a capital budget was reached. The total net present value for projects identified for inclusion in the capital budget was determined. Then, finally, the total net present value using the heuristic approach was compared with the total net present value obtained in the optimization approach to determine the relative shortfall resulting from the use of a heuristic approach rather than an optimization approach for selecting investment candidates. While this approach served as the basic instrument for analysis, several alternative mutations of this design were taken.

Single-Period Comparisons

To begin, several designed simulations employed a single-period capital constraint only. Subsequent simulations allowed for the multiperiod case.

1. *Number of projects.* Three situations were developed for the number of projects or investment candidates considered for inclusion in the capital budget: 50, 100, and 150. The simulation simply identified a series of projects: 1, 2, 3, . . . up to 50 or 100 or 150 in total. Subsequently characteristics for each and every project were determined.

2. *Distribution of net present values.* The net present values of the investment candidates were generated randomly from triangular distributions. Three cases were used: a symmetrical triangular distribution, a triangular distribution skewed right, and a triangular distribution skewed left. In each case, the net present value for each and every previously labeled project was determined.

The triangular distributions were straightforward transformations of readily available, uniformly distributed random variables. Apart from the computational ease of using triangular distribution, it was also a simple matter to investigate the impact of skewness.

3. *Distribution of capital requirements.* Likewise, the capital required to implement each and every project was generated randomly from a triangular distribution for both the symmetrical and asymmetrical cases as described above.

4. *Capital availability.* In the simulation, the capital available for implementation of investment candidates was expressed as a percentage of the total capital that would be required to implement all the capital investment proposals. Then in the simulations the budget constraint—expressed as the ratio of capital availability to total capital requirements—was allowed to vary incrementally.

The phenomenon of "lumpiness" of capital investments was examined by allowing the capital availability to vary so that for any given number of investment candidates the relative lumpiness of the candidates varied.

Multiperiod Comparisons

The multiperiod case was examined in several different ways. These approaches reflected changes from the basic design for the single-period case.

1. *Distribution of capital requirements.* Using three cases for randomly generating capital requirements from a triangular distribution, as given above, the capital requirements for a given project were identified for both a first and a second period.
2. *Capital availabilities.* Again, as a mutation on the single-period cases, capital availability as a percentage of capital requirements was expressed for both the first and second period.
3. *Heuristic decision rules.* While the mathematical programming model could handle the multiperiod case as a straightforward extension of the single-period case, it was necessary to provide some decision rules for the heuristic approach. Specifically, two types of decision rules were expressed.

First, the net present-value index for the multiperiod case was used exactly as applied in the single-period case in the sense that the second-period capital requirements were simply ignored. Thus ranking of investment proposals and the subsequent selection of a set of proposals for implementation were based solely on the capital requirements for the first period. Clearly, such a shortcut decision rule was capable of producing nonfeasible solutions because the second-period capital requirements were ignored.

Second, the previously given decision rule was modified by simply aggregating the capital requirements for a given project for both periods while ignoring the difference in timing of the requirements. Similarly, the capital availability by period was aggregated to give the total availability over two periods. In essence, the two-period scenario was collapsed into the familiar one-period scenario.

STUDY RESULTS

As a means of collapsing the considerable quantity of data from the simulation studies, the basic simulation study can be examined in detail, while the results from the variations of the basic simulation can be summarized.[2]

Case 1.11

The basic simulation study had the following set of distinct characteristics:

- Single-period budget constraint with capital availability, as a percentage of total capital requirements, allowed to vary in five-point increments
- Fifty investment candidates
- Symmetrical distributions for both net present values and capital requirements
- Expression of the output measurement in percentage form as the relative difference between the total net present value of the investment candidates selected by the mathematical programming model and the total net present value of the investment candidates selected by the heuristic approach. The denominator required to provide the measurement of the relative difference was the total net present value of the investment candidates selected by the mathematical programming model. See Table 1.

Table 1

Capital Availability Relative to Total Capital Requirements	Relative Difference in Total Net Present Values
5%	4.83%
10%	1.89%
15%	0.00%
20%	2.00%
25%	0.89%
30%	0.79%
35%	1.75%
40%	2.14%
45%	0.86%
50%	0.15%
55%	0.22%
60%	1.09%
65%	0.77%
70%	1.44%
75%	0.76%
80%	0.00%
85%	1.54%
90%	1.34%
95%	0.26%

The simulation results showed that the relative difference between the two sets of investment candidates was less than 2 percent in seventeen of nineteen cases. While the effect of varying the capital availability was to vary the lumpiness of the individual project, there appeared to be no systematic relationship between lumpiness and the relative difference between the selections.

Case 1.12. This was the same as Case 1.11 except that the distributions from which net present values and capital requirements were drawn were both skewed to the right. The simulation results showed that the relative difference between the two approaches was less than 2 percent in fifteen of the nineteen cases. The maximum relative difference was 9.79 percent. No systematic relationship with lumpiness appeared to exist.

Case 1.13. This was the same as Case 1.11 except that net present-value distributions and capital requirement distributions were both skewed left. The simulation results showed that the relative difference between the two approaches was less than 2 percent. No systematic relationship with lumpiness appeared to exist.

Case 1.14. This was the same as Case 1.11 except capital requirements distribution was skewed right and net present-value distribution was skewed left. The simulation results showed that the relative difference between the two approaches was less than 2 percent in seventeen of the nineteen cases. The maximum relative difference was 4.13 percent. No systematic relationship with lumpiness appeared to exist.

Case 1.15. This was the same as Case 1.11 except capital requirements distribution was skewed left and net present-value distribution was skewed right. The simulation results showed that the relative difference between the two approaches was less than 2 percent in seventeen of the nineteen cases. The maximum relative difference was 3.9 percent. No systematic relationship with lumpiness appeared to exist.

Case 1.21. This was the same as Case 1.11 except that 100 projects were used and the capital availability constraint as a percentage of total capital requirements varied in increments of 10 percentage points. The simulation results showed that the relative difference between the two approaches was less than 2 percent in all ten cases. The maximum relative difference was 0.87 percent. No systematic relationship with lumpiness appeared to exist.

Case 1.22. This was the same as Case 1.12 except that 100 projects were used. The simulation results showed that in all cases the relative difference between the two approaches was less than 2 percent. The maximum relative difference was 0.77 percent. No systematic relationship with lumpiness appeared to exist.

Case 1.23. This was the same as Case 1.13 except 100 projects were used. The simulation results showed that the relative difference between the two approaches was less than 2 percent in all cases. The maximum relative difference was 1.77 percent. No systematic relationship with lumpiness appeared to exist.

Case 1.24. This was the same as Case 1.14 except 100 projects were used. The simulation results showed that in all cases the relative difference between the two approaches was less than 2 percent. The maximum relative difference was 1.38 percent. No systematic relationship with lumpiness appeared to exist.

Case 1.25. This was the same as Case 1.15 except 100 projects were used. The simulation results showed that the relative difference between the two approaches was less than 2 percent in nine of the ten cases. The maximum relative difference was 2.64 percent. No systematic relationship with lumpiness appeared to exist.

Case 1.31. This was the same as Case 1.11 except that 150 projects were used with the total capital available equal to 50 percent of the total capital required. The simulation results showed that the relative difference between the two approaches was 0.06 percent.

Case 2.1 Series

This was the same as Case 1 series except that two budget constraints were given and two capital requirements for each project were determined—one for each period. The decision rule for the heuristic ranking approach was simply to ignore the second-period budget constraint. The simulation results for all cases, that is, for the symmetrical and the four asymmetrical distributions, formed the same pattern. When the projects were relatively lumpy—the capital availability was less than 50 percent of the total capital requirements—there were major differences between the two approaches.

However, as long as the total capital availability was more than 50 percent of the total capital requirements, the relative difference between the two approaches was less than 5 percent. Moreover, as can be anticipated, when the projects were relatively lumpy, the solutions generated by the heuristic ranking approach were not feasible in terms of the implications for the second-period capital requirements.[3] In other words, the mathematical programming approach showed its superiority in producing feasible solutions with lumpy investments. However, there was essentially no difference between the results using the mathematical programming approach and the heuristic ranking approach when the projects were small in scale relative to the total capital availability.

Case 2.2 Series

This was the same as Case 2.1 series except that 100 projects were used. The same observations hold for this case as in the former instance except that lumpiness was less significant in terms of the relative differences between the two approaches.

Case 3.1 Series

This was the same as Case 2.1 series except that the heuristic ranking approach used the total capital requirements over the two periods while ignoring the timing of the capital requirements. In this case, and for distribution combinations, the results using the heuristic ranking approach were essentially the same as the results using the mathematical programming approach.

In summary, in the single-period case, the results obtained by using the heuristic ranking approach were essentially the same as the results obtained by using the optimizing mathematical programming approach. The differences in the results using these two approaches were small, indeed. Lumpiness appeared to be irrelevant, as did the nature of the distributions of net present values and capital requirements.

In the multiperiod case, the two approaches produced essentially the same results under two conditions: (1) when the projects were small in scale relative to the total capital available, and (2) when the heuristic approach aggregated the total capital requirements and total capital availability over the two periods while simultaneously ignoring the timing of the capital. In other words, in the multiperiod case, the two approaches did result in markedly different solutions when projects were relatively lumpy and when the heuristic approach ignored the second-period capital requirements.

IMPLICATIONS FOR MANAGEMENT AND
DIRECTIONS FOR FURTHER INVESTIGATION

Notwithstanding the strength of the theory underlying mathematical programming approaches and the power of the algorithms for solving such models, the results obtained through their use in this study do not appear to provide any significant benefit to management over a heuristic approach—except in one set of circumstances. In the two-period case, the mathematical programming approaches were superior to the heuristic ranking approach when projects were lumpy and when the heuristic approach ignored capital availability constraints beyond the first period. However, in all other circumstances in this study, it appears that management can make use of the net present-value ranking approach and obtain results that are essentially identical to those that would be obtained with mathematical programming models. Indeed, the ranking approach offers substantial benefits. Using the ranking approach, one can make the selection of capital investment proposals with nothing more than a pencil and the back of an envelope. There is absolutely no need to invest in any expensive computer program. Moreover, as one considers the accuracy of the data estimates in any capital management process, one has to question the use of a very sophisticated technique that offers very little improvement over the heuristic approach.

Some comments regarding the circumstances under which the mathematical programming approach is superior are warranted. It appears that when projects are lumpy and the two-period capital requirements are ignored by a naive decision rule, the mathematical programming approach is superior. However, the heuristic approach could be improved upon readily by developing some decision rules that would allow for the protection of feasibility. And, as feasibility is protected, it may very well be that the heuristic approach produces improved results.

In conclusion, this study does not offer support for the complete rejection of mathematical programming approaches on the basis of overkill in the development of a capital budget. However, the study does offer some evidence as to when use of the mathematical programming approach is not warranted.

Presumably, the power of the mathematical programming approaches would improve — on a relative basis — as the number of constraints increased. Constraints involving multiperiod resource requirements and constraints allowing for project interdependence would, intuitively, increase the efficacy of mathematical programming approaches. However, one cannot push such approaches too far. Instead, further study of decision rules for use with heuristic approaches to capital rationing is very apt to support the use of naive approaches to capital management on the part of business organizations.

APPENDIX

Case 1.11

> Single period
> 50 projects
> Symmetric distributions

Results Minimum relative difference in total net present values = 0%

Maximum relative difference in total net present values = 4.83%

Average relative difference in total net present values = 1.20%

Case 1.12

Single period
50 projects
Asymmetric distributions
    Capital requirements – skewed right
    Net present values – skewed right

Results Minimum relative difference = 0%

Maximum relative difference = 8.79%

Average relative difference = 1.37%

Case 1.13

Single period
50 projects
Asymmetric distributions
    Capital requirements – skewed left
    Net present values – skewed left

Results Minimum relative difference = 0%

Maximum relative difference = 2.81%

Average relative difference = 0.43%

Case 1.14

Single period
50 projects
Asymmetric distributions
    Capital requirements – skewed right
    Net present values – skewed left

Results   Minimum relative difference =   0%

Maximum relative difference = 4.13%

Average relative difference   = 0.76%

Case 1.15

Single period
50 projects
Asymmetric distributions
  Capital requirements — skewed left
  Net present values — skewed right

Results   Minimum relative difference =   0%

Maximum relative difference = 3.90%

Average relative difference   = 0.72%

Case 1.21

Single period
100 projects
Symmetric distributions

Results   Minimum relative difference = 0.10%

Maximum relative difference = 0.87%

Average relative difference   = 0.32%

Case 1.22

Single period
100 projects
Asymmetric distributions
  Capital requirements — skewed right
  Net present values — skewed right

Results Minimum relative difference = 0.0%

Maximum relative difference = 0.77%

Average relative difference   = 0.42%

Case 1.23

Single period
100 projects
Asymmetric distributions
  Capital requirements – skewed left
  Net present values – skewed left

Results Minimum relative difference = 0.0%

Maximum relative difference = 1.77%

Average relative difference   = 0.40%

Case 1.24

Single period
100 projects
Asymmetric distributions
  Capital requirements – skewed right
  Net present values – skewed left

Results Minimum relative difference = 0.0%

Maximum relative difference = 1.38%

Average relative difference   = 0.47%

Case 1.25

Single period
100 projects
Asymmetric distributions
  Capital requirements – skewed left
  Net present values – skewed right

Results   Minimum relative difference = 0.0%

Maximum relative difference = 2.64%

Average relative difference   = 0.65%

Case 1.31

Single period
150 projects
Symmetric distributions

Results   Relative difference = 0.06%

Case 2.11

Two period
50 projects
Heuristic approach ignored second budget constraint
Symmetric distributions

Results   Minimum relative difference =   0.76%

Maximum relative difference = -70.46%

Average relative difference   =   11.47%

Heuristic approach produced some nonfeasible solutions due to second budget constraint being ignored.

Case 2.12

Two period
50 projects
Heuristic approach ignored second budget constraint
Asymmetric distributions
  Capital requirements—skewed right
  Net present values—skewed right

Results Minimum relative difference =   0%

Maximum relative difference = –81.93%

Average relative difference   = 11.04%

Heuristic approach produced some nonfeasible solutions due to second budget constraint being ignored.

Case 2.13

   Two period
   50 projects
   Heuristic approach ignored second budget constraint
   Asymmetric distributions
      Capital requirements—skewed left
      Net present values—skewed left

Results Minimum relative difference = 0.07%

Maximum relative difference = –28.74%

Average relative difference   =   8.61%

Heuristic approach produced some nonfeasible solutions due to second budget constraint being ignored.

Case 2.14

   Two period
   50 projects
   Heuristic approach ignored second budget constraint
   Asymmetric distributions
      Capital requirements—skewed right
      Net present values—skewed left

Results Minimum relative difference =   0.18%

Maximum relative difference = –52.72%

Average relative difference   =   7.67%

Heuristic approach produced some nonfeasible solutions due to second budget constraint being ignored.

Case 2.15

Two period
50 projects
Heuristic approach ignored second budget constraint
Asymmetric distributions
  Capital requirements — skewed left
  Net present values — skewed right

Results Minimum relative difference =   0.15%

Maximum relative difference = −48.71%

Average relative difference   = 10.49%

Heuristic approach produced some nonfeasible solutions due to second budget constraint being ignored.

Case 2.21

Two period
100 projects
Heuristic approach ignored second budget constraint
Symmetric distributions

Results Minimum relative difference =   0.49%

Maximum relative difference = −29.68%

Average relative difference   =   9.11%

Heuristic approach produced some nonfeasible solutions due to second budget constraint being ignored.

Case 2.22

Two period
100 projects
Heuristic approach ignored second budget constraint
Asymmetric distributions
  Capital requirements — skewed right
  Net present values — skewed right

Results Minimum relative difference =   0.30%

Maximum relative difference = –29.68%

Average relative difference   =   9.11%

Heuristic approach produced some nonfeasible solutions due to second budget constraint being ignored.

Case 2.23

Two period
100 projects
Heuristic approach ignored second budget constraint
Asymmetric distributions
  Capital requirement–skewed left
  Net present values–skewed left

Results Minimum relative difference =   0.13%

Maximum relative difference = –66.70%

Average relative difference   =   12.88%

Heuristic approach produced some nonfeasible solutions due to second budget constraint being ignored.

Case 2.24

Two period
100 projects
Heuristic approach ignored second budget constraint
Asymmetric distributions
  Capital requirement–skewed right
  Net present values–skewed left

Results Minimum relative difference =   0.13%

Maximum relative difference = –27.21%

Average relative difference   =   12.88%

Heuristic approach produced some nonfeasible solutions due to second budget constraint being ignored.

Case 2.25

Two period
100 projects
Heuristic approach ignored second budget constraint
Asymmetric distributions
  Capital requirement—skewed left
  Net present values—skewed right

Results Minimum relative difference =   0.21%

Maximum relative difference = −36.87%

Average relative difference   =   10.77%

Heuristic approach produced a nonfeasible solution due to second budget constraint being ignored.

Case 2.31

Single period
150 projects
Heuristic approach ignored second budget constraint
Symmetric distributions

Results   Relative difference = −7.81%

Heuristic approach produced a nonfeasible solution due to second budget constraint being ignored.

Case 3.11

Two period
50 projects
Heuristic approach incorporated all capital requirements but ignored timing
Symmetric distributions

Results Minimum relative difference =   1.75%

Maximum relative difference = −12.66%

Average relative difference   =   0.52%

Heuristic approach produced some nonfeasible solutions due to timing of capital requirements being ignored.

Case 3.12

Two period
50 projects
Heuristic approach incorporated all capital requirements but ignored timing
Asymmetric distributions
   Capital requirements – skewed right
   Net present values – skewed right

Results   Minimum relative difference = 1.58%

          Maximum relative difference = -3.40%

          Average relative difference   = 0.12%

Heuristic approach produced some nonfeasible solutions due to timing of capital
requirements being ignored.

Case 3.13

Two period
50 projects
Heuristic approach incorporated all capital requirements but ignored timing
Asymmetric distributions
   Capital requirements – skewed left
   Net present values – skewed left

Results   Minimum relative difference = 2.71%

          Maximum relative difference = -6.86%

          Average relative difference   = 0.27%

Heuristic approach produced some nonfeasible solutions due to timing of capital
requirements being ignored.

Case 3.14

Two period
50 projects
Heuristic approach incorporated all capital requirements but ignored timing
Asymmetric distributions
   Capital requirements – skewed right
   Net present values – skewed left

Results Minimum relative difference =   2.54%

Maximum relative difference = –10.88%

Average relative difference   =   0.34%

Heuristic approach produced some nonfeasible solutions due to timing of capital requirements being ignored.

Case 3.15

Two period
50 projects
Heuristic approach incorporated all capital requirements but ignored timing
Asymmetric distributions
  Capital requirements – skewed left
  Net present values – skewed right

Results Minimum relative difference = 2.12%

Maximum relative difference = –3.11%

Average relative difference   =   0%

Heuristic approach produced some nonfeasible solutions due to timing of capital requirements being ignored.

Case 3.21

Two period
100 projects
Heuristic approach incorporated all capital requirements but ignored timing
Symmetric distributions

Results Minimum relative difference = 0.77%

Maximum relative difference = –3.21%

Average relative difference   = 0.52%

Heuristic approach produced some nonfeasible solutions due to timing of capital requirements being ignored.

Case 3.22

Two period
100 projects
Heuristic approach incorporated all capital requirements but ignored timing
Asymmetric distributions
  Capital requirements—skewed right
  Net present values—skewed right

Results Minimum relative difference = 0.63%

         Maximum relative difference = -1.00%

         Average relative difference   = 0.15%

Heuristic approach produced some nonfeasible solutions due to timing of capital
requirements being ignored.

Case 3.23

Two period
100 projects
Heuristic approach incorporated all capital requirements but ignored timing
Asymmetric distributions
  Capital requirements—skewed left
  Net present values—skewed left

Results Minimum relative difference = 0.98%

         Maximum relative difference = -3.85%

         Average relative difference   = 0.32%

Heuristic approach produced some nonfeasible solutions due to timing of capital
requirements being ignored.

Case 3.24

Two period
100 projects
Heuristic approach incorporated all capital requirements but ignored timing
Asymmetric distributions
  Capital requirements—skewed right
  Net present values—skewed left

Results Minimum relative difference = 0.98%

Maximum relative difference = -2.56%

Average relative difference   = 0.33%

Heuristic approach produced some nonfeasible solutions due to timing of capital requirements being ignored.

Case 3.25

Two period
100 projects
Heuristic approach incorporated all capital requirements but ignored timing
Asymmetric distributions
   Capital requirements—skewed left
   Net present value—skewed right

Results Minimum relative difference = 0.12%

Maximum relative difference = -3.54%

Average relative difference   = 0.55%

Case 3.31

Two period
150 projects
Heuristic approach incorporated all capital requirements but ignored timing
Asymmetric distributions

Results Relative differences = -0.17%

Heuristic approach produced a nonfeasible solution due to timing of capital requirements being ignored.

NOTES

1. The algorithm for solving the mathematical programming model was the property of Bell Canada. As such, the algorithm was a modified version of CAMIO (Capital Allocation Model Integrated Optimizer) purchased from Analysis, Research and Computation, Inc., of Austin, Texas.

2. The appendix contains a summary of the simulation results.

3. In terms of significance of the nonfeasible solutions, the violation of the budget constraint was not a serious problem. In virtually all cases, elimination of the violation would be realized if the second-period budget constraint were increased by 5 percent.

REFERENCES

[1] Balas, Egon. "An Additive Algorithm for Solving Linear Programs with Zero-One Variables," *Operations Research* 13, No. 4 (July–August 1965), pp. 517–549.

[2] Dean J. *Capital Budgeting.* New York: Columbia University Press, 1951.

[3] Fogler, H. Russell. "Overkill in Capital Budgeting Technique?" *Financial Management* 1, No. 1 (Spring 1972), pp. 92–62.

[4] Hirshleifer, J. "On the Theory of Optimal Investment," *Journal of Political Economy* 65, No. 4 (August 1958), pp. 329–52.

[5] Lorie, J.H., and Savage, L.J. "Three Problems in Rationing Capital," *Journal of Business* (October 1955), pp. 229–39.

[6] Weingartner, H. Martin. *Mathematical Programming and the Analysis of Capital Budgeting Problems.* Englewood Cliffs, N.J.: Prentice-Hall, 1963.

EPILOGUE

The theme of this book was stated in the introduction as current investment problems in a variety-rich and changing world. In a broad sense, this was also the major subject of the conference of which the papers included in this volume represent a not insignificant part. There appeared to be a consensus among the participants of the conference that environmental dynamics are evolving in ways that call for more explicit recognition of diversity in corporate decision models. It was our objective in putting together this volume to focus on the issues of complexity and change in ways that would highlight this need for greater recognition of diversity.

We believe that three major points are evident from the essays in this book. First, the environmental indifference that is often assumed implicitly by many financial theories and models is not a reasonable assumption for the future. Sociopolitical incursions into the marketplace to reorder priorities and to redistribute wealth according to criteria other than pure supply and demand render traditional viewpoints less viable than they were in the past. Failure to incorporate these external considerations into the resource allocation process can lead to decisions that are at best inappropriate considering the circumstances. Thus, decision makers cannot afford to assume the existence of benign governments and indifferent reactions by groups other than shareholders in making resource allocation decisions.

Second, informational requirements or assumptions of most existing financial models are unrealistic or unreasonable. What is needed is a realization that the data required by current theories to form the basis for choosing from among several alternatives may not be available or cannot be estimated reliably. Likewise, managers are generally unable to process environmental signals before the fact and to obtain all intelligence from them that can be extracted after the fact. These informational limitations must be realized and incorporated into models of choice if they are to be made operational.

Third, the assumption of altruistic behavior on the part of decision makers should be weakened if useful theories are to be forthcoming. Self-interest on the part of various stakeholder groups defines the operating boundaries for corporations. Unless this self-serving behavior is recognized and the power structures that facilitate divisiveness are dealt with adequately, decision models cannot capture the essence of the resource allocation process. Misplaced altruism might buy conceptual simplification and mathematical tractability for financial theories, but it is becoming increasingly clear that the price of these virtues in terms of the usefulness of the resultant models for allocating resources is too high.

No pretext is being made that the essays in this volume can overcome the difficulties enumerated above. That is not the purpose of this book. Rather, these papers serve to identify problem areas and to indicate promising directions for further research. We believe that the suggestions for future development contained herein are keys for the successful evolution of financial management to meet the challenges of the 1980s.